BEETHOVEN

& THE

SPIRITUAL PATH

BEETHOVEN

& THE

SPIRITUAL PATH

DAVID TAME

The Theosophical Publishing House
P.O. Box 270
Wheaton, IL 60189-0270

A publication of the Theosophical Publishing House,
a department of the Theosophical Society in America.

*This publication made possible with
the assistance of the Kern Foundation.*

Library of Congress Cataloging-in-Publication Data

Tame, David.
    Beethoven & the spiritual path / David Tame.
        p.   cm.
    Includes bibliographical references and index.
    ISBN 0-8356-0701-1 : $14.00
    1. Beethoven, Ludwig, van, 1770–1827—Criticism and interpretation.
2. Music—Moral and ethical aspects.   3. Music, Influence of.   4. Music—
Philosophy and aesthetics.   I. Title.   II. Title: Beethoven and the
spiritual path.
ML410.B43T35   1994
780′.92—dc20   93-48496
                                                                              CIP
                                                                              MN

9 8 7 6 5 4 3 2 1 * 94 95 96 97 98 99

Cover design and art work by Scott Fray after a portrait by Josef
Steiler, "Beethoven composing the Missa Solemnis," c. 1819.

Illustration on page 31 is an engraving by Johann Josef Neidl, c. 1801,
after a drawing by Gandolph Ernst Stainhauser von Treuberg, 1800.

Printed in the United States of America by Versa Press

Again,
   to the seventh angel
   to the two olive trees
   and to all who will sing the new song

   . . . and to Faith Collingwood, with deep
gratitude, for word-processing the manuscript
a time, half a time, and then some

CONTENTS

PART I

The Mission

There is no loftier mission than to approach the Godhead more nearly than other mortals and by means of that contact to spread the rays of the Godhead through the human race.
—BEETHOVEN, IN A LETTER OF 1823[1]

The Importance of 1
Beethoven Today

"MUSIC," SAID BEETHOVEN, "should strike fire from a man."[2] This is the story of that music which strikes fire from us and of the life of the man who gave it to the world.

Conventional biographies have never sufficiently emphasized the essentially spiritual nature of Beethoven's life. And conventional scholarly musicological commentaries have never sufficiently brought out the fundamentally metaphysical nature of Beethoven's music. In truth, Beethoven was a disciple treading the spiritual path. His life and his music can only be understood and appreciated correctly when seen from this perspective.

Beethoven's life story depicts the archetypal striving of the human soul to overcome all outer adversity and inner imperfection during the sacred adventure of the quest for union with God. Despite a poor start in life, he still managed to chart a course to victory in a way which can inspire us all. In the midst of disaster in his personal life, he nevertheless created works of magnificence that will thrill and uplift people of all nations for as long as the world endures. His story is told in Part II of this book.

Beethoven's music, in itself, tells the story of the path all spiritual pilgrims must tread, each major composition depicting

1

a certain stage on the Way. His works are among the greatest music for meditation in existence. Part III of this book is therefore intended to be a piece-by-piece guide to understanding and using the music of Beethoven toward the goal of self-transformation.

As Ernest Newman wrote, it is "the peculiarity of Beethoven's imagination that again and again he lifts us to a height from which we reevaluate not only all of music but all life, all emotion, and all thoughts."[3] The crucial point here is that Beethoven's music can *change* us. Ultimately, this music is capable of revolutionizing our consciousness.

Beethoven was a true revolutionary who lived in a revolutionary age. However, his personal revolution was primarily psychological and spiritual. Even as the cannon of another revolutionary, Napoleon Bonaparte, were bombarding Vienna, Beethoven was taking shelter in that very city, in a friend's cellar, and was halfway through composing his Fifth Piano Concerto, the *Emperor*. The flesh-and-blood emperor, Napoleon, was to sweep across and overcome most of Europe—but later would meet his Waterloo. Ultimately, it was the revolution of Beethoven and his "intangible" art which was to prove the more tangibly effective and permanent.

For Beethoven knew the power of music to touch the soul of the individual. And being touched, it is transformed. While Napoleon chose to conquer by cannon, Beethoven chose the composer's pen as his instrument for world change. He was, and still is, a conqueror of hearts.

Throughout the ages, the wisest of sages and philosophers have known that music is among the most potent of all means through which the human consciousness is altered—for better or worse, according to the music. It may be that a civilization can rise no higher than the spiritual and moral level of its music. As Andrew Fletcher, author and orator, stated in the Scottish Parliament of 1704, "I knew a very wise man who believed that if a man were permitted to make all the ballads, he need not care who should make the laws of a nation."[4]

Beethoven thoroughly understood this principle. As a youth he had read Schiller's call to all artists: "The dignity of mankind is committed into your hands—take care of it! For with you it declines or rises!" Beethoven sought consciously to manifest a music capable of raising humanity above its former state, lifting

2

human minds into contact with the Mind of God. Through music he sought to bring the matrices of Spirit into Matter, to place seeds of Christ consciousness into the humanity he so loved. The extent to which he succeeded can be measured from the fact that he is generally considered to have been the world's greatest composer.

Even in childhood Beethoven was aware of the inner power of music, its power to transform consciousness. His earliest letters tell of a young man already composing not for himself but for others and in the service of humanity. Once, the child Beethoven incredulously asked his early music instructor, Friar Willibald Koch, "Why, when you are so good a musician, have you vowed yourself to solitude?"

By listening to his works, we can follow Beethoven in the unrelenting progress of his musical/spiritual ascent. (At their core, musicality and spirituality are one and the same.) In doing so, our own spiritual awareness is opened more and more—as he intended. Like the hand of a Tibetan monk on his prayer wheel, Beethoven's music spins and quickens our chakras (spiritual centers), lifts up our moods, and even, to some extent, lastingly transforms who we are. Elements of the consciousness of God, present in the tones, are absorbed and taken on by us.

Moreover, through the transformation of consciousness, individual by individual, Beethoven played a vital, necessary role in the alteration of social consciousness in general, forging a bridge toward the twentieth and twenty-first century modes of thought. Though he effected this through the medium of music, his influence has been subtly disseminated throughout all of art and all of society.

Beethoven's artistic perception was so in advance of his own time that in composing his greatest works, he was doing so quite consciously for posterity. As he wrote to his music publisher regarding the *Hammerclavier* piano sonata, "Here is a sonata for you that will keep the pianist busy, and which will be played fifty years hence."[5] Especially in the case of his later works, Beethoven already knew when composing them that they would not be appreciated, or even understood, by the majority of his contemporaries. Not all of his last great string quartets were even performed at all during his lifetime, and until the onset of the twentieth century, none of these late quartets were widely apprehended to be the

3

The Inner Power
of Music

TO UNDERSTAND the profound ability Beethoven's music possesses to change consciousness—the consciousness of the individual and of society—we need to go back to the inner nature of all music, and indeed of sound itself. According to the materialist worldview of the twentieth century, music is an intangible art form (it cannot be seen or touched) of little practical significance. But in Beethoven's day, there were still strong echoes of the viewpoint on music held by the sages and philosophers of antiquity. According to the ancients, music is the most powerful of all artistic mediums, through which the consciousness of the artist can reach and affect the thoughts and characters of others. And more than this, the wise of ancient times, from China to Egypt, and from India to the classical age of Greece, believed there is something fundamental about music—something which, they believed, made music as much a science as an art.

The ancients believed music to have the power sublimely to evolve or utterly to degrade the individual psyche—and, since the individual is the basic building block of all societies, music could make or break entire civilizations, according to the kind widely played. Music was even thought capable of producing significant effects upon matter itself, and so was employed to guarantee good harvests, to change the weather, and to influence the outcome of military campaigns. The Bible records how the walls of the besieged city of Jericho were toppled by the scientific use of sound produced in numerologically significant ways with ram's horns (while the rest of the army, interestingly, were commanded by Joshua to remain completely silent). In the hands of the malevolent or ignorant, music, it was believed, could lead a civilization to ultimate doom, so great was its persistent effect. Yet in the hands of the wise and benevolent, the art of music was a practical tool of beauty and power capable of leading a society into a golden age of peace, prosperity, and brotherhood. Beethoven understood this thoroughly, agreed with it, and consciously used his art to change for the better the characters, thoughts, and aspirations of all who heard it.

Certainly, we know today that music is far, far from being intangible or of insignificant practical effect. Music has been shown by many modern researchers to exert a powerful influence upon the health and state of the mind, the emotions, and the physical body. Music can change metabolism, affect the strength of the muscles, raise or lower blood pressure, and influence digestion.[1] Different kinds of music can either calm the nerves or make them discordant, speed up or slow down the heartbeat. Dr. Howard Hanson, Director of the Eastman School of Music at the University of Rochester, states: "Music can be soothing or invigorating, ennobling or vulgarizing, philosophical or orgiastic. It has powers of evil as well as for good."[2]

6

What is the source of music's great power? Almost everywhere throughout the ancient world (and even in some parts of the earth today) we find the power of music explained by the same basic conception: *music releases into the material world a fundamental, superphysical energy from beyond the world of everyday experience.* Music was conceived as being a specialized, scientific (even more than artistic) use of *sound*, and, in the view of ancient thinkers, sound was the most metaphysical and mystical force in all of nature. The ancient Vedas of India assert that divine vibrational force— referred to as the OM—is the source of all matter and all creation. This Primal Sound exists everywhere and is beyond mortal hearing, but within the tangible universe of time and space, the OM manifests in a stepped-down, lower-frequency form not only as audible sound, but also as light, color, and every kind of energy and substance. In the Vedic language Sanskrit, this Cosmic Sound was called *anahata*, and audible sound *ahata*.

This same concept is found in various guises throughout the ancient world. Primal Sound, called variously OM, AUM, AMEN, HU, YAHWEH, the Logos or Word of Christianity, the Lost Word, or the music of the spheres, was believed to be the means by which all creation was formed and the means by which it is preserved—and altered—by God from moment to moment. As we find in the book of Genesis, God enacts creation by "speaking" the Word ("And God said . . .").

The OM, or Word, was the source of all things, and in no way did it manifest more powerfully in the everyday world than through sound; in no way could humanity harness and utilize its energies more potently than through music. Thus, music and magic were virtually synonymous: all music was believed to have a "magical" effect, and very little magic was not based upon some kind of music. (And do we not still speak today of the "magic of music"?)

The effect achieved would differ according to the type and quality of music played: as in music, so in life. And, therefore, in the great civilizations of antiquity, laws sometimes dictated what music could or could not be played—not out of an authoritarian spirit of repression, but because wrong music was believed to be more dangerous in the long run than any military threat or economic debacle. The ancient Chinese text, *Shu King*, records how Emperor Shun traveled through his various territories to test the exact pitches of musical notes. Back in his palace, he had court songs, folk songs, and the music of the different Chinese instruments played to him in order to ensure that the music was all in perfect attunement with the five notes of the ancient Chinese scale. This scale, in turn, was believed to be attuned to the cycles and rhythms of the heavens. Hence, so long as the kingdom played music which was aligned with the immutable heavens, its own permanence and vigor was believed to be assured. When a gift of female musicians was sent by the people of Ts'e to the kingdom of Loo, Confucius protested to Loo's ruler that the new sounds could spread throughout the kingdom and alter the entire society. When the ruler did not heed his advice, Confucius stormed out of the court in protest.[3]

7

Good music, on the other hand, was believed in antiquity not only to preserve but also to enhance the state and all aspects of life. Musicians, therefore, had a sacred duty to perform good music to the best of their ability, for the benefit of all. They were carefully trained by experienced teachers who were usually also their spiritual teachers or gurus—a tradition especially strong in India. Thus music education and spiritual education were very closely connected.

Good music was defined as that which was a perfect or near-perfect audible manifestation of the music of the spheres. It was capable of creating states of consciousness and aspects of society which were in alignment with the Will of God, and would dissolve all that was not. The ancient Chinese text, *The Spring and Autumn of Lu Bu Ve*, states:

> The origins of music lie far back in time. It arises out of proportion and is rooted in the Great One. . . . That from which all beings arise and have their origin is the Great One. . . . The bodily shape belongs to the world of space, and everything spatial has a sound. . . . When the world is at peace, when all things are at rest . . . then music can be brought to perfection. Perfected music has its effects. When desires and emotions do not follow wrong paths, then music can be perfected.[4]

The ritualized use of sound and music, aligned musically through a system of correspondences with astrological cycles, was used by the ancient Chinese, the Druids of Britain, and in other ancient societies to preserve and assure the prosperity and progress of their civilizations for hundreds or even thousands of years. John Michell has recounted how one of the Welsh Triads, verses of great age which incorporate oral traditions from bardic historians of pre-historic times, states that long-ago Britain possessed three perpetual choirs of chanting saints. The three choirs were at three locations equidistant on an arc, at Glastonbury, Stonehenge, and Llantwit Major in Glamorgan. At each location twenty-four hundred saints maintained a tag-chant, a hundred for each of the twenty-four hours. The chants guided the ritual order of life on earth, invoked spiritual blessings for the perfecting of the society, and were verbal

8

formulas which are said to have varied with the hours, seasons, and years.[5]

On the other hand, wrong music was defined in antiquity as that which was not an expression of the music of the spheres, but only of imperfect mortal intellect and feelings. Bad music would inevitably instill regrettable habits of consciousness and directions of life into the individual and society, and was therefore to be shunned. The music of immoral, ego-centered, proud, undisciplined, and rebellious musicians would, it was believed, tend to produce similar character traits in the minds of many who heard them, with the result that such undesirable traits would gradually become widespread throughout society.

In this respect, we have the comparatively recent historical example of the rock music revolution which appeared so dramatically and seemed to change society so swiftly in the sixties. Rock and its effect is a huge and complex subject. But one thing which can be stated is that there are many authorities both within and without the popular music industry who are certain the sixties revolution—its permissiveness, its drug use, its rebellion against society, its hedonism, and its politics—did not *produce* the music of the era, but was largely *caused by* it. According to this view, rock music, in its sound, its lyrical content, and its semiology, was the catalyst from which other aspects of the sixties revolution sprang up throughout society. Simon Frith, one of the world's foremost sociologists of rock music, has stated that "[Rock's] cultural effects have musical causes."[6] Mick Jagger of The Rolling Stones apparently agrees that not only rock, but all music, can act as such a catalyst, saying:

> Music is one of the things that changes society . . . you get different attitudes to things . . . even the way you walk . . . and the way you talk. Remember the Twenties when jazz in Europe changed a lot of things? People got more crazy . . . and it made profound changes in that society.[7]

While it was all happening, during the sixties themselves, Jagger stated: "We are moving after the minds, and so are most of the new groups."[8]

Moreover, the sixties' musical revolution was not at all unique historically. For instance, philosophers in ancient Greece were aware of the inner power of music and were concerned about the

9

grave implications of the relatively sudden anarchistic musical revolution which beset their society from around 444 B.C. to beyond 400 B.C. Through their writings the philosophers sought to help reason to prevail. In his *Republic* Plato was clear in his views that music molded character, that musical innovation led to political innovation and anarchy, and that it was the duty of all statesmen and educators to condemn bad music (and to be sufficiently educated to be able to discern good music from bad). Plato further insisted that the characters of the young are particularly malleable, and therefore particularly susceptible to moral corruption—that the music they hear is of the utmost importance for themselves and for the state. On the other hand, of good music he wrote: "Rhythm and harmony enter most powerfully into the innermost part of the soul and lay forcible hands upon it, bearing grace with them, so making graceful him who is rightly trained."[9]

Aristotle agreed, stating that "emotions of any kind are produced by melody and rhythm; therefore by music a man becomes accustomed to feeling the right emotions; music has power to form character, and the various kinds of music based on the various modes may be distinguished by their effects on character—one, for example, working in the direction of melancholy, another of effeminacy; one encouraging abandonment, another self-control, another enthusiasm, and so on through the series."

Or, as Confucius put it from the other side of the globe: "If one should desire to know whether a kingdom is well governed, or if its morals are good or bad, the quality of its music will furnish the answer."[10]

That the tones of music communicate emotions has been established in more recent times in works such as Gurney's *The Power of Sound* (1880), John Hosper's *Meaning and Truth in the Arts* (1946), Leonard Meyer's *Emotion and Meaning in Music* (1960), and a number of other works. Certainly music is more than just "sounds." And if music does communicate, then we might well ask of each piece, *what* is it communicating?

Deryck Cooke, the British musicologist and author of *The Language of Music*, affirms that highly specific emotions are conveyed by music. These can be recognized, identified, and even classified. Cooke's argument that music is a language of the emotions is strongly supported in his book by hundreds of examples ranging from plainsong to Stravinsky. The creative act in music is, says Cooke, "the transformation of a complex of emotions into musical form." Repetitively, different musicians express the same emotions through similar musical forms, styles, and even specific melodies. For example, Cooke demonstrates that a phrase of just two notes (the minor sixth of the scale falling to the fifth) conveys a very similar emotion in specific parts of the music of Josquin, Morley, Bach, Mozart, Schubert, Mussorgsky, Verdi, Wagner, Schoenberg, Stravinsky, Britten, and others.[11]

At last, today, some inkling of the true inner power locked within music and of the widespread nature of its effects are coming to be recognized once more. Music therapy, once used extensively by the ancients but shunned by nineteenth- and twentieth-century materialism, is again on the rise and has cured or helped in the treatment of mental and physical ailments such as hysteria, depression, anxiety, nervousness, insomnia, high blood pressure, headaches, asthma, brain damage, cancer tendency, heart weakness, Parkinson's disease, tuberculosis, and many other conditions of mental and physical dissonance.

Moreover, even if we are not ill, let us not forget that there is no limit to how far we can improve ourselves physically, mentally, and spiritually and that we can still use good music to—as the ancient philosophers would have put it—influence for the better the rhythm of our thoughts, the melody of our emotions, the harmony of our bodily health, our immunity from disease, and our grace of movement, thus improving the whole person. For in the view of the flautist and exponent of New Age music Tim Wheater, music "affects both body and psyche, and its potency has barely been tapped."

The mysteries of music have indeed barely been tapped. Even the once "hard" science of physics has now largely paralleled in its findings what the ancient wisdom has always told us about the nature of matter itself: that matter does indeed appear to be a form of crystallized tone. Underlying all of physics we discover the same laws of harmony and of frequency correspondence to be found in music. As H. P. Blavatsky put it over a century ago, "Atoms are called Vibrations in Occultism."[12]

And the idea that music exerts an objective influence upon life seems borne out by experiments into the effects of different

11

kinds of music upon plants. In studying the effects of music upon human beings, it is hard to be certain that the results are due to the objective effects of the sounds, since they may be caused by the individual's subjective reactions. In plant research, however, any effects of the music upon the plants are almost certainly due to the objective influence—good or bad—of the tones directly upon the cells and processes of the life-form. Such research has been carried out in America, in the former USSR, and in India, but the most well-known series of experiments were those of Dorothy Retallack at Temple Bell College, Denver, Colorado, in 1970, which attracted great media interest at the time.

Dorothy Retallack studied the effects of different types of music upon a wide variety of plants under strict laboratory conditions where all other conditions except the music were identical. Plants in silent control cabinets grew normally. Rock music stunted the growth and even killed the plants in some rock-exposed cabinets. Classical music, Indian ragas, and devotional music enhanced plant growth beyond that of the control groups. Amazingly enough, plants exposed to classical music even grew toward the speaker, as if toward light, and would even twine themselves around it. Plants exposed to rock music tended to grow away from the speaker.[13]

The fascinating and mysterious realms to which a study of the inner nature of music takes us are seemingly endless, and the subject is dealt with at length in my *The Secret Power of Music*.[14]

It is because of music's actual power over the physical world and because of its influence over character and civilization that the music of Beethoven takes on such significance. To study his works is not to study dry, academic facts concerning notes and musical structure, but it is to study consciousness and its changes. For if music is such a powerful a force, in revolutionizing it as he did, just what other wide-ranging and profound impacts must Beethoven have exerted upon humanity? For as the twentieth-century composer and author Cyril Scott wrote, "An innovation in musical style has invariably been followed by an innovation in politics and morals."[15] Beethoven is acknowledged to have been a great composer, but beyond the world of music, just how different might the world now be had he not lived? His aesthetics became the gospel of Romanticism, and the movement of Romanticism in all of the arts went on to change how many people thought and lived.

12

As the musician and esotericist Dane Rudhyar has written, "Music is the innermost layer, the body of power, the inner strength of civilization." And he continues:

> Civilization is born of Tone and perpetuates itself through the syntonic ritual celebrated day in and day out in the homes and temples of the race. This syntonic ritual must be understood again in its deep spiritual sense and performed not only perfunctorily or by lips, but with the energy of the Self pervading all tones . . . Vegetation and civilization; these are the two terms of a nearly perfect analogy . . . and music is to civilization what the flow of sap and magnetic growth are to the plant. Civilization patterns itself upon music, as the sand spread upon a vibrating disc falls into geometrical shapes under the impact of tones. [16]

What a whole new light such a perspective sheds on the meaning of what the great composers achieved. The great composers of the eighteenth, nineteenth, and twentieth centuries created music which transformed the consciousness of Western humanity, gradually and progressively bringing it into alignment with the spirit of the coming age of Aquarius in all its many forms and facets. Could it be that the composers and their music were preparatory—part of a plan conceived beyond the matter-world?

13

For no Golden Age such as many are expecting to come forth in Aquarius can ever appear spontaneously or out of the blue. It must be forged and won by men and women themselves; hence the necessity for their preparation. And hence the appearance of the mighty wave of great composers, who ultimately were composers of new thought-processes and new modes of perceiving and dealing with reality—not only Beethoven, but also J. S. Bach, Chopin, Handel, Haydn, Wagner, Liszt, Mozart, Mendelssohn, Mahler, Vaughan Williams, Rachmaninoff, Bruckner, and many others who each brought forth a portion of the music of the spheres.

One and all, they created their art with the conscious intent of helping those who heard it accelerate and raise their consciousness. Said Handel to a friend, "I should be sorry if I only entertained them; I wished to make them better." And in the words of J. S. Bach, "The aim and final reason of all music should be nothing else but the glory of God and the refreshment of the spirit." Mozart held with the Masonic belief that the purpose of art was to promote peace, brotherhood, and harmony in all who experienced it, and devoted his music to this cause. And, to quote just one such line from Beethoven, on the score of his stupendous *Missa Solemnis* he wrote: "From the heart, may it reach other hearts."

Beethoven, then, was a musical avatar, born to initiate new and higher vibrations of thought and feeling in the hearts of the people of his own day, of our day, and of untold centuries to come.

14

Whence Came the Music?

 AT FIRST SIGHT it seems so easy to say that Beethoven "composed" his music. But just what does this really mean? From where did his ideas actually originate? And, for that matter, where does any great music come from?

The materialist will answer that it comes from the neurons in the brain of the musician. There is a long-standing esoteric belief, however, that much great music is inspired by spiritual sources, who are able to "give" to the sufficiently attuned musician a portion of the music of the spheres. This basic idea surfaces in many cultures throughout history, such as in the tradition of the Muse of ancient Greece; in medieval paintings of St. Cecilia, the saint of music, depicted with an inspiring angel leaning over her shoulder; and in the Hindu concept of the Gandharvas, the angels who inspire music in humanity.

Musicians themselves have very often put on record their own belief that they had been inspired from beyond their own consciousness. There are many such accounts; for instance, Robert Schumann wrote music which he said had been dictated to him by angels, and certainly his wife, for one, believed him, saying after his death that, "It is in the music of Robert Schumann that the angels sing."[1] Handel, likewise, believed that his incredible masterpiece, the *Messiah*, was revealed to him. During its composition he felt that the gates of heaven had been opened to him and he was able to see and hear the sublime chorusing of divine beings. As he later declared: "I think I did see all Heaven before me and the great God Himself."[2] As though he was indeed the listener and recipient of the music rather than its creator, as the notes came to him, he was so moved that his tears flowed and blotted the ink. And the fact that a work of such unearthly quality, and also great length, was composed by Handel in but three weeks further attests to its being inspired. Why, three weeks is scarcely long enough to have written down the notes!

The English composer Cyril Scott also wrote quite specifically about occasions during which heavenly inspiration took place. Scott was in his heyday as a composer and acknowledged as among the greatest in England at the time, during the early decades of the twentieth century. In Debussy's estimate he was then "one of the rarest artists of the present generation."[3] In his book, *The Initiate in the Dark Cycle*, the third of a classic occult trilogy Scott always insisted to be a factual account, he records a fascinating description of revealed music taking place during a visit to the house of a spiritual Master in England:

16

> From far away I heard the strains of an organ with which
> was mingled the sound of voices so pure and ethereal as
> to suggest the chanting of a celestial choir, wafted on a
> peaceful evening breeze. The music was unlike any music
> I had heard before.

In the book, Scott continues his description of the music which was being heard clairaudiently, and then records the words of the Master who was present: "My Brother Koot Hoomi playing on His organ . . . and the voices you hear are those of the Gandharvas . . . Listen well, and remember, for one day you shall give forth such music to the world." [4] (Incidentally, Scott was acutely aware of the effects of music on the individual and society, and wrote the first modern, path-breaking book on the subject, *Music, Its Secret Influence Throughout the Ages.*[5])

It should, however, at this point be stressed that "received music" certainly does not mean that the composer who brings it forth has, like some trance medium, no control over what comes through. Far from it. The process is impossible unless the musician is musically educated and talented enough first to receive the sounds, then to comprehend them, and finally to organize and shape them into a work. It is a process of (usually unconscious) cooperation. That the musician was inspired takes nothing away from his or her own achievement at all: a person truly *must* be a great artist in order to receive great art. Before we can receive the "message," we must have mastered the medium, and we must in our own heart and soul be reaching and striving to bring forth such great works.

All kinds of musicians, not only classical composers, have some experience of this. For example, singer/songwriter Van Morrison has stated:

> There are certain songs that I do write that way, particularly the *Astral Weeks* album. All the material on that album, and a lot of my early albums, were just channelled. They just came through. I mean, I'd get whole lines, whole verses just coming through. And it's almost like automatic writing—*not* automatic writing, I want to emphasize that—but similar. I'd just write them down. I got whole songs like that.[6]

17

There are more than a few signs of such inspiration in Beethoven. For example, so transcendent are the strains of the tremendous *Eroica* Symphony that it is not uncommon to find illumined musicologists speaking of it as something surely inspired from the beyond. Beethoven's sketches for the *Eroica* still exist, and from them the genesis and evolution of the work can be traced. Of them, the respected musicologist Ernest Newman said: "Here, more than anywhere else, do we get that curious feeling that in his greatest works Beethoven was 'possessed'—the mere human instrument through which a vast musical design realized itself in all its marvelous logic."[7] In his *Sketches of Eroica*, Gustav Nottebohn was also of the opinion that in composing his third symphony, the *Eroica*, Beethoven must have been veritably "possessed."[8] Berlioz also declared of Beethoven's Eighth Symphony that its pattern was formulated in heaven and dropped into the brain of its composer.[9]

This tallies with Beethoven's own best account of how he received his musical ideas. This account is in a letter of 1823 to Louis Schlosser, which shows that the process of composing was a cooperative venture combining Beethoven's initial reception of the basic themes with his own hard work to develop them into a coherent piece:

> I carry my thoughts about me for a long time, before I write them down. Meanwhile my memory is so tenacious that I am sure never to forget, not even in years, a theme that has once occurred to me. I change many things, discard and try again until I am satisfied. Then, however, there begins in my head the development in every direction . . . and there remains for me nothing but the labor of writing it down, which is quickly accomplished when I have the time . . .
>
> You will ask where my ideas come from. I cannot say for certain. They come uncalled, sometimes independently, sometimes in association with other things. It seems to me that I could wrest them from Nature herself with my own hands, as I go walking in the woods. They come to me in the silence of the night or in the early morning, stirred into being by moods which the poet would translate into words, but which I put into sounds; and these go through my head ringing and singing and storming until at last I have them before me as notes.[10]

A cautionary note about inspiration is necessary here for the musicians and artists of today. We must always be aware of how active a party Beethoven was in the composing process, as is evident from his words above. We frequently find today that those who are open to a nonmaterialist worldview nevertheless harbor erroneous concepts of the real nature of divine inspiration. A great deal of contemporary "channeling," whether of spoken or written messages or of music, has, in fact, nothing to do with divine guidance, but is instead a low and unwholesome form of spiritualism. More often than not, those who believe they have been singled out for special guidance are, unfortunately, the victims of their own overactive imaginations and of what in esotericism is called *glamour*, which in this context means the susceptibility of the imperfect human ego to self-aggrandizement. There is, unfortunately, a lot of what is simply self-delusion in the psychic movement.

True guidance from above has nothing to do with spiritualism (or what is today called *channeling*). Rather, it has to do with the sacred adventure of achieving oneness with the Mind of God. This takes work to achieve—and effort, determination, and a genuine commitment to self-growth.

This hard truth parallels the teachings of the great yogis to their disciples to avoid the allure of *siddhis* or "supernatural powers." Those who seek these above all else may acquire them, but may in the process be sidetracked from the only truly worthwhile goal— union with the Godhead. Similarly, I have observed that musicians and psychics who become obsessive about being "guided" invariably do start to hear voices, but the voices they hear are likely those of their own unconscious. Thus they are of an unhealthy "forced" psychological nature rather than of divine value.

Divine inspiration can take place, but it is not to be found through a passive "opening up" as in channeling, nor through an obsessive seeking after such inspiration. The best and most practical way to win such help is to work creatively on one's compositions as though they depended in their entirety upon one's own efforts for their conception and completion—for indeed they do. Leave otherworldly and impractical hopes for guidance quite aside. If it is to come, such aid will come through one's own work and abilities, and one may not be aware of being guided at all. The creative process is, as the saying goes, ninety percent perspiration. We need only put in our ninety percent, and the other ten percent will look after itself!

Whatever the manner of true inspiration coming from beyond ourselves, from the present writer's experience it enters one's consciousness in a manner very similar to telepathy—for I have also had the interesting experience of acting as "receiver" for telepathic experiments conducted by parapsychologists. And such receptions "flash," as it were, in the mind, as though static electricity had been connected to us from its source and discharged in a split second. Like one's recollections of a dream upon awakening, after a few moments the memory can be lost. So it is very interesting that from boyhood Beethoven was in the habit of jotting ideas into a sketchbook whenever they came to him. He carried a sketchbook

19

with him constantly. Beethoven also advised other composers to use sketchbooks, because, he said, "In this way not only is one's own imagination stimulated but *one learns also to pin down immediately the most remote ideas.*"[11] These are my italics, for I believe this line gives profound insight into why Beethoven was so successful in tapping the music of the spheres. From boyhood he trained himself as a cooperative, highly attuned "receiving station" for inspiration at any hour of the day or night.

Ultimately, I am suggesting, Beethoven's music is far more than the creation of any mortal. It is "given" music, intended for all of us, a gift through the use of which the consciousness of the race can evolve. Originating, I believe, beyond the physical universe, Beethoven's music was given to humanity from on high.

PART II

The Man

I would have ended my life—The only thing that held me back was my art. For indeed it seemed impossible to leave this world before I had produced all the works that I felt the urge to compose; and thus I have dragged on this miserable existence— truly wretched for so susceptible a body, which can be thrown by a sudden change from the best condition to the very worst.— Patience, they say, is what I must now choose for my guide, and I have done so—I hope my determination will endure until it pleases the inexorable Parcae to break the thread. Perhaps I shall get better, perhaps not; I am ready.—Forced to become a philosopher already in my twenty-eighth year,—oh it is not easy, and for the artist much more difficult than for anyone else.—Almighty God, who looks down into my innermost soul, you see into my heart and you know that it is filled with love for humanity and a desire to do good.

—BEETHOVEN, TESTAMENT OF 1802[1]

Before the Eroica

 THE LESSONS OF ADVERSITY are sometimes learned from an early age. Beethoven's upbringing was far from perfect. The family, though of quite cultured Moselle stock, never had a great deal of money. Maria Magdelena, Beethoven's mother, was warm and loving ("My best friend," Beethoven called her[2]). But she could not totally shield him from his father, a court musician who had taken to drink in the face of misfortune, and who sometimes beat young Ludwig.

When Ludwig was five, his father, Johann, gave him his first music lessons. It has since been suggested that he did so out of selfish motives, hoping to exploit his son as a child prodigy. A long-standing belief has it that to this end he claimed that the boy had been born two years later than he actually had. The truth is that the confusion was inexplicably Beethoven's own. As a result, even into maturity Beethoven believed that he had been born in 1772, and not, as was the case, in 1770.

It is nonetheless true that Johann von Beethoven could be a cruel taskmaster. It is hardly short of miraculous that young Ludwig grew up to love music, considering the conditions under which he was first taught it: at times locked in the cellar by his drunken father as a "punishment," at other times forced to practice at all hours to the point that he would weep while playing.

A schoolfriend, Wurzer, later recalled "Luis" at this age as follows: "Apparently his mother was already dead at the time [actually, she was alive, but unable to cope with her family], for Luis von Beethoven was distinguished by uncleanliness, negligence, etc. Not a sign was to be discovered in him of that spark of genius which glowed so brilliantly in him afterwards."[3] Others recollected young Ludwig as a withdrawn, solitary, lonely figure, shy of social contact and unable to learn anything at school. (These are all classic symptoms of the badly raised gifted child.)

Within a year of commencing music lessons, however, Beethoven had made swift progress with the piano and the violin. Though not in actuality the child prodigy legend has it that his father sought to display to the world after the manner of Mozart, Beethoven adhered tenaciously to his practicing, and in his early teens something of his inner talent did begin to appear. At the age of eleven he left school to concentrate fully upon music. Within a year he had published his first composition.

At the age of sixteen, Beethoven traveled to Vienna and met the thirty-one-year-old Mozart. Vienna was the musical center of Europe; several orchestras were based there, and all the best Viennese families nurtured chamber music. But after only two weeks there, his mother's illness and impending death from tuberculosis unfortunately forced Beethoven to cut short his stay and return home. Five years later he was to become the student of Haydn, even as Mozart had been. But for the time being, the young composer had enough troubles at home to keep him occupied. Still only seventeen, his mother was now dead, and his father's alcoholism worsened. So in 1789 Beethoven went to his father's employer and requested, and obtained, half of his father's salary, to be paid to Ludwig as guardian and manager of the family. Dutifully, he looked after the family consisting of an alcoholic father, two younger brothers, and a short-lived infant sister for five years. He was not free to return to Vienna until November, 1792. He was by then in his early twenties, determined to study, experiment, and bring his creative faculties to their full maturity as a pianist and composer.

One aspect of Beethoven's life during his teens and twenties of particular interest to the esoteric student is that many of his closest friends and associates were Freemasons, and others were members of the Bavarian Illuminati.

Freemasonry in those days was not so much the insiders' network by which to advance one's career that it often tends to be nowadays, but was still a young and vital organization, genuinely concerned with the development of character and with fostering universal emancipation. The Illuminati were an offshoot movement from mainstream Freemasonry, founded in 1776 by Adam Weishaupt and others. At first sight the Illuminati shared similar goals with the Masons, and many individuals became members of both orders, believing the two to be complementary in purpose. Only after a number of exposures in 1784–86 was the true nature of the Illuminati revealed. The organization consisted of a series of concentric circles of initiation and membership, and the real goals of its inner-core members were virtually the antithesis of those of Freemasonry. Adam Weishaupt and his closest workers were in fact totally opposed to religion, seeking rather to stamp it out, and their ultimate goal was apparently world domination to be achieved through secretly infiltrating the echelons of power.

In the twentieth century the story of the Illuminati has caught the imaginations of many, such as in Robert Anton Wilson's and Robert Shea's *Illuminatus!* trilogy. The word *Illuminati* has become synonymous with the idea of a collection of anonymous evil men secretly plotting conspiracies on a global scale. It must be borne in mind, however, that many of the actual nineteenth-century Illuminati members were themselves altruistic and quite ignorant of the order's true goals.

In Beethoven's day Freemasonry was also something of a threat to the established order, but for the opposite reason. Masonry supported democracy and human rights, such as are more than hinted at in Beethoven's opera, *Fidelio*. But Europe was almost entirely ruled at that time by monarchical systems of power. Nevertheless, many prominent people of the day were Masons, and many major movements and historical events of the eighteenth and nineteenth centuries were influenced by Masons working either overtly or from behind the scenes. The American Revolution is a case in point: Washington and his chiefs of staff, as well as many of the signers of the Declaration of Independence, were reputed to be members of the order.

Mozart was a Freemason, and his later music was consistently influenced by the order. *The Magic Flute*, for example, is a

Masonic piece of music through and through. Masonry is infused into Mozart's music not only through Masonic spiritual or moral ideals contained within the operas he composed, but also in the numerological and tonal symbology half-hidden in the music itself. Many of Mozart's Masonic friends and associates were also Illuminati, and it is not impossible that Mozart might have joined the Illuminati himself. Goethe was another great artistic mind of Beethoven's day who was also both a Mason and an Illuminist.

It is against this background that we note with interest Beethoven's own association with Masons and Illuminists. Christian Gottlob Neefe, the German composer, organist, and conductor who was Beethoven's tutor throughout his teens and early twenties (the 1780s and early 1790s) was a leader of the Illuminati in Bonn. Yet Beethoven gained greatly from his close association with Neefe, and not only musically. Neefe introduced the young musician to those ideals of brotherhood, universal liberty, and the spiritual progress of civilization which both Freemasons and many well-intentioned Illuminists believed in. If Neefe did have darker aspects of character, or was privy to the real goals of the Illuminati, then Beethoven seems not to have been exposed to them. Other Illuminati members known to Beethoven included his pupil, friend, and biographer Ferdinand Ries, his Bonn publisher Nikolaus Simrock, Johann Joseph Eichoff, Bonn's Court Marshall von Schall, and Johann Peter Eichoff; one comes across these names a number of times in detailed biographies of Beethoven.

When the truth about the Illuminati was exposed in 1784–86 —that its leaders sought to overthrow the states of Europe—its lodges were outlawed and forced to dissolve. Some lodges attempted to reemerge under other guises, however. It is common to hear even modern-day conspiracy theorists talking about the Illuminati as a secret elite still in existence and still holding high positions of economic and political power. It must be said, however, that such claims are unsubstantiated. There is as yet no positive evidence that the Bavarian Illuminati *per se* survived even into the 1800s. But lodges certainly did continue under various guises until the late 1790s. For their part, the Bonn group reemerged in the 1790s as a "Reading Society" of thirteen members, a number which soon swelled to over a hundred, including a number of Beethoven's friends and acquaintances. It was this "Reading Society" that commissioned, in 1790, one of Beethoven's earliest works, the *Cantata on the Death of Emperor Joseph II.* One key member of the society was Count Waldstein, who became Beethoven's intimate friend and patron and to whom the wonderful Piano Sonata in C Major of 1803–4 is dedicated.

Beethoven's close association as a young man with those believing in Masonic ideals had an influence upon him which was to be lifelong, its echoes still unmistakable in the choral movement of the Ninth Symphony. The absorption of Masonic ideals aided Beethoven in the development of his own spiritual and moral views and his belief in the basic good of humanity. Masonic thinking also emerges in Beethoven's own view of the role of the arts as a fundamental method of promoting brotherhood, joy, and the ideal of universal freedom. As Freemason L. F. Lenz wrote, music should "inculcate feelings of humanity, wisdom and patience, virtue and honesty, loyalty to friends, and finally an understanding of freedom."

When Beethoven became free to return to Vienna in 1792, his Illuminati tutor, Neefe, was replaced by the great Franz Joseph Haydn. Haydn was also a Freemason, having been introduced to the order by Mozart. While in Vienna, Beethoven lived for several years with the noble Lichnowsky family at their invitation, Prince Karl Lichnowsky also being a member of the order. From 1800, Lichnowsky granted Beethoven the invaluable gift of an annual stipend of six hundred florins, which gave him the freedom to concentrate entirely on composing.

It is unclear whether Beethoven himself joined Freemasonry, or whether its influence upon him was less direct, coming through his association with so many of its members. Karl Holz, his violinist friend, did state that Beethoven joined the order, but there is no further evidence for this. The question is largely academic in any case, for even if he were not a member, Beethoven had so many friends who were Masons that he must have learned something of its philosophy; on the other hand, if he did become a member, it would have been characteristic of him to have remained very much an independent, free spirit.

The growth of Freemasonry and the Illuminati in Beethoven's time were symptomatic of a broader trend toward self-assertion and individuality in the worlds of politics, philosophy, religion, and art.

This trend was in contradiction to the general subservience of the individual to class structures, to monarchs, to the Church, and to tradition, such as had been the case in earlier centuries. This resurrection of conscious individuality was influenced vibrationally, and in other ways, by the early preparatory influence of the coming New Age of Aquarius. As this book will indicate, it was the destiny of Beethoven to be this resurrection's most important musical spokesman, both in his music and in his life. His music sounded out in tone the story of the individual on the Path of soul-evolution. In life Beethoven looked up to no mortal and was in many ways the first truly freelance composer in Western music.

Beethoven's radical independence of thought also sealed him off from the more outwardly revolutionary and subversive tendencies of his time. While the Illuminati and others worked behind the scenes to foment revolution throughout Europe, Beethoven's interest was apparently not engaged. Once he stated laconically, "I believe that so long as an Austrian can get his brown ale and his little sausages, he is not likely to revolt."[4]

As the eighteenth century approached its close, Beethoven was entering his late twenties. He was by now a musician of obvious and outstanding promise, both as a composer and as a pianist. In character he was powerful, confident, and extremely self-assertive. But his forceful ego tended to advance its own personal will rather more than that of its Maker. Beethoven's words in a letter to Court Secretary Von Zmeskall in 1798 reveal something of his real attitude showing through the humor: "The devil take you. I don't want to know anything about your whole system of ethics. *Power* is the morality of men who stand out from the rest, and it is also mine."[5]

And Beethoven *was* powerful. His compositions were not as yet of a quality to rank him with Mozart or Haydn, yet while even musical geniuses such as these ranked as servants of the nobility, Beethoven entered the high society of Vienna without deference or constraint. In public contests on the piano, he invariably emerged the victor. His irrepressible force of character caused even many among the nobility to accept him as at least an equal. He was nobody's lackey or paid entertainer, but came as himself, as Beethoven, expecting to be accepted as such—and he was.

In later years he would be the champion of humanity, composing to exalt all people, and he would strive daily to act as the

28

servant of God. Yet in his early twenties, feeling his inner power and realizing his musical potential, his goals were at first those of personal fame and personal glory. Inasmuch as his greatest music would concern itself with the sublimation of human will to a higher purpose, his major compositions could never have come forth if Beethoven had remained forever self-oriented.

This sublimation of the human will to the Greater Will is the prime challenge of the spiritual Path. In fact, this transference of one's allegiance from self to Self, and to God, *is* the essence of the spiritual Path. All other aspects of this Path—all practices, all tests and trials, all teachings and disciplines, and all of the love and the adversity are a part of the great drama of the gradual fusing of the mortal, lesser self with that which is immortal and immutable.

But in order to become one with God, the soul itself must first possess an identity, rounded out and matured as a worthy offering to give back to its Creator. The lukewarm personality, "neither hot, nor cold,"[6] does not have anything to offer to God or to the Path. But both the "hot" (determinedly good soul) and the "cold" (determinedly bad soul) have much to offer, because even the radically bad soul has developed a strong ego, so that if the soul is turned about and converted, the powerful ego, now surrendered to the Supreme, will be a great driving force on the Path. The lukewarm individual, lost in the mass consciousness, has no flame of willpower to offer to God, whereas the personality of powerful will, once having surrendered the lesser will to the Greater, has everything.

29

The misdirected self-will of the mortal ego is the core source of all that separates us from God and Reality. It is the source of pride, interpersonal strife and dislike, hardness of heart, disobedience to God, jealousy, greed, and all sense of disunity, mortal problems, and *maya*. Hence the core challenge of the Path: can the mortal ego agree to "die," that it might live again and forever in Christ consciousness? In his early twenties, Beethoven's ego had not yet done so. But the story of his ensuing years is one of the greatest examples of a person's overcoming the lesser self and thus winning a spiritual victory.

Beethoven's heart, touched by his Higher Self, was already anything but devoid of altruistic love for humanity. Intimations of the spiritual mission which lay ahead grew in him daily; yet still he could be exceedingly arrogant. In 1801 he referred to his friends as "merely instruments on which to play when I feel inclined."[7] These same friends were often victims of Beethoven's moods and outbursts, though afterwards he could be deeply penitent and apologetic. The young Beethoven displayed traits reminiscent of the lives of many saints and sages in the years before the full realization of their life-mission came upon them. As in the case of the young St. Francis, Beethoven's episodes of evening merriment with his young friends alternated with periods of solitary, solemn contemplation or wonder at the glory of life. Though as yet he did not know precisely where it would lead him, he studied and practiced his music for long hours. Of one thing he was certain: an almost infinite potential was his to express in music, if he remained true and faithful to his art.

In appearance the young Beethoven was short, broad, and black-haired, with a wide forehead and chin. His eyes are said to have been very expressive. Though he dressed most smartly at this age, later he was to become more negligent in appearance as he became more solitary and the direction of his attention more otherworldly. Often cold and haughty to strangers and of uncultured manners, Beethoven was described by Italian composer Luigi Cherubini as "an unlicked bear."[8] But usually his magnetic strength of personality and musical genius attracted admirers more than his uncouthness repelled them.

Mixing in Vienna's social life, the youthful Beethoven was always in love with one pretty girl or another, and at times thought of starting a family of his own. Once, his feelings were deep enough for him to propose, but he was refused. His friend, Franz Wegeler, amusingly records that though Beethoven's passions were always of the highest degree, they "left impressions as little deep as were those made upon the beauties who had caused them."[9]

At this stage in his life Beethoven still hoped to be a virtuoso pianist, but this dearest hope was soon to crash forever. At first he dismissed the problem as imagination or absent-mindedness, but within a year or two of its onset, the great, glaring truth could only be faced in horror and painfully acknowledged: *He was becoming deaf!* He, whose very *life* lay in music!

The first problematic signs appeared around 1794, but by 1800, when Beethoven was twenty-nine, the reality of encroaching deafness was unmistakable. Because when addressed from a

31

Beethoven in 1800, at the age of twenty-nine

distance Beethoven often did not hear and respond, he acquired a reputation for arrogance. To avoid the embarrassment of people discovering his affliction, he began to abstain from all social gatherings, becoming as much a recluse as possible. Only to his very closest friends could he bring himself to reveal the tragedy.

A letter from Beethoven to his friend, Karl Amenda, dated July 1, 1801, reveals his growing despair: "How often would I like to have you here with me, for your B is leading a very unhappy life and is at variance with Nature and his Creator. Many times already I have cursed Him for exposing His creatures to the slightest hazard, so that the most beautiful blossom is thereby often crushed and destroyed. Let me tell you that my most prized possession, *my hearing*, has greatly deteriorated."[10] At first, the worst thing to Beethoven about his malady was social embarrassment, not the disruption of his music, and he continued in the letter: "I beg of you to keep the matter of my deafness a profound secret *to be confided to nobody no matter who it is.*"[11]

The degree of the deafness did not increase swiftly, however. For ten more years Beethoven was able to perform as solo pianist in the concert hall and could still hear speech or music unaided and clear enough for most purposes, if he was not too far from the source of sound. But in its early years, the deafness itself was less serious than was the bleak despair and harrowing anxiety to which it led him. For Beethoven, this malady, ever worsening, was an unrelenting source of anguish. Whatever dreams he had held of life now seemed shattered into fragments.

Around this time there ended what is now regarded as Beethoven's first period of musical creation. But such was his unstoppable will and attunement to the music of the spheres that even the tragedy of deafness marked the beginning of an infinitely greater, second period.

The loss of one's perceptive faculties has symbolic and mythical overtones in mysticism. In raja yoga, concentration and samadhi are achieved partly by cutting off one's awareness of the senses. In the early stages this can be assisted not only by closing the eyes, but also by putting the fingers over the ears and by concentrating one's attention upon a mantra or visualization. When all awareness of the outer world is gone, meditation becomes potently effective and samadhi, the experience of divine union, closer to attainment.

In *Music: The Keynote of Human Evolution*,[12] Corinne Heline writes: "Ancient [Chinese] tradition always depicts a true Chinese musician as blind. Esoterically, this implies that his gift of the divine art is so completely guided by, and dedicated to, hosts of celestial guardians that both his sight and consciousness are focused above and beyond the objective world." The same tradition held true in the West, Carolan and so many other great Irish and Scottish harpists of the past having been blind. On the one hand, there was a practical reason for this: children born blind or who became blind were, if the family could afford it, taught to play the harp so that they did not need to beg for a living. Nevertheless, an air of mystique came to surround these blind musicians, and in the case of harpists such as Carolan, who was so amazingly talented and prolific, it does indeed seem that the loss of his sight heightened his ability to create and perform in the world of sound.

Beethoven, having retreated from almost all social contact, now dwelt alone. But from the depths of despair he found the seeds of a new determination that there would yet be something to live for. Audible sound, which is called *ahata* in Sanskrit, was becoming progressively lost to him, but it was as though he began to hear, deep within himself, the physically inaudible *anahata* or unstruck Cosmic Sound. To Wegeler he now wrote:

> Plutarch has shown me the path of *resignation*. If it is at all possible, I will bid defiance to my fate, though I feel that for as long as I live there will be moments when I shall be God's most unhappy creature—I beg you not to say anything about my condition to anyone, not even to Lorchen. I live entirely in my music; and hardly have I completed one composition when I have already begun another. At my present state of composing, I often produce three or four works at the same time.[13]

33

He was still young, physically vigorous, and darkly handsome, and between the summer and November of 1801, a change came which infused Beethoven with the will to live and to absorb all the beauty that the world could bring to him. Love! How it infuses life into the soul as though by its very stirring of the heart. Beethoven wrote again to Wegeler, his friend from his home town of Bonn:

> I am now leading a slightly more pleasant life, for I am mixing more with my fellow creatures... This change has been brought about by a dear charming girl who loves me and whom I love. After two years I am again enjoying a few blissful moments; and for the first time I feel that— marriage might bring me happiness. Unfortunately, she is not of my class—and at the moment—I certainly could

not marry. . . Oh, if only I could be rid of [the deafness]
I would embrace the whole world—

The letter continues with a passage which we can surely interpret as the awakening within him of the path of spiritual attainment,
in which he writes of *the goal which he feels but cannot describe*:

My youth, yes, I feel it, is only just beginning, for was I
not always a sickly fellow? For some time now my physical
strength has been increasing more and more, and therefore
my mental powers also. Every day brings me nearer to the
goal which I feel but cannot describe. *And it is only in
that condition* [i.e., of continual soul-progress] *that your
Beethoven can live* [my italics]. There must be no rest. . . If
only I can be partially liberated from my affliction, then—
I will come to you as a complete and mature man, and
renew our old feelings of friendship. You will find me as
happy as I am fated to be on this earth, not unhappy—no,
that I could not bear—I will seize Fate by the throat; it
shall certainly not bend and crush me completely—Oh, it
would be so lovely to live a thousand lives.[14]

34

The "dear charming girl" of Beethoven's letter was probably
the noble-born Giulietta Guicciardi, who was taking lessons from
him. His new sense of hope also sprang from the fact that he
was undertaking new treatment for his deafness and had some
expectations of at least a partial cure.

But the summer of 1802 found Beethoven in an unimproved,
and in fact worsened, condition. Added to this tragic disappointment was the marriage of Giulietta to one Count Gallenberg, a
man of her own class. With this double blow to his mind, the
body also deteriorated. By autumn the composer was gravely ill.
Either the illness or a despair that led him even to contemplate
taking his own life led Beethoven to feel his end to be near. It is
from this background that the Heiligenstadt Testament comes to
us, the most famous and moving document of Beethoven's life.
Dated October 6, 1802, it reads:

O my fellow men, who accuse me of being malevolent,
stubborn or even misanthropic, how greatly do you wrong

me. For you do not know the secret reason which makes me seem that way to you. Ever since my childhood my heart and soul have been imbued with the tender feeling of goodwill; and I have always been inclined to accomplish great things. But just think, for the last six years I have been afflicted with an incurable complaint which has been made worse by incompetent doctors. From year to year my hopes of being cured have gradually been shattered and finally I have been forced to accept the prospect of *a permanent infirmity* (whose cure will take years or, perhaps, be impossible). Though born with a fiery, active temperament, even susceptible to the diversions of society, I was soon compelled to withdraw myself, to live life alone. If at times I tried to forget all this, oh how harshly I was flung back by the doubly sad experience of my bad hearing. Yet it was impossible for me to say to people, "Speak louder, shout, for I am deaf." Ah, how could I possibly admit an infirmity in the *one sense* which ought to be more perfect in me than in others, a sense which I once possessed in the highest perfection, a perfection such as few in my profession enjoy or ever have enjoyed.—Oh I cannot do it; therefore forgive me when you see me draw back when I would have gladly mingled with you. Moreover my misfortune pains me doubly, inasmuch as it leads to my being misjudged. For me there can be no relaxation in human society, no refined conversations, no mutual confidences. I must live quite alone and may creep into society only as often as sheer necessity demands; I must live like an outcast. If I approach near to people a hot terror seizes upon me, and I fear being exposed to the danger that my condition might be noticed. Thus it has been during the last six months which I have spent in the country. By ordering me to spare my hearing as much as possible, my intelligent doctor almost fell in with my own present frame of mind, though sometimes I ran counter to it by yielding to my desire for companionship. But what a humiliation for me when someone standing next to me heard a flute in the distance and *I heard nothing*, or someone heard a *shepherd singing* and again I heard nothing . . .

35

And it is now that the deep inner nature of Beethoven as a soul born to discipleship to the Will of God reveals itself to us:

> Such incidents almost drove me to despair;—a little more of that and I would have ended my life—The only thing that held me back was *my art*. For indeed it seemed to me impossible to leave this world before I had produced all the works that I felt the urge to compose; and thus I have dragged on this miserable existence—truly wretched for so susceptible a body, which can be thrown by a sudden change from the best condition to the very worst. — *Patience*, they say, is what I must now choose for my guide, and I have done so—I hope my determination will remain firm to endure until it pleases the inexorable Parcae [Fates] to break the thread. Perhaps I shall get better, perhaps not; I am ready.—Forced to become a philosopher already in my twenty-eighth year,—oh it is not easy, and for the artist much more difficult than for anyone else.—Almighty God, who looks down into my innermost soul, you see into my heart and you know that it is filled with love for humanity and a desire to do good . . .

And to his brothers he added:

> Urge your children to be *virtuous*, for virtue alone can make a man happy. Money cannot do this. I speak from experience. It was virtue that sustained me in my misery. It was thanks to virtue and also to my art that I did not put an end to my life by suicide . . . If [death] comes before I have had the chance to develop all my artistic capacities, it will still be coming too soon despite my harsh fate, and I should probably wish it later—yet even so I should be happy, for would it not free me from a state of endless suffering?—Come *when* thou wilt, Death, and I shall face thee with courage.— Farewell and do not wholly forget me when I am dead; I deserve this from you, for during my lifetime I was thinking of you often and of ways to make you happy—please be so—
> LUDWIG VAN BEETHOVEN

36

Four days later, Beethoven left Heiligenstadt, a little village outside Vienna, and added the tragic postscript:

Heiglnstadt [Heiligenstadt], October 10th, 1802. Thus I bid thee farewell—and indeed sadly.—Yes, that fond hope —which I brought here with me, to be cured to a degree at last—this I must now wholly abandon. As the autumn leaves fall and wither, likewise—that hope has faded for me. I am leaving here—almost in the same condition as I arrived—Even that high courage—which has so often inspired me on fine summer days—has vanished—Oh Providence—do but grant me one day *of pure joy*—For so long now the inner echo of real joy has been unknown to me—Oh when—Oh when, Oh, Divine One—shall I be able to hear and feel this echo again in the temple of Nature and in contact with humanity—Never?—No—Oh, that would be too hard.[15]

Confirmation that the Testament may have been written as he contemplated suicide comes from a letter written to Wegeler eight years later:

I should be happy, perhaps one of the happiest of men, if the demon had not taken possession of my ears. If I had not read somewhere that a man may not voluntarily part with his life so long as a good deed remains for him to perform, I should long ago have been no more—and indeed by my own hands. O, life is so beautiful, but to me it is poisoned.[16]

The Heiligenstadt Testament marked the nadir of Beethoven's despair. Thereafter he began to learn increasingly how to submit to his destiny, whatever it might be. And after all, one can imagine how nearly inconceivable it must have seemed to him not to live on in order to crystallize and put down on paper the new compositions which were already in his head. He knew that these were his greatest works so far—yet, ironically, only *he* could hear *this* music, and it was the rest of the world which was deaf to it. The idea of forsaking the world without penning the stupendous Third Symphony must indeed have seemed unthinkable.

And so he worked on. The Second Symphony was completed at Heiligenstadt; the Third pressed to come forth. Even the core ideas of the Fifth stem from this period. He must have felt tremendous satisfaction at what was now coming forth from his pen. His must have been an intense eagerness to climb the heights of ascending creativity he could sense ahead. To live with his fate was still far from easy. But for the sake of others, Beethoven went willingly to this crucifixion, and found that it led to the resurrection of the meaning of his life.

He now plunged into the composition of the magnificent Third Symphony, the *Eroica*. Its tones sang of individual heroism and victory. In its highest and truest level of interpretation, the symphony told of the individual soul's tests and trials on the Path, and of its courage, determination, and triumphant overcoming. Truly, nobody could have composed music of such individual heroism and such victory over tribulation unless they had first experienced the same firsthand in life.

Of Life and Love

IF THE HEILIGENSTADT TESTAMENT marked an emotional point lower than which it was impossible to fall, then the only way left for Beethoven to go was up. And as the early years of the nineteenth century unfolded, it became obvious that his increasing deafness was not, as might have been expected, detracting from his composing at all. Moreover, through his thirties and early forties, Beethoven could hear sufficiently for communication, if with difficulty, so that the condition did not wholly bar him from engaging in social life.

In fact, Beethoven was usually in love with one girl or another during these middle years. And though his loves may have been at least several, each of them during its span was genuine and deeply felt. Among the most important of these attachments were a series of three over the years with his pupils Giulietta Guicciardi, her cousin Countess Josephine von Deym, and finally with Josephine's sister, Countess Therese von Brunswick.

These three relationships, were, if anything, of ascending levels of seriousness. The first, to Giulietta, is probably the one referred to in a letter we have already quoted, in which he speaks of a "dear charming girl." The second, with Josephine, an attractive young widow of much finesse, spanned the years 1804 to 1806. Charlotte, the younger sister of Josephine, described the composer's visits as follows: "He comes every day and stays with Pepi [Josephine] for hours"; and a month later, "This is becoming a little dangerous . . . Beethoven is here almost every day."[1]

The big problem was their difference in class. Beethoven was of the common people, Josephine of the nobility, as indeed were her cousin Giulietta and her sister Therese. So Josephine's family would certainly have opposed the affair; but there was no ultimate reason why the two could not have married, and the reason for the relationship's eventual cooling is uncertain. Quite possibly, Josephine felt bound by duty to her four children. And being only recently widowed, Beethoven's entreaties may have come too soon.

From around 1806 or 1807, it was Josephine's sister, Therese, who captured the composer's heart. If not the equal of Josephine's beauty, Therese appears to have been the more attuned to him mentally, and by all accounts the fact that they did not marry was due not to her indecision but to vacillation on the part of Beethoven. One possible factor contributing to Beethoven's repeated inability to marry lies in his personal astrology, a subject examined in the next chapter.

However, it was in the company of Josephine and Therese that Beethoven returned for a while into the rounds of social gaiety. Simultaneously he thereby won an important moral victory over his deafness, determining to keep it a secret no longer. If it should be that the condition was incurable, then he would live with it as best he could.

Magnificent works now flooded forth. The period between 1805 and 1812 saw the creation of, to name only the most significant pieces: the opera *Fidelio* and its *Leonore No. 3* Overture; the *Appassionata* and F-sharp Major Piano Sonatas; the three *Rasumovsky* and the fine *Harp* and F Minor String Quartets; the Mass in C Major; the grand Fourth and Fifth Piano Concertos; his only Violin Concerto; and the Fourth, Fifth, Sixth, Seventh, and Eighth of the total nine symphonies.

Prior to the *Eroica*, Beethoven's works had been accomplished pieces, but similar in style and content to those of other contemporary musicians. In his second period, however, he revolutionized musical forms and styles, largely, we might conjecture, as a result of his new mental outlook. In a world of increasing deafness, to socialize with ease or to continue as a virtuoso pianist was impossible; but if his condition shattered his dreams of success in the outer world of society, it also caused him to turn within. And while human relationships came and went, Beethoven was discovering God, the eternal companion. This reorientation of his soul is, in my view, the primary reason for the higher level of composition in his second period creations. Even his innovations of style and form largely stem from a fundamental need to express through music new and deeper worlds of soul-experience. Whereas before he composed for himself, in his second period Beethoven was consciously striving to become the musical servant of God.

Beethoven's behavior was not always godlike, however. The reader will recall that Beethoven was receiving an annual stipend of six hundred florins from his most stalwart supporter, Prince Lichnowski. In October 1806, officers of Napoleon's army were guests at the prince's country seat, Gratz Castle. The prince promised that Beethoven would play for them. Beethoven refused—he would not play for officers of Napoleon! Lichnowski insisted. Beethoven again refused, locking himself into a room. Lichnowski broke down the door. At this, Beethoven grabbed a chair and was about to break it over the head of the prince when a third party intervened. Beethoven then ran out, furious, into the pouring rain. Instead of returning, he sent Lichnowski a message: "Prince! What you are, you are by chance and by birth. What I am, I am by myself. There have been, there will be thousands of princes. There is only one Beethoven."[2]

41

Beethoven's point may have been made, but Lichnowski also made a point by stopping the yearly six hundred florins. Financially as well as literally, in storming out of the castle, Beethoven had put himself out in the cold. For over a year he existed on the income from his works' performances and from giving lessons. A point was reached where it seemed he would have to leave Vienna to seek employment. Then the Viennese aristocracy rallied round; three wealthy patrons would provide a total of four thousand florins annually for the rest of his life, provided Beethoven remained in Vienna. This was no huge amount, but enough to free him to live on as a composer. Were it not for these three generous souls, humanity may never have received many of the works Beethoven went on to bring forth for us, for the annual grant once more freed him to concentrate on composition. Nevertheless, his finances were never much more than sufficient to cover basic needs, especially since Austrian currency had within a few years been devalued.

What pattern did a typical day in the life of Beethoven follow at this time? He would get up at dawn, have breakfast, and then go straight to his desk, where he would compose until midday. Specifically, he usually used the mornings for the largely mechanical activity of transcribing. The rest of the day then remained for the genesis, ordering, and developing of ideas. After lunch he liked to take a long walk, often not arriving back until late afternoon. Depending on where he was living at the time, his walk would either be through fields, woods, or several times around the city of Vienna. The evenings were spent in talking with friends and reading newspapers in taverns, in going to the theater, in playing music, or in doing more composing. Though he usually retired at about 10 P.M., if a flood of musical ideas overcame him as they sometimes did, he would stay up until late to write them down. Throughout the day, while walking alone or talking with friends, he would always have his notebook with him in which musical ideas and experiments could be jotted down and worked out whenever he felt the need.

42

His mental prowess and forceful personality were chiefly directed into his art, so that the organization of his more earthly affairs at times received scant attention. Others frequently had to manage his finances, business transactions, and even the running of his household. Visitors to the famed composer rarely found the man or the lifestyle they had expected. Major General Kyd discovered this for himself when he called on Beethoven in September, 1816. The great man was shaving when they arrived, which was always a major operation for him. He greeted Kyd and Dr. Bertolini with his face a mess of razor cuts, bits of paper, and daubs of soap. Major General Kyd took a seat, and it collapsed beneath him and sprawled him across the floor. Observing Beethoven's poverty, Kyd offered him two hundred ducats to compose a symphony, but stipulated that it should be composed in the more conventional style of Beethoven's earlier days. He should have known better than to impose any limitations whatsoever upon this composer. The next day, Beethoven, walking in the street with a friend, saw Kyd and exclaimed: "There's the man whom I threw downstairs yesterday!"[3]

Beethoven could be careful about his dress and general appearance, but increasingly as the years went on, while deeply involved in an important work (as he frequently was), he would allow his appearance to degenerate. When his head swam with the concentration of composing, to refresh himself, not prone to doing things in half-measures, he would empty a jug of water over his head, most of the water frequently ending up over the floor. In 1822, Johann Rochlitz, a music critic and friend of Beethoven, described him as giving the impression of being a "very able man reared on a desert island and suddenly brought fresh into the world."[4] The "desert island" reference is also reminiscent of Karl Czerny's first impression of Beethoven from nineteen years earlier. Beethoven was only about thirty-three at the time, but Czerny, coming as his pupil and then but a child, seeing a man attired in a hairy suit and with an unkempt growth of hair and beard, naturally thought he must be Robinson Crusoe!

Despite the many trying episodes during Beethoven's life, it would be wrong to believe that he was naturally a melancholy person. The majority of his works could not have been composed by a man without inner resources of joy and placidity of mind. Most of his letters are either quite natural and straightforward or, occasionally, actually exuberant. Those who knew him before his deafness became acute stated that among his close male friends, he would be "droll, lively, indeed, voluble at times, and fond of giving play to all the arts of wit and sarcasm."[5] Even afterwards, during his thirties, Beethoven is described by his friend Ignatz von Seyfreid to have been "merry, ready for any jest, happy, full of life, witty and not seldom satirical." True, his inherent stubbornness and lack of malleability caused some to find him very hard to get on with. Nor did his frustration at his deafness do anything to improve his temper. Yet his friends *were* and remained his friends precisely because they had seen beyond the mere exterior and were aware of the Real Man of his interior heart.

In his social relationships there were certain patterns which repeated themselves. Though having no wife or children of his own, Beethoven several times became attached to what might be called "surrogate families," becoming so close a friend as to live near or even with them and partaking of their life as though a family member. With women another pattern occurred even more

43

frequently: those he became attracted to were almost invariably unattainable in one way or another. Some, as we have seen, were of a higher class. Others were already married or courted by others, and so could only be his friends. A few who were eligible rejected him. The composer cannot be said to have enjoyed a normal, deep, lasting, and reciprocated courtship with any woman. Biographer Maynard Solomon may be correct when he comments, "It seems clear that there was some element of pretence or at least self-deception in Beethoven's continual series of flirtations which bordered upon, but never became, love affairs."[6]

One romantic episode in Beethoven's life was, however, of greater importance to him than any other. In this he perhaps even achieved for a short time a reciprocated and genuine relationship. In a concealed drawer after his death was found a letter addressed to an unnamed lady referred to by Beethoven as his "Eternally Beloved." (The term *Unsterbliche Geliebte* is usually translated literally, but not rationally, as "Immortal Beloved." The concept of eternalness is clearly what Beethoven intended.) This letter is a veritable outpouring of the composer's heart. It seems certain that it was written to a person with whom Beethoven came closer to uniting than with any other. Yet for well over a century the identity of the Eternally Beloved was to biographers either one of the great mysteries of Beethoven's life, or else, as often happened, her identity was incorrectly assumed on scant evidence. Only quite recently, in the late 1970s, following an impressive and detailed Sherlock Holmes-style investigation of the Eternally Beloved controversy, did Maynard Solomon in his biography of Beethoven put forth an extremely strong argument that Beethoven's Eternally Beloved was Antonie Brentano.[7]

Antonie von Birkenstock (1780–1869) was married at the age of eighteen to Franz Brentano, a Frankfurt merchant who was fifteen years her senior, and with whom she had four children. Franz was a loving and considerate husband, yet Antonie suffered many years of silent, unspoken unhappiness: she apparently could not return his deep love; furthermore, Brentano worked very long hours at his business. Antonie also missed her hometown of Vienna desperately, which she visited only every two years. So deep was her unhappiness and her sense of being unfulfilled that she suffered a number of periods of severe depression and physical illness prior to her meeting with Beethoven.

44

Then Antonie's father died in Vienna. Heartbroken, she returned with her husband to the city and eventually prevailed upon him to remain, as events turned out, for three years. It was through Bettina Brentano, her sister-in-law, a poetess who already knew Beethoven, that Antonie first called to visit the composer in May, 1810. His acquaintance with them led Beethoven to become close friends with the Brentano family—a deep friendship which extended not only to Antonie, but also to her husband, Franz. But at some time during 1811, the friendship with Antonie developed into something more. To Antonie, disappointed in life, Beethoven was representative of all that was high, noble, and fulfilling. We know that while she was ill in Vienna, he would visit regularly, seat himself at the pianoforte in her room without a word, and improvise; then he left as he had arrived, taking notice of no other person.

The weight of evidence suggests that it was Antonie who offered herself to Beethoven, being the first to voice the idea of marriage.[8] Considering his own deep love for her, this suggestion would have presented to the highly honorable and idealistic composer a serious dilemma of the soul. Not only was Antonie already married, but Franz was Beethoven's own good friend. The ecstasy and the agony of true love combined with the challenge of morality and honor are captured in the uniquely candid Eternally Beloved letter which, due to Maynard Solomon's research, we now know is from 1812, Beethoven's forty-second year.

The letter begins:

July 6, in the morning.

My angel, my all, my very self—Only a few words today and at that with pencil (with yours)—Not until tomorrow will my lodgings be definitely determined upon—what a useless waste of time—Why this deep sorrow when necessity speaks?—can our love endure except through sacrifices, through not demanding everything from one another; can you change the fact that you are not wholly mine, I not wholly thine?—Oh God, look out into the beauties of nature and comfort your heart with that which must be— Love demands everything, and that very justly—*thus it is to me with you, and to you with me.* But you forget so easily

45

that I must live *for me* and for you; if we were wholly united you would feel the pain of it as little as I—My journey was a fearful one; I did not reach here until 4 o'clock yesterday morning. Lacking horses the post-coach chose another route, but what an awful one; at the stage before the last I was warned not to travel at night; I was made fearful of a forest, but that only made me the more eager— and I was wrong. The coach must needs break down on the wretched road, a bottomless mud road. Without such postilions as I had with me I should have remained stuck in the road. Esterhazy, travelling the usual road here, had the same fate with eight horses that I had with four—Yet I got some pleasure out of it, as I always do when I successfully overcome difficulties—

Beethoven was writing of his journey from Prague to Teplitz, but note how his account is deeply suffused with the symbolism of a mythic rite of passage: the journey was "fearful"; he was warned of a forest, and not to travel at night; the mud was "bottomless," but he "successfully [overcame all the] difficulties." Maynard Solomon, who uncovered the identity of the Eternally Beloved and who has a background in psychoanalysis, attempts to relate the journey symbolically to Beethoven's conflicting emotions regarding Antonie's love. This theory may have validity, but the account of the journey also resonates strongly with the Path of the individual undergoing initiation, and the difficulties of the seeker on the road to the Self. Mircea Eliade, the world-renowned anthropologist, has written on the "difficult road leading to the center" which is found in many mythologies the world over; he summarizes the road as being "from the profane to the sacred, from the ephemeral and illusory to reality and eternity, from death to life, from man to the divinity." Eliade cites as examples the "Danger-ridden voyages of the heroic expeditions in search of the Golden Fleece, the Golden Apples; the Herb of Life, wanderings in labyrinths."[9] (Even Beethoven had to take "another route.")

We must beware of reading too much into these few lines which he jotted down hurriedly; nevertheless, they contain unmistakable impressions, conveyed unconsciously: images of Beethoven the overcomer, Beethoven the victor over life's adversities.

The coach journey becomes a concentrated representation of the spiritual Path.

Then, as the letter continues, the torn heart of Beethoven is laid bare for us:

> Now a quick change to things internal from things external. We shall surely see each other soon; moreover, today I cannot share with you the thoughts I have had during these last few days touching my own life—If our hearts were always close together, I would have none of these. My heart is full of so many things to say to you— ah—there are moments when I feel that speech amounts to nothing at all—Cheer up—remain my true, my only treasure, my all as I am yours. The gods must send us the rest, what for us must and shall be—
>
> Your faithful Ludwig
>
> Evening, Monday, July 6

47

> You are suffering, my dearest creature—only now have I learned that letters must be posted very early in the morning on Mondays—Thursdays—the only days on which the mail-coach goes from here to K.—You are suffering— Ah, wherever I am, there you are also—I will arrange it with you and me that I can live with you. What a life!!! thus!!! without you—pursued by the goodness of mankind hither and thither—which I as little want to deserve as I deserve it—Humility of man towards man—it pains me—and when I consider myself in relation to the universe, what am I and what is He—whom we call the greatest—and yet— herein lies the divine in man—I weep when I reflect that you will probably not receive the first report from me until Saturday—Much as you love me—I love you more—But do not ever conceal yourself from me—good night—As I am taking the baths I must go to bed—Oh God—so near! so far! Is not our love truly a heavenly structure, and also as firm as the vault of heaven?—

Good morning, on July 7.

Though still in bed, my thoughts go out to you, my Eternally Beloved, now and then joyfully, then sadly, waiting to learn whether or not fate will hear us—I can live only wholly with you or not at all—Yes, I am resolved to wander so long away from you until I can fly to your arms and say that I am really at home with you, and can send my soul enwrapped in you into the land of spirits— Yes, unhappily it must be so—You will be the more contained since you know my fidelity to you. No one else can ever possess my heart—never—never—Oh God, why must one be parted from own whom one so loves. And yet my life in V[ienna] is now a wretched life—Your love makes me at once the happiest and the unhappiest of men— at my age I need a steady, quiet life—can that be so in our connection? My angel, I have just been told that the mailcoach goes every day—therefore I must close at once so that you may receive the l[etter] at once.—Be calm, only by a calm consideration of our existence can we achieve our purpose to live together—Be calm—love me—today— yesterday—what tearful longings for you—you—you—my life—my all—farewell.—Oh continue to love me—never misjudge the most faithful heart of your beloved.

ever thine
ever mine
ever ours

L.[10]

In the weeks following the writing of the Eternally Beloved letter, Beethoven stayed with Antonie and Franz Brentano in Karlsbad and Franzensbad. We simply do not know exactly what took place at this time between the three, but Antonie and Franz did remain married and Beethoven remained their friend. Obviously either Antonie, or Beethoven, or both, could not bring themselves to break up the existing marriage. I believe that whatever Antonie's decision, Beethoven was ultimately not able to take this step at the expense of Franz and his family. Maynard Solomon writes that "in some way the trio managed to pass through the crisis into a new stage of their relationship. Passion had been sublimated into exalted friendship. Beethoven was visibly elated during these months, as evidenced by his correspondence and his productivity." But in late 1812 Franz decided that he could no longer put off returning to Frankfurt. Thus the Brentanos left Vienna. There is no record of Beethoven ever journeying to see them again, or of Antonie ever returning to Vienna.

Surviving descriptions of Beethoven in 1813 describe a man in mourning. He had "neither a decent coat nor a whole shirt" to wear, we are told, and became negligent to the point of being dirty.[11] He kept to himself almost exclusively and produced no work of note throughout the whole year. It was probably during this same year that a reported episode took place which some interpret as a strange kind of suicide attempt. While staying at the country palace of Countess Marie Erdödy, Beethoven disappeared and was presumed to have left. But he was eventually found in a distant part of the palace gardens—three days later. Some believed he had been intending to starve himself to death. If this was an attempt at suicide, then it was certainly a bizarre one. There may be another explanation altogether; now it is impossible to recover the truth. Perhaps he had simply wandered off and submitted himself to an indefinite period of dazed, solitary grief and ascetic contemplation.

The evidence for Beethoven's Eternally Beloved as having been Antonie Brentano is only circumstantial, it is true. And to tantalizingly confuse the issue, it so happens that his earlier love Josephine had recently been abandoned by a second husband and was also traveling somewhere at this time; it is not recorded where. About nine months after the time Beethoven wrote the letter, Josephine gave birth to a baby girl. Nevertheless, the case for Antonie is much stronger.

Antonie Brentano seems to have retained a place in Beethoven's heart for the rest of his life. Five years after their last meeting, he is thought to have caught sight of Antonie's daughter Maximiliane, which brought all the memories of the affair flooding back to him, and led to his writing down the diary note: "Love—yes, love alone can make your life happy! O God, let me find someone whose love I am allowed. Baden, 27 July, when M passed by and, I think, looked at me."[12] Perhaps it is not coincidental that his song cycle (a rarity for him) of 1816 was entitled *To The Distant*

49

Beloved. Certainly Maximiliane and Antonie Brentano were the only women to whom he dedicated any compositions during the 1820s (Beethoven's fifties)—the Piano Sonata in E Major, Op. 109 (1820), the English publication of the Piano Sonata in C Minor, Op. 111 (1821–22), and the Thirty-three Variations in C Major on a Waltz by Anton Diabelli, Op. 120 (1823). To the day he died, and through all his many moves of lodgings, Beethoven retained along with his memories a miniature portrait of Antonie and the Eternally Beloved letter.

In September 1816 Beethoven was visited by his nephew's schoolmaster, who also brought his two daughters. One of them overheard Beethoven and the schoolmaster talking as the party took a walk, and records these words from Beethoven: "Five years ago, he said, he had made the acquaintance of a person, union with whom he would have considered the greatest happiness of his life. It was not to be thought of, almost an impossibility, a chimera— nevertheless it is now as on the first day . . . It had never reached a confession, but he could not get it out of his mind."[13]

Following the Brentanos' departure, Beethoven entered into what has been called his "dry" period. No compositions of major importance were to come through him until the *Hammerclavier* Sonata, begun in 1817. Though other factors also helped cause this comparatively dry spell of several years' duration (as we shall recount in Chapter 10), the Eternally Beloved affair and its conclusion surely contributed. However, he had lived through a similarly critical period of nearly unbearable grief before, during the Heiligenstadt confrontation with his encroaching malady. Now, difficult though the years of 1813–18 were for him, they were once again to conclude in the emergence of a yet greater artist, and in what is arguably the most profound and advanced music yet composed.

Beethoven as a Sagittarian

 AGAIN BEETHOVEN had loved, and again he had lost. But again, the decision not to carry through to complete union in marriage was at least partly his own.

After Beethoven's death a friend of the Brunswick family, Fräulein Karoline Languider, claimed that his earlier relationship with Countess Therese Brunswick actually led to an engagement, and she continued:

> That was decidedly his profoundest love [she did not know of his affair with Antonie Bretano], and that it did not result in marriage, it is said, was due to the—what shall I call it— real artistic temperament of Beethoven, who, in spite of his great love, could not make up his mind to get married. It is said that Countess Therese took it greatly to heart.[1]

Why, we might well ask, could not this man of such forceful character "make up his mind to get married" when he so evidently loved Therese? (Her portrait which she gave him, painted by Lampi, always hung upon his wall.)

Conventional biographers have always been hard-put to explain such contradictions of Beethoven's character. Biographers are, for example, mystified at his propensity to be writing the most sublime, ethereal music at one moment, then throwing people down the stairs at the next—such artistic finesse, they marvel, from a man once seen to pick his teeth in public with a candlestick! The paradoxes presented by his personality have been called one of the most difficult subjects in the entire field of biography. It is even suggested by some scholars that Alexander Thayer, Beethoven's most important biographer, who spent thirty years in the preparation of the first three volumes of his exacting five-volume work, never completed the final two due to his inability to reconcile for himself Beethoven's more sacred characteristics with his negative traits. Over a period of many years, whenever Thayer tried to write the final volumes, he would develop a splitting headache in less than an hour, though he was perfectly able to do other work and to write other books—a most curious phenomenon probably psychosomatic in origin. Perhaps Beethoven's unpredictable temper was still causing headaches from beyond the grave!

Examining Beethoven's personality from a less conventional, more esoteric perspective may solve many of its riddles, however. For his colorful character traits are largely explained by his astrology. If the reader knows any Sagittarians of the Beethoven type, the chances are that while reading Beethoven anecdotes you'll have felt more than a little *déjà vu!*

Ludwig could never firmly establish his precise birthdate. He was christened on December 17; in Catholic Bonn, it was customary to baptize on the day after birth; thus his date of birth was probably December 16, 1770. Since this date is not definite, however, and since there is no record of the time of birth, a complete and accurate natal chart for Beethoven is not possible. But he was certainly a Sagittarian.

A good proportion of the baffling elements of Beethoven's personality may be explicable in terms of his Sun sign. Rare indeed, for example, would be the Pisces, the Cancer, the Virgo, or the Libra who could exhibit such a flashing temper. The Taurus might well do so (less frequently), but would then never back off and repent so quickly afterwards. Beethoven's Sun sign does not explain everything about him—no more than does anybody's Sun sign. There are elements of personal karma to consider also. Childhood experience is also a major factor in character development, and any developmental psychologist would recognize that some of Beethoven's traits must at least partly have been due to the abusive treatment he received from his father. Perhaps he even unconsciously emulated his father's aggressive behavior. On top of this, the influence of one's Sun sign is mitigated and modified by all the other aspects of one's natal chart, so that we do not, of course, find ourselves with only twelve standard character types living in the world. Thus there are clear differences between all individuals who share the same Sun sign. Some Sagittarians, for example, are not at all argumentative. Others are actually introverted (though one would have to search some before locating such a specimen). It might be said that there are subtypes within each sign. Yet despite all this, it is difficult from the esoteric viewpoint to avoid the conclusion that his belonging to a particular Sagittarian subtype goes a long way toward explaining many of Beethoven's behavior patterns. He seems, in fact, to have been an almost painfully overt example of a particular type of archer.

His bluntness of speech and lack of tact are typically Sagittarian, as was his total incomprehension of their effects on others. Sagittarians are honest folk, so from Beethoven's point of view, he was only telling people what he thought about them—in all honesty. But blunt Sagittarian "honesty" usually has other signs cringing. Sagittarius is a fire sign, and Beethoven was true to form in being extraverted and in having the potential to flare up in fiery temper. But it is also typically Sagittarian to feel remorse afterwards and to try to make amends, and again there are many recorded examples of Beethoven doing so. Two letters to his composer friend J. N. Hummel, on two consecutive days, read:

53

> Do not come to me any more. You are a false fellow, and the knacker take all such.[2]

> You are an honorable fellow, and I see you were right. So come this afternoon to me. You will also find Schup-panzigh, and both of us will bump, thump and pump you to your heart's delight.[3]

Sagittarian temper tantrums are rarely genuinely malicious, and may even have their amusing side; for example, the following incident recorded by Beethoven's pupil, Ries:

> One day we were eating our noonday meal at the Swan Inn; the waiter brought him the wrong dish. Scarcely had

Beethoven spoken a few words about the matter, which the waiter answered in a manner not altogether modest, when Beethoven seized the dish (it was a mass of lungs with plenty of gravy) and threw it at the waiter's head. The poor fellow had an armful of other dishes (an adeptness which Viennese waiters possess in a high degree) and could not help himself; the gravy ran down his face. He and Beethoven screamed and vituperated while all the other guests roared with laughter. Finally, Beethoven himself was overcome with the comicalness of the situation, as the waiter who wanted to scold could not, because he was kept busy licking from his chops the gravy that ran down his face, making the most ridiculous grimaces the while.[4]

To be born under any sign does not, however, mean that one is "fated" or "doomed" to exhibit forever that sign's negative characteristics. This is an incorrect understanding of the nature of astrology. As Beethoven himself knew, life itself can be seen as a test; we are born in order to grow through overcoming adversity. In this view, our Sun sign largely determines what specific types of tests we are intended to face and overcome in a particular lifetime. Thus, for example, Sagittarians are not "naturally" blunt of speech and are not "fated" always to be so; rather, one of the tests or initiations for that lifetime is to learn how to be tactful to others, to become more aware of the effects of their words on others, and to study the laws of how to keep harmony. (Meanwhile, Sagittarians' sometimes blunt speech is also a test of harmony to individuals of other signs!) Our Sun sign is our teacher and our initiator, as is our entire natal chart. As I propose below, Beethoven did strive with great determination to advance on the path of self-mastery. If he happened to be less harmonious than many spiritual people, or than many other composers, it may be because his temper was one of his soul's especially prominent tests in that life, and he did not always pass with top marks.

Sun signs also have their positive sides, however, and these provide us with the opportunity of manifesting the beneficial, creative aspects of our sign to the greatest possible extent. Beethoven was as adept at incarnating good Sagittarian characteristics as he was the less fortunate traits. This is shown in his love of the countryside, his desire to be frequently outdoors, the attraction faraway places held for him (he never actually traveled far afield, but always desired and had plans to do so), his love of a good joke, and, so typical of the archer, his natural optimism and joy (which *was* Beethoven's natural inclination, his periods of melancholia being the result of circumstances).

Physically, Sagittarians are either very tall and athletic in appearance or below average height with stocky, sturdy forms. Beethoven was the latter, and his large skull and high, broad forehead was also standard for an archer's face. Sagittarian trouble spots in the body include the intestines and the liver: Beethoven suffered for years from malfunctioning intestines, and liver failure probably played a large part in his death. In this respect, excessive drinking can also be a Sagittarian tendency, and Beethoven was never one to say no to a glass or four; for example, his once saying that he "only" had one bottle of wine with his meals. Nevertheless, his intake was somewhat the norm for the times, and he was never an alcoholic.

Some, though not all, Sagittarians are physically clumsy, and Beethoven could be a walking disaster area: delicate furniture was always at risk in his presence; he was always likely to knock something over or to spill his inkwell into the piano. His refusal to bow to tradition and authority is also typical of the fiery archer.

55

Exuberance, quick fury, clumsiness—all these inclinations rolled into one were demonstrated all too publicly on an occasion when Beethoven performed his "new piano concerto" (No. 4 or 5) in 1808. According to composer Ludwig Spohr's account:

> Beethoven was playing a new piano concerto of his, but already at the first tutti, forgetting that he was a soloist, he jumped up and began to conduct in his own peculiar fashion. At the first sforzando he threw out his arms so wide that he knocked over both the lamps from the music-stand of the piano. The audience laughed and Beethoven was so beside himself over this disturbance that he stopped the orchestra and made them start again. Segfried, worried for fear that this would happen again in the same place, took the precaution of ordering two choirboys to stand next to Beethoven and to hold the lamps in their hands. One of them innocently stepped closer and followed the

music from the piano part. But when the fatal sforzando burst forth the poor boy received from Beethoven's right hand such a sharp slap in the face that, terrified, he dropped the lamp on the floor. The other, more wary boy, who had been anxiously following Beethoven's movements, succeeded in avoiding the blow by ducking in time. If the audience had laughed the first time, now they indulged in a truly bacchanalian riot. Beethoven broke out in such a fury that when he struck the first chord of the solo he broke six strings. Every effort of the true music lovers to restore calm and attention remained unavailing for some time; thus the first Allegro of the Concerto was completely lost to the audience. After this incident Beethoven wanted to give no more concerts.[5]

Though Alexander Thayer doubted the truth of this anecdote, other biographers accept its general veracity, particularly since there are several better authenticated stories along the same lines.

Sagittarians are frequently impulsive in love, as was Beethoven. They are not shy of affairs, but can suddenly become extremely shy when wedding bells are mentioned. If they do marry, it may not always be a wise choice. In this respect, Beethoven did propose on at least two occasions, rather on the spur of the moment and to younger women who refused him, and who he later realized were quite unsuitable for him. On the other hand, archerlike, he himself did prove hard to catch, and stopped short suddenly at the prospect of marriage with Countess Therese and probably even with Antonie herself, his Eternally Beloved. Antonie, incidentally, was a Gemini, and Sagittarian-Gemini matches usually prove most successful. But concerning matters of the heart, the inherently dualistic nature of the Gemini can show itself in the desire for or acceptance of simultaneous relationships—literally, two-timing— and Antonie, we have seen, was possibly the female part of a love-triangle with Beethoven and her husband.

For the transmission into the physical world of the music that came through him, Beethoven's Sagittarian mind was exactly what was required. Another composer, no matter how skilled, born under another sign, may not have been suited to the task; in addition to Beethoven, the only other great composer to have been a Sagittarian was Jean Sibelius (1865–1957), whose culture and time period was totally different. Sagittarians tend to have both a religious streak and a soaring imagination: precisely the combination required for a composer who was to bring forth the nine symphonies and other works of Beethoven's genius. The Sagittarian is also well-suited to the task of penning the music of the spiritual seeker and of the victory of the soul on the Path. For example, writing on the mind and character of the Sagittarian, Derek and Julia Parker, in *The Compleat Astrologer*,[6] could easily be writing about Beethoven and his music:

> He will set his sights on an objective which seems beyond him ["Every day brings me nearer to the goal which I feel but cannot describe," wrote Beethoven]; as it comes within reach, he will raise his sights still higher and be anxious to start on a new project almost before he has completed the old one. . . . The Sagittarian is versatile and, like the Geminian, needs to have more than one task on hand at a time [". . . hardly have I completed one composition when I have already begun another . . . I often produce three or four works at the same time"]. . . . Once trained and disciplined, his mind is capable of a great deal. He is at his best dealing with old problems on new lines; each difficulty will be approached from several angles, perhaps unusual ones [a perfect description of Beethoven's approach to the art of composition]. . . . The challenge of a problem is a delight to a Sagittarian ["Yet I got some pleasure out of it, as I always do when I successfully overcome difficulties"], for it caters to his pleasure in exploration, in pushing his mind ever outward.

The description of Sagittarian qualities given here derives from the most standard form of astrology. However, perhaps the most important reason why Beethoven as a Sagittarian was ideal for the composing of his music is explained by a less well-known but higher form of astrology. In "Cosmic" or "Karmic" astrology, it is not the astrology of the limited, human personality that is studied, but rather it is the astrology of the potential of the soul to express the Higher Self. Under this system, each Sun sign expresses its own particular divine quality or spiritual keynote, and a measure

57

of a soul's success on the spiritual path is the extent to which it manifests the divine qualities of all twelve signs of the zodiac, but in particular those of its own Sun sign.

The divine quality of Sagittarius is "God-Victory," and what more apt term would there be to describe Beethoven's music? For the glorious, initiatic victory of the one who overcomes became the core theme of his mature, fourteen-year "heroic" or second period, and was expressed again in the third period at a still more exalted level. Whatever their astrology, it is essential for *all* spiritual pilgrims to take on this Sagittarian quality as they tread the Homeward Path; and truly Beethoven's art was and is the successful and faithful rendition in tonal form of what it means to hear, to manifest, and to know God-Victory.

The Religion
of Beethoven

 ONE SENTENCE in a Beethoven letter of 1823 perfectly encapsulates his views on the meaning of life and what he sought, throughout his life, to achieve with his music:

> There is no loftier mission than to approach the Godhead more nearly than other mortals and by means of that contact to spread the rays of the Godhead through the human race.[1]

Of this "mission" Beethoven specifies here two stages: "to approach the Godhead" and "to spread the rays of the Godhead." The second of these he accomplished through his art, by allowing others to hear and experience that which he, too, had experienced from his ever closer proximity to the Divine. But how did he go about the first stage of this mission, without which the second would have been impossible? What was Beethoven's concept of God, and what was the manner of his spiritual path of "approach"? To Bettina Brentano he said: "When I open my eyes I must sigh, for what I see is contrary to my religion."[2] What, then, was Beethoven's religion?

Beethoven was formally raised a Catholic, but as a child received no substantial religious training. Formally he remained a

Catholic all his life, but he was not an active churchgoer. Whereas other composers such as Bach, Handel, Haydn, and Mozart embraced Christian beliefs, Beethoven seems not to have been inspired by either the Church's doctrine and dogma, nor by what to a person of his own inner zeal for God would have seemed the lukewarm spiritual commitment of most of the clergy. In once writing, "Socrates and Jesus were my masters,"[3] Beethoven was accepting Jesus himself as his master (and also Socrates) rather than the institutionalized religion.

Anton Schindler, a friend who at one time also acted as a kind of secretary and general aide to Beethoven, wrote in his early biography of the composer: "It was one of his peculiarities that he never spoke on religious topics or concerning the dogmas of the various Christian churches in order to give his opinion about them. It may be said with considerable certainty, however, that his religious views rested less upon the creed of the church, than that they had their origin in deism. Without having a manufactured theory before him he plainly recognized the existence of God in the world as well as the world in God."[4]

Some of Beethoven's metaphysical outlook would have been formed early. During his teens he encountered Masonry, as we have seen, and also Kantian morality. Though not formally enrolled, he attended lectures in Bonn relating Immanuel Kant's philosophy to Catholicism. He frequently read the poetry of Friedrich von Schiller and decades later used Schiller's "Ode to Joy" within his Ninth Symphony. Beethoven and his generation also took up the writings of Plutarch, who inspired them to treasure freedom and never to relent in the effort to forge a new and better world. At the age of nineteen Beethoven composed his cantata "On the Death of Joseph II" in memory of the Habsburg Emperor who had used his reign to bring about reform according to the principles expressed in the *Philosophes*. We also know from Beethoven's own words that during his formative years he took Socrates and Jesus as his models. Like Jesus, Socrates, too, was more of an avatar and a sage than a philosopher. If Beethoven strove seriously to emulate the lives and characters of these two, then the earnestness with which he approached self-progression, even at this age, is impressive. By twenty-one he was writing: "Help others, whenever one can. Love Liberty. Above all, never deny the Truth, not even at the foot of a throne."[5]

60

So what, to Beethoven, was Truth? Certainly it was not the dogma of orthodox religion, but was sufficiently independent and nonconformist a definition that Haydn, a Freemason and devout Catholic, once called Beethoven "an atheist." He was far from that, however. While composing the *Missa Solemnis*, he penned worded notes in the scoresheet margins in reference to the music, containing lines such as: "Come from the heart, may it reach other hearts . . . God above all others . . . God has never abandoned me . . . Prayer for inner and outer peace . . . One must pray, pray, pray . . . "[6] And an 1816 journal entry reads: "It was not the fortuitous meeting of the chordal atoms that made the world; if order and beauty are reflected in the constitution of the universe, then there is a God."

What seems evident from this man's life and work is that his religious views cannot be defined in merely intellectual terms, for his experiences of God were deep and profound enough to have been mystical experiences. He was above all else a mystic, and therefore unlikely to have been much concerned with the particulars of what this or that religious institution believed in. Beethoven went straight to God.

His notes in the margins of the *Missa Solemnis* demonstrate what a unity Beethoven felt between his music and the act of prayer. For him the two were synonymous: his music *was* his prayer and his meditation. What, for him, could be the attraction of attending churches where the divine spark had gone out, when he perceived God as All in all, and when he could contact the Divinity more easily during his sojourns within the temple of Nature? At the age of forty-three, he wrote: "In the country it seems as if every tree said to me "Holy! Holy!"—who can give complete expression to the ecstasy of the woods! O, the sweet stillness of the woods!"[7]

All this is not to say that Beethoven did not study scripture. It is known that he read not only the Bible, but also the Hindu Vedas, Persian poetry, and other ancient writings, and even the Apocrypha. In fact, Beethoven possessed his own copy of the Apocrypha, the pre-Christian and Christian texts which were not included in the Bible. These were highly controversial and rarely read in Beethoven's day, and it is typical of his free spirit that he should feel the need to own a copy. Upon Beethoven's death the Apocrypha were still a sufficiently sensitive subject for the censor to ban the volume from being sold at auction.

61

From his own inner, personal experience with God, Beethoven was able to recognize spiritual truth wherever he found it, whatever the source or the religion. Thus, we can well understand that the simplistic, unenlightened dogmas of his local church possessed no attraction for him.

Concisely stated, Beethoven's religion was that which is called the Ancient Wisdom—that system of Truth Eternal which has existed at the esoteric heart of all religion since time immemorial. Esoteric teachings were not widespread or widely known during Beethoven's lifetime, but on the occasions that he did come across them, they appear to have held great personal importance to him, because they corresponded to his own inner experiences. For example, on one of his manuscript pages, he copied out the following passages from Hindu scripture:

> God is immaterial; as He is invisible, He can therefore have no form. But from what we are able to perceive in His works we conclude that He is eternal, omnipotent, omniscient and omnipresent. The mighty one, He alone is free from all desire or passion. There is no greater than He.
>
> Brahman; His mind is self-existent. He, the Almighty, is present in every part of space. His omniscience is self-inspired, and His conception includes every other. Of His all-embracing attributes the greatest is omniscience. For it there is no threefold kind of being—it is independent of everything—O God! Thou art the true, eternal, blessed, unchangeable light of all time and space.
>
> . . . What moved Thee to manifest Thy power and boundless goodness? What brilliant light directed Thy power? Wisdom beyond measure! How was it first manifested? Oh! direct my mind! Oh! raise it up from this grievous depth.[8]

62

Certain sentences from an essay of Schiller's were also copied out and framed by Beethoven, and stood always on his desk. Anton Schindler said that Beethoven considered them to be the sum of the loftiest and purest religion. They are words which constitute the essence of the mystical perception of the Supreme. I reproduce below the entire passage from which Beethoven took them, with the words he copied in capitals:

The epoptae [Egyptian priests] recognized a single, highest cause of all things, a primeval, natural force, the essence of all essences, which was the same as the demiurge of the Greek philosophers. There is nothing more elevated than the simple grandeur with which they spoke of the creator of the universe. In order to distinguish him the more emphatically they gave him no name. A name, said they, is only a need for pointing a difference; he who is only, has no need of a name, for there is no one with whom he could be confounded. Under an ancient monument of Isis were to be read the words: "I AM THAT WHICH IS," and upon a pyramid at Sais the strange primeval inscription: "I AM ALL, THAT IS, THAT WAS, THAT WILL BE; NO MORTAL HATH EVER ME UNVEILED." No one was permitted to enter the temple of Serapis who did not bear upon his breast or forehead the name Iao, or I-ha-ho—a name similar in sound to the Hebrew Jehovah and of all likelihood of the same meaning; and no name was uttered with greater reverence in Egypt than this name Iao. In the hymn which the hierophant, or guardian of the sanctuary, sang to the candidate for initiation, this was the first division in the instruction concerning the nature of the divinity: "HE IS ALONE BY HIMSELF, AND TO HE ALONE DO ALL THINGS OWE THEIR EXISTENCE."9

Such truth appeals to those of mystical consciousness, such as Beethoven possessed, speaking as it does of God as being in all, and all in God, yet God still remaining fundamentally beyond mortal sight or comprehension. For if God is everywhere and in all things, God is not in reality separated from us at all. The only thing separating us from the Godhead is our own mortality, our own untransmuted and impure consciousness. And so by our progressive self-purification, and by the gradual sanctifying of ourselves through prayer, self-sacrifice, right motive, and good deeds, we can grow closer to the One, for day by day we are becoming more of what we really are, for we are ourselves God; our Real Self is the God within.

This truth was known by all the great sages and avatars. As we read in the Upanishads, "Thou art That": Thou, the disciple, art That, the Godhead. As St. Paul queried Christ's followers at Corinth: "Know ye not that ye are the temple of God, and that the Spirit of God dwelleth in you?"[10] (Evidently they didn't, but Beethoven is unlikely to have missed the deep implications of such lines in scripture.) Thus, even Paul was a pantheist, perceiving no duality between God and the individual, but writing to the Corinthians of "the One who subjected all things to him, so that God may be all in all."[11] Similarly, when the Jews challenged Christ for saying God was in himself, he replied by quoting the Psalms: "Is it not written in your law, I said, Ye are gods?"[12] (The original, Psalm 82:6, states: "I have said, ye are gods . . . all of you.") In quoting this, Jesus was justifying his own Sonship on the basis that *all* people are (potential) gods, or Sons and Daughters of God. This Sonship, for the mystics of all cultures and ages, has been the goal of life: the summoning of *more of God* into this world of time and space through the sublimation of one's personality and the raising and redeeming of human consciousness by its becoming one with the Divine.

64   To reach this goal there is a Path to tread: the purpose of life is to actualize more of our own inner Reality, which is God. Every good thought or deed counts towards progress on this Path, and every harmful or negative thought or deed keeps us from the goal. Thus, rightly used, every activity and every minute of the day can propel us toward becoming more Godlike and infuses our life with purpose and meaning. This surely was Beethoven's philosophy, for life as a spiritual Path is the one major conceptual theme which both runs through his major compositions and describes how he lived his life.

Beethoven and the Spiritual Path | 8

All things flowed clear and pure out of God. Though often darkly led to evil by passion, I returned, through penance and purification, to the pure fountain—to God—and to your art. In this I was never impelled by selfishness; may it always be so.
                                        —Beethoven, JOURNAL of 1815

AS MUSICOLOGIST J. W. N. Sullivan once noted,[1] the two chief characteristics of Beethoven's attitude towards life were the realization of *life as suffering* and the realization of *the heroism of achievement*. The first is life's fundamental problem; the second, its fundamental solution.

The realization of the nature of mortal life as suffering was also arrived at by Gautama Buddha. The Buddha saw that life, subject as it is to illness, aging, and death, is inherently impermanent and therefore must contain suffering. He formulated the Eightfold Path by which to rise from mortality into the expansive consciousness of Nirvana. The Buddha also pronounced three ways of treading this path: the long way of knowledge, the shorter way of faith, and the shortest way, through action. Of these three, Beethoven chose the latter.

His journal records from his twenty-fifth year the following entry: "Courage! In spite of all bodily weaknesses my spirit shall rule. Twenty-five years have come: This year must determine the mature man. Nothing must remain undone."[2] An entry from 1814 strikes a note common in the thoughts of all disciples—the urgency of making the optimum use of time: "There is much on earth to be done—do it soon! I must not continue my present everyday life,—art asks this sacrifice also. Take rest in diversion [only] in order to work more energetically."[3] In the 1820s Johann Sporschil, a historian and publicist who knew Beethoven, described him as "one of the most active men who every lived," saying that "deepest midnight found him still working."[4]

World servers have *purpose*. There is, in fact, no limit to the amount of service they can render, save the limitations marked by time itself. And so, as modern research has shown, self-actualized people tend to sleep less than others. As Beethoven himself wrote to Wegeler: "Not a word about rest! I know of none except in sleep, and sorry enough am I that I am obliged to yield up more to it than formerly."[5] In his copy of Homer's *Odyssey*, he underlined the words "too much sleep is injurious."

Beethoven's journals and letters contain many indications of his pursuit of self-perfection. In 1807 he told Frau Marie Bigot: "From childhood I learned to love virtue, and everything beautiful and good."[6] In 1816 when Countess Erdödy was suffering from incurable lameness, Beethoven wrote a letter to her which included a passage again revealing his belief in the attainability of perfection: "It is the fate of mortals, but *even here one's power should become manifest, i.e., to endure unconsciously and to feel one's nothingness, and so attain that perfection* of which the Almighty through such means will deem us worthy."[7]

66

The human soul's potential to become perfect, though denied by the doctrines of orthodox Christianity, is an attainable goal and has been recognized by all who, like Beethoven, have drawn sufficiently close to God to receive such truths directly from the source. So it was that St. Paul could say that God "revealed his Son in me."[8] So it was that even Christ taught: "Be ye perfect, even as your father in heaven is perfect."[9] So it was that St. John of the Cross could say in the life of the greatest devotees, "the body feels such glory in the glory of the soul that it magnifies God after its own manner, perceiving that He is in its very bones . . ."[10] And so it is that Beethoven could say that a human being's destiny is to "reach his perfection again"—a perfection which in 1801 he had referred to as "the goal which I feel but cannot describe."[11]

Beethoven attained the perfection he sought most nearly in his music, even if he did not attain it completely in himself as a man. His propensity for flashes of fury was never completely overcome.

He could also be remarkably childlike. Hummel once played on this naïveté when he wrote to him with feigned seriousness that a lamp for the blind had been invented. Beethoven immediately told all his friends about it, insisting it was true!

So it would be a mistake to idealize Beethoven the man, even as it is a mistake to idolize any human personality. I do not propose that we should, like Thayer, suffer headaches because of our inability to reconcile the godlike prowess of Beethoven the composer and the somewhat less godlike level of harmony reached by the man. This is the great mystery of the incarnation of the Word in all people, the great mystery of the indwelling Christos: perfection is attainable, but it is a perfection of the heart. The mortal flesh can never be totally perfected—even as the Buddha recognized that life is suffering, that *mortal* life is inherently imperfect. Who among us can boast the perfect form? Who among even the most spiritual of individuals on earth has never taken a misstep or said the wrong thing? Who has never erred in any way? No, the perfection, the God, is within—even as Beethoven, in the Heiligenstadt Testament, pleaded that we see: "O my fellow men, who accuse me of being malevolent, stubborn or even misanthropic, how greatly do you wrong me . . . Almighty God . . . you see into my heart and you know that it is filled with love for humanity and a desire to do good."

67

In his service to humanity, one of Beethoven's most amazing abilities was the degree to which he could put aside the lesser self, with all of its problems and pains in life, in order that the Higher Self might come through. In the midst of some of his own greatest personal difficulties, he wrote music which was infinitely joyous and inspiring. The beautiful Second Symphony was composed around the fateful time of the Heiligenstadt Testament. Beethoven's greatest piano concerto, the *Emperor*, was written while he was living in spartan conditions in Vienna near to the time that the city was being besieged and bombarded by the army of Napoleon.

It is instructive to compare the life and achievements of Beethoven with those of Bonaparte. Napoleon was only a matter of months older than the composer, and it was to him that Beethoven originally intended to dedicate his Third Symphony. These contemporaries lived only a couple of centuries before the astrological Age of Aquarius would dawn; it was already a revolutionary time, with change in the air. Though one was a musical revolutionary and the other a military revolutionary, each was entrusted with a mission which could aid and ease the dawn of the new era. But while one succeeded, the other failed.

Through his brilliant strategy and popular appeal, Napoleon could have formed a democratic United States of Europe, much as Washington had done across the Atlantic. But Napoleon failed to pass that challenge on the Path which provided the spiritual theme for several of Beethoven's major works: the bowing of the will of the human ego to that of the Supreme. (In esotericism, the term *ego* is not used in its Freudian sense but as referring to that portion of human consciousness which is still apart from and has not surrendered to God. Hence it is that portion of the soul which is still egocentric, rather than theocentric.) Exhilarated by his victories, Napoleon took the glory for himself, failing to consecrate it to God. In May 1804 he assumed the title of Emperor, thus exalting the human ego and ending the possibility of Europe becoming a divinely guided democratic republic such as the United States became under the leadership of Washington and other God-loving leaders. Napoleon's failure can be viewed as a setback to the real, inner destiny of Europe from which it has not even now recovered.[12]

Beethoven's reaction to the news of Napoleon's assumption of the title was to stride over to his copy of the symphony and cross out the name "Bonaparte" with such violence that (as can still be seen, for the page survives) his pen tore a hole in the paper. He then ripped the title page, with the dedication, out of the score, and flung it to the floor, crying: "He, too, then, is nothing better than an ordinary man! Now he will trample on all human rights only to humor his ambition; he will place himself above all others— become a tyrant!"[13] To the symphony he gave a more general theme, naming it simply *Eroica*.

Napoleon would have done well to have understood the ancient esoteric maxim which advises all who tread the Way: "Kill out ambition, but live like one ambitious." For the ambitious frame of mind is essential if one is to thrust forward and succeed in any divine calling; but where thought of self remains, one will always, sooner or later, meet one's Waterloo. Beethoven understood this perfectly.

68

Mabel Collins, an early Theosophist, expounded upon this maxim with words of the deepest wisdom published in 1885:

Ambition is the first curse: the great tempter of the man who is rising above his fellows. It is the simplest form of looking for reward. Men of intelligence and power are led away from their higher possibilities by it continually. Yet it is a necessary teacher. Its results turn to dust and ashes in the mouth; like death and estrangement, it shows the man at last that to work for self is to work for disappointment. But though this first rule seems so simple and easy, do not quickly pass it by. For these vices of the ordinary man pass through a subtle transformation and reappear with changed aspect in the heart of the disciple. It is easy to say: "I will not be ambitious"; it is not so easy to say: "When the Master reads my heart, He will find it clean utterly."

And as she continues, it is impossible not to see the relevance of her words to Beethoven's dark nights of the soul, when encroaching deafness and the loss of his Eternally Beloved pierced his heart, and yet he found strength to live on, for the sake of goals higher than self-reward:

69

Seek in the heart the source of evil and expunge it. It lives fruitfully in the heart of the devoted disciple as well as in the man of desire. He who will enter upon the path of power must tear this thing out of his heart. And then the heart will bleed, and the whole life of the man seem to be utterly dissolved. This ordeal must be endured . . . Live neither in the present nor the future, but in the Eternal. This giant weed [the source of evil, the self-centered ego] cannot flower there; this blot upon existence is wiped out by the very atmosphere of eternal thought.[14]

These words were not published during Beethoven's life, but similar precepts were, and he embodied them immaculately. His journal contains what appears to be a quotation followed by his own comment:

"Blessed is he who has overcome all passions and then proceeds energetically to perform his duties under all circumstances careless of success! Let the motive lie in the deed, not in the outcome. Be not one of those whose spring of action is the hope of reward." Do not let your life pass in inactivity. Be industrious, do your duty, banish all thoughts as to results.

On one occasion in Beethoven's later years, a copyist happened to fawn on him and praise him. Jesus, when called "good master," made of it a lesson in the denial of personal praise, answering "Why callest thou me good? There is none good but God."[15] Beethoven did likewise, though in his own inimitable style, replying: "Go to the devil with your 'gracious Sir'! There is only one who can be called gracious and that is God." In 1815 he wrote to the Countess Erdödy, "No news from me—that is to say *nothing from nothing*"[16]—a marked denial of the worth of the human ego.

Mlle. de Girardi once praised Beethoven in her poetry. He replied: "It is a singular sensation to see and hear one's self praised, and then to be conscious of one's own imperfections as I am. I always regard such occasions as admonishments to get nearer the unattainable goal set for us by art and nature, hard as it may be."[17] (The goal being "unattainable" only in the sense that the potential for progress is infinite.)

We see from this that to him the "goal" of "nature" (life) and the goal of art (or whatever one's divine calling may be) were for Beethoven one and the same: forging his art enhanced his spiritual progress, and his spiritual progress enhanced his art. There was no dichotomy between his music and his Path. Even at a young age we find him uniting the two, asserting that (Beethoven's emphasis) "*Freedom* and *progress* are the purpose of art and of all life." And it is here that we bear witness to the God within him: it is in his art that we discover absolute perfection—a divine outpouring from a man.

H. E. Krehbiel wrote: "To Beethoven music was not only a manifestation of the beautiful, an art, it was akin to religion. He felt himself to be a prophet, a seer." When in his youth Beethoven vowed, "I will only use my art for the benefit of the poor," he was referring more than anything to the poor in Spirit. He once wrote in a letter: "From my earliest childhood my zeal to serve suffering humanity with my art was never content with any kind

70

of a subterfuge; and no other reward is needed than the internal satisfaction which always accompanies such a deed."

As early as the age of twenty-two, he had clearly recognized the purpose of his music, calling it "my divine art." He sometimes referred to God as the "great Tonemaster above" (a phrase fraught with esoteric truth). Beethoven was furious whenever he encountered any example of pseudo-art—music professed to be serious yet actually intended only to entertain, not to improve; or virtuosity devoid of the divine spark. He once related that "From childhood I have been striving to grasp the meaning of what is wise and good in each age." And he continued: "Shame on the artist who does not feel duty bound to do this at least."

Beethoven's unrelenting impulse towards progress, always the hallmark of the disciple, is evident in a number of his recorded statements. Still young, he was writing in his diary lines such as, "I am happy only when I have overcome a difficulty." In his sacred labor, too, the composition of music was a meaningless exercise to him if it did not represent aesthetic and technical progression. To the poet Friedrich von Mathisson, Beethoven wrote in 1800: "You yourself know what a change is wrought by a few years in the case of an artist who is continually pushing forward. The greater the progress which one makes in art, the less one is satisfied with one's old works."[18] And on another occasion: "Art demands of us that we shall not stand still."[19]

71

Indeed, Beethoven never did stand still and was always, as he put it, "continually pushing forward." But though his progress was constant, by far the most distinctive feature of his evolution as an artist was his relatively sudden transition, at two times during his life, into new heights of technical accomplishment and spiritual vision. These two distinct leaps of inner growth raised him each time into a new dimension of consciousness, out of which came a sudden flowering of composition.

So different was the music which followed these two evolutionary leaps that it is common to speak of Beethoven's music as belonging to three periods. To the first period belongs everything composed prior to the *Eroica* Symphony. The *Eroica* was an unprecedented revolutionary advance not only for Beethoven but for the whole world of music, and beyond music, for its effect on the consciousness of all who heard it. Thus this seminal work signaled the opening of Beethoven's second period, from which many of his most famous works derive. (When speaking of Beethoven's music, it is the second period works which most people have in mind.) Then, after over fifteen years, again his music was lifted quite suddenly into the third period's still more exalted levels of art and metaphysical supremacy as expressed in the *Missa Solemnis* and the Ninth Symphony.

Beethoven's three periods should not be mythologized into having been *absolutely* distinct from each other, or *absolutely* clear-cut in their chronology. But nevertheless, they are distinct from each other and sudden in the transition from one to the other to a surprising degree. What, then, caused these transitions? What caused these expansions of consciousness?

A clue to the answer is that the second and third periods each emerged Phoenixlike from the ashes and the tribulation of what were probably the two most painful and difficult periods in Beethoven's life. The second period works only began after his first great dark night of the soul at the time of his confrontation with encroaching deafness between 1799 and 1802. The onset of the third period came only after the second great dark night of 1815–20, corresponding with his "dry period" during which he experienced separation from Antonie Brentano, court cases, financial worries, and great anxiety over the welfare of his nephew, for the custody of whom Beethoven fought lengthy legal battles against the boy's mother, who did not enjoy a high reputation (a full account of this story is given in Chapter 10).

Each new period signaled a man not only renewed, but who viewed the world from higher vistas than ever before. This expanded perspective was possible because he himself had risen in consciousness. But he was able to do so only after undergoing a fiery trial. When the ego is buffeted and pained by life's adversities (understood by esotericists to be the result of karma), it may react in one of two ways. Some blame God and become even more self-righteous, even more self-centered in their separation from the Divine, thus failing the test. Others recognize the ultimate futility of selfhood lived apart from God and realize that it often takes such adversity to "shake" the human ego into seeing life from a new angle, opening its perceptions, and acknowledging that all that is meaningful is in the One. In successively surrendering the limited human ego, or the idolization of one's human self, a vacuum is created into which God can enter. Gradually, stage by stage on the Path, the individual becomes God in human form, being literally Godlike. Such an individual becomes the anointed one, becoming (in the New Testament's Greek) "the Christos."

This process was touched upon in Jesus' teachings recorded in the Book of Hebrews: "My son, despise not thou the chastening of the Lord [or of the Lord through the guru], nor faint when thou art rebuked of him: For whom the Lord loveth he chasteneth, and scourgeth every son whom he receiveth. If ye endure chastening, God dealeth with you as with sons; for what son is he whom the father chasteneth not?"[20]

Beethoven's reaction to his dark nights was to surrender the lesser self and to affirm Divine authority. Therefore music containing more of God's light and energy could be and was initiated. And *initiated* is indeed the word, for Beethoven's resurrections into his second and third creative periods were likely the results of initiatory experiences of some form.

The concept of initiation conjures for some people only the image of ceremony and outer display. And it is indeed true that in many esoteric schools and religious traditions, initiations amount to nothing more than this. But in the case of the only genuine form of initiation, ceremony is the least important aspect of the process. Ceremony cannot give to the novice that which the novice has not forged within. Initiation correctly understood is therefore primarily and essentially an activity of the initiated himself or herself. The disciple must be self-purged of mortal desire and imperfection, expanding by self-effort the capacity to contain and utilize inner Light. The disciple must prove attainment in the maintenance of faith, harmony, constancy, and all other qualities necessary for the path of initiation. A disciple is unlikely to be given more Light or God-consciousness by initiation until a chalice of consciousness has been forged within capable of securing and containing that Light; otherwise this precious illumination could be misused and "spilled upon the ground."

Some seekers may look in error to their guru or master for initiation. Yet all the while, God is looking to them to initiate the fire of freedom on earth, to initiate the correct use of free will in their lives and the correct use of God's laws. *To initiate* is "to begin, to start, to set in motion, to introduce." For every gift that is received, a gift must be given. Those who would receive the gift of initiation from God should ask themselves: What gift will I give to God in return?

Beethoven gave to God the gift of himself—to serve selflessly at a higher level of devotion, purity, and determination than before. When we listen to the magnificent *Eroica* which Beethoven received in return in his second period, or to the unsurpassed *Choral* Symphony of his third period, how could we ourselves ever desire to give less to God than Beethoven did? For if we offer up the chalice of a transmuted, purified selfhood, we all shall receive like blessings, according to the nature of our life's calling, which we in turn may then offer as a blessing to humanity. With what measure ye mete, it shall be measured unto you again and again and again.

The various esoteric schools of thought and religious traditions each have their own terminology for initiations which test and strengthen the disciple's inner mettle by adversity. To Catholic mystics, for example, this is the Purgatory Way. St. John of the Cross wrote of spiritual purgation:

74

> God, Who is all perfection, wars against all the imperfect habits of the soul, so that He may transform it in Himself and make it sweet, bright and peaceful, as does the fire when it has entered the wood.
>
> This severe purgation comes to pass in few souls—in those alone whom the Lord desires to raise to a higher degree of union; for he prepares each one with a purgation of greater or less severity, according to the degree to which He desires to raise it.[21]

In the terminology of modern esotericism, the initiation of which St. John wrote would be understood as a process directed by the inner-plane spiritual hierarchy of our world. This same spiritual hierarchy, who initiated Beethoven by bestowing new energy and Light upon him, are the source of the true initiations experienced by others and of the inspiration behind the music of Beethoven and all of the great composers. This inner-plane spiritual hierarchy of ascended masters and cosmic beings has been known throughout the ages, sometimes being called the angels or the heavenly hosts. In the Vedas they are called the Immortals. Buddhists know them as the liberated ones, those who have attained Nirvana. To the Rosicrucians they were the Invisible College. Modern esoteric teachings refer to them variously as Hierarchy, the White Lodge, or as the Great White Brotherhood (*White* referring not to color or race, but to the white light of their auras). They are our elder brothers and sisters on the Path—the very best teachers and gurus we could have, because having graduated from earth's schoolroom through all races and religions, they have already attained mastery over time and space to become one with God.

Did Beethoven, then, have a guru? And did he know he was being initiated?

According to the modern esoteric viewpoint, those who are actually members of an outer, physical movement formed by the Brotherhood could well be aware of having a guru at inner levels; but many people on earth are in actuality disciples of the Brotherhood and do work great deeds for humanity, while in their physical, waking lives, they have little or no awareness or knowledge of events at inner levels. According to the esoteric viewpoint, almost all of the great composers were disciples of the Great White Brotherhood and took incarnation specifically to carry out the missions for music which they accomplished. Often in their letters or memoirs we discover that they did indeed feel a great sense of "mission," that they felt they were here for a purpose, and certainly most of them had great reverence and devotion to God. But few if any were aware of events at inner levels.

In his outer, conscious mind, Beethoven would not have been aware of his initiations specifically as such. But he cannot have failed to have felt the changes. After all, he participated in initiating them. Further, he would have been quite aware of the results—of his expanded consciousness and more sublime levels of composition. And he knew he was becoming more at one with God.

One of Beethoven's favorite books was Sturm's *Observations Concerning the Works of God in Nature.* From this he copied out the following passage, which must have struck a familiar chord with him and is evidence that he did know he was undergoing spiritual purgation:

In praise of Thy goodness I must confess that Thou didst try with all Thy means to draw me to Thee. Sometimes it pleased Thee to let me feel the heavy hand of Thy displeasure and to humiliate my proud heart by manifold castigations. Sickness and misfortune didst Thou send upon me to turn my thoughts to my errantries.—One thing, only, O Father, do I ask: cease not to labour for my betterment. In whatsoever manner it be, let me turn to Thee and become fruitful in good works.

If, as a man, Beethoven never attained the pinnacle of perfection (in that particular life), nevertheless his was a lifetime of striving for the good, and he advanced mightily. And, in a sense, "perfection" is only discovered within any mortal in this way—that one *does one's very best*, day by day and year by year.

There are occasions when the greatest and most shining examples of spiritual attainment, such as the lives and teachings of Jesus Christ, Gautama Buddha, and Confucius, seem almost too glorious and perfect for us to identify with. And it is then that we may find comfort, courage, and inspiration from a life such as Beethoven's—for he was so obviously flawed, as we are also born flawed, but in life he progressed unrelentingly, and in his art even this man of rugged demeanor was able to bring to the ears of humanity the harmonies of the heavens.

Moreover, his compositions are themselves the music of his progressive initiations. In his magnificent music we can actually hear what it feels like to have consciousness raised to such levels as his. And his music's progress was by no means restricted to the most obvious transformations leading into the second and third periods. Rather, it is almost true to say that every major composition was more advanced and supreme than those which had gone before. In meditating on these works, the energies and states of consciousness necessary for spiritual attainment and initiation are transferred to us. From higher octaves of existence, Light-energy is actively transferred to our own beings as we listen. He trod the Path, but left the record of his footsteps for us to follow. Through his music, we can follow Beethoven in his ascent.

Bride and Bridegroom

9

IN 1823 THE DEAF COMPOSER conversed in writing with his first biographer, Anton Schindler, about his romance of years before with Giulietta Guiciardi. "I was loved by her very much, and more than her husband ever was," he wrote. But the pair broke up, prior to her marriage. Later, while Giulietta found herself staying in Vienna, she went again to visit the composer. "But I scorned her," he told Schindler. "If I had wasted my vital forces in that way, what could have been left for the best and most noble of myself?"[1]

An important question in the lives of all who would be the brides of the Divine, treading the path of union with the Bridegroom, the Higher Self, is whether or not to marry in the exoteric sense, entering into wedlock with another human soul. The path of the single celibate and the path of the sanctified marriage partner are each valid for the spiritual seeker, but each offers very different ways of life.

St. Paul taught early Christians the acceptability of marriage for those on the Path—but only those who would otherwise be troubled by desire. To the Corinthians he wrote:

> Now concerning the things whereof ye wrote unto me: It
> is good for a man not to touch a woman. Nevertheless, to

avoid fornication, let every man have his own wife, and let every woman have her own husband . . . But I speak this by permission, and not of commandment. For I would that all men were even as I myself. But every man hath his proper gift of God, one after this manner, and another after that. I say therefore to the unmarried and widows, It is good for them if they abide even as I. But if they cannot contain, let them marry: for it is better to marry than to burn.[2]

These teachings of St. Paul were appropriately oriented to his Piscean age. They are not necessarily so appropriate for the Aquarian age now upon us.

Marriage is a sacred relationship of God the Father (incarnate in man) with God the Mother (incarnate in woman). Among the spiritually advanced, marriage is also important for bringing children into incarnation who are at least as advanced and possibly even more divinely endowed than their parents. In the Aquarian age, souls of great Light are waiting to be born. Others may also choose to practice the "third way" of celibacy or self-restraint *within* marriage, a way of life which can be practiced with results by those on a spiritual path. Ramakrishna is often cited as an example of an advanced individual who was celibate throughout his marriage.

However, the musical composers of the past were not heirs to the esoteric traditions and knew only the choice between the single life and the normal life of wedlock. Among the advanced souls who, in preparation for the coming New Age, brought to earth the music of the spheres during the eighteenth and nineteenth centuries, the large majority did marry. Most of these marriages perfectly fulfilled the only criterion which justifies marriage from a spiritual point of view: that the partners are able to serve God more creatively and productively together than singly. Clara Schumann, through the years of her marriage to Robert Schumann, upheld and strengthened him during his periods of nervous disorder. Not only did she provide the stable home environment in which he could best compose, but she also took up his music upon his death, becoming herself one of the most respected pianists of the time and seeing to it that Schumann's music became known and appreciated around the world through her years of touring as a concert pianist.

Beethoven never married, and indeed he was sometimes not only unmarried but literally quite alone. One way or the other this fact is bound to have had a very important effect upon his life, outlook, and music. Would marriage have distracted him from his mission? Would it have taken the edge off the power and grandeur of his works? Or could it, through bringing him greater joy, as well as stability, actually have improved his creativity?

By all accounts, his sometimes wish to be married stemmed from real attachments of the heart and from the need for companionship, rather than from physical desire. He strove to be pure and moral even from his teens. So opposed was he to the practice of cohabitation outside of wedlock that he would sometimes refuse to visit or even to speak to anyone whom he thought had done so.

It would be unrealistic, though, to imagine that Beethoven forever remained celibate. While maintaining high moral opinions in his youth, in his forties he became resigned to the ways of the flesh and behaved much as any other Viennese man of the time. He lived during a period as permissive in its morality as our own and so was quite surrounded by bad example. In the wake of the Eternally Beloved affair, lightly coded correspondence with his friend Baron von Zmeskall makes it clear that they visited prostitutes at that time,[3] usually at Zmeskall's prompting—but lines in Beethoven's journals apparently testify to his subsequent revulsion: "Sensual enjoyment without the union of souls is and always will be bestial," he wrote. "After it there is no trace of exalted sentiment, rather one feels remorse."[4]

Still, given his celebrity, surprisingly little is known about this aspect of his life. As a result, some biographers have idealized him as more pure than he may actually have been, while, on the other hand, there was a tendency in the early twentieth century to believe that his various ailments, including his deafness and eventual death, were all the result of syphilis contracted in his youth, for which there is not a shred of evidence.

Beethoven's friend Stephan von Breuning, who knew him well, did say that in his youth Beethoven always had "a great deal of success" with women; other contemporaries apparently suspected that he was of exceptional virility; and his friend Franz Wegeler stated he was capable of amorous conquests that would have been difficult if not impossible for many an Adonis. On the evidence, this was quite an exaggeration. Moreover, we should not confuse amorous conquests with sexual ones. Neither is there any actual record of any casual sexual indulgences in Beethoven's youth. What is most likely is that being an emotional and artistic man, his heart was won by many a woman, but despite all the sweethearts whose names have come down to us, his relationships may well have been purely of the heart. There is, however, a strange account recorded by his pupil Ferdinand Ries, but as we might expect from the larger-than-life Beethoven, the scene is so bizarre as to leave us, ultimately, more puzzled than before. Ries visited the composer one evening to find

> a handsome young woman sitting on the sofa beside him. Thinking that I might be intruding I wanted to go at once. But Beethoven detained me and said: "Play, for the time being." He and the lady remained seated behind me. I had already played for a long time when Beethoven called out: "Ries, play some love music;" a little later, "something melancholy," then "something passionate," etc. From what I heard I came to the conclusion that in some manner he must have offended the lady and was trying to make amends . . . At last he jumped up and shouted: "Why, all those things are by me!" The lady soon went away; to my great amazement Beethoven did not know who she was.[5]

Whatever action "offended the lady" seems likely to have been paralleled by the manner of his advances toward the young widow Josephine von Deym, who wrote to him in 1805:

> This favor you have accorded me, the pleasure of your company, would have been the finest ornament of my life if you had been able to love me less sensually. . . . I would have to break holy vows were I to listen to your desire.[6]

Yet a diametrically different kind of story is related by horn player Nikolaus Simrock. Once Beethoven and his friends, traveling to Mergentheim, stopped at a certain place to dine. Simrock says that then "some of the young men prompted the waiting-girl to play off her charms upon Beethoven. He received her advances and familiarities with repellent coldness; and as she, encouraged by the others, still persevered, he lost his patience, and put an end to her importunities with a smart box on the ear."[7]

Perhaps the deepest insight comes from words we were never meant to see (and one feels almost to be prying beyond decency to recount them, for they were communicated in privacy between the soul and God), but a journal entry in 1817 or 1818 cries out:

> Love alone—yes only love can give you a happier life—O God—let me—let me finally find one—who will strengthen me in virtue—who will lawfully be mine.[8]

So let us allow that at times an individual can be lonely. Yet let us also allow to Beethoven's great merit that no attraction to a human woman was ever anything but secondary to his attachment to the Divine, and no inner pain of the soul was ever allowed to long interfere with his mission to humanity.

For certain souls, who have incarnated in order to fulfill a particular kind of life-mission, the celibate state is the most productive. The font of all humanity's creative genius—the sacred energy anchored at the base of the spine at nonphysical levels, which in Hinduism is referred to as *kundalini*—is expended during the physical act of love but retained by the celibate. This kundalini energy is in fact present throughout all of nature and is the evolutionary force, as yet undiscovered by science, within all forms of life. In humans, when the physical, emotional, and mental levels of being are purified and a selfless devotion to God and humanity is present, the kundalini energy can ascend the "spinal altar" to invigorate and energize one's whole being with Light. This state imbues one with vastly increased wellsprings of altruistic love, illumination, devotion, creativity, joy, spiritual intuition, and divinely directed willpower.

To say that such blessings are granted only to the unmarried devotee would be a great oversimplification, however. Physical celibacy lacking in emotional and mental control, and deficient in sincere altruism and devotion, will achieve little if any awakening of this sacred energy within. On the other hand, many a joyfully married couple are so pure in heart and disciplined in their spiritual practices that they have far greater inner resources of creativity and spiritual light than the less sincere and less disciplined single devotee.

81

Another positive factor about marriage from the point of view of the Path is that it typically offers one a crash course in the art of understanding and getting along with another soul—a course which one *has* to pass if the marriage is to work and survive. Throughout this same learning process, one may glean insights into one's own psychological and spiritual weaknesses, which the single person may take a great deal longer to discover.

But the single disciple, if capable of self-discipline, tends to find it easier to be more *intense* in many activities of the Path. Being more alone, such a person is able to arrange his or her time so as to use every minute usefully; and without an earthly beloved to commune with, the tendency is more towards holding continual inner communion with God. As St. Paul said to the early Christians of Corinth:

> But I would have you without carefulness. He that is un-married careth for the things that belong to the Lord, how he may please the Lord: but he that is married careth for the things that are of the world, how he may please his wife.[9]

Paul's words were for a certain people at a certain time of history, and ask to be read not in a spirit of fanaticism, but with a more expansive understanding. Nevertheless, these words seem to apply most pointedly to Beethoven, for whom the question of marriage was a life-theme of decades' duration. For Beethoven, Pauline passages such as these must have loomed large:

> Nevertheless he that standeth steadfast in his heart, having no necessity, but hath power over his own will, and hath so decreed in his heart that he will keep his virgin[ity] doeth well . . . And this I speak for your own profit; not that I may cast a snare upon you, but for that which is comely, and that ye may attend upon the Lord without distraction.[10]

I have attempted in this discussion to make the point clearly that it is neither right nor wrong on the Path to choose to marry. There are so many factors involved, both of a general and of a personal nature, and either way can be advantageous, depending on circumstances and on the individual.

Beethoven's turned out to be the path of the unmarried, and on the weight of the evidence one is even tempted to say that he was *destined* to remain unmarried. Beethoven was to be one of the—and many would say *the*—greatest transmitter of the music of the spheres of the entire period of classical and romantic tonal art. Only J. S. Bach could possibly be said to have composed music of equal greatness or of an equally potent molding and shaping effect upon society. So perhaps Beethoven's life-mission was of such great and demanding proportions that he could only fulfill it by the renunciation both of his hearing and of a normal family life.

The single spiritual pilgrim frequently discovers that because of the lack of worldly distraction in such a life, every experience and perception becomes more intense and deeply felt. It is clear from his letters and journals that Beethoven knew this. Days at a time went by without his conversing at length with another person or experiencing social pleasures. During such periods, the Divine Presence is, perhaps, felt more clearly. The consciousness inclines naturally towards prayerfulness. The mind becomes very still. A little scene of nature might fill one with transcendent ecstasy. All these experiences can serve to enhance creative art, and all did so in the case of Beethoven's music. In his particular case, upon reflection, it is very difficult to believe that he would have brought forth the music that he did had he been married. His second-period music was, after all, "heroic" music representing the individual Piscean-style spiritual initiate, and in order to compose his third-period work, his relationship to God had to become intimate to a point beyond even the imaginations of most people.

83

Not that his steadfastness was not assailed from time to time. For example, his journal of 1812 and 1813 contains entries in which the struggle is clearly revealed. This was soon after the ending of his apparent tie with Antonie Brentano, and his reflections upon the affair and its conclusion are here shot through with broader, archetypal concerns of the spiritual Path:

> Submission, absolute submission to your fate, only this can give you the sacrifice . . . to the servitude—O, hard struggle! Turn everything which remains to be done to planning the long journey—you must yourself find all that your most blessed wish can offer, you must force it to your will—keep always of the same mind.
>
> Thou mayest no longer be a man, not for thyself, only for others, for there is no longer happiness except in thyself,

in thy art—O God, give me strength to conquer myself, nothing must chain me to life. This way, everything with A. is finished.

To forgo a great act which might have been and remain so—O, what a difference compared with an unstudied life which often arose in my fancy—O fearful conditions which do not suppress my feeling for domesticity, but whose execution O God, God look down upon the unhappy B., do not permit it to last thus much longer—11

The first paragraph is a self-exhortation to relinquish all lesser concerns of life than those of the Path—"the long journey." The second paragraph is again a self-exhortation to surrender, to conquer the lesser self. Beethoven writes: "Thou mayest no longer be a man," meaning that, for him, to live an ordinary life would place him apart from the Will of God. He continues, "nothing must chain me to life." This is a powerful line, but what exactly does he mean by *life*? The answer is given earlier in the sentence: that he can no longer live for himself, only for others; he must not be chained to ordinary mortal life lacking higher purpose. "This way, everything with A. is finished." These journal entries point to a time of tortuous pain.

Elsewhere, we find two further short entries in which the "T" referred to by Beethoven is surely Antonie, who was often known to people as "Toni":

In the case of T. there is nothing to do but to leave it to God, never to go where one might do a wrong through weakness—to Him, to the all-knowing God, be all this committed.12

And again:

Be as kind as possible to T. Her attachment deserves never to be forgotten even if the results could never prove advantageous to you.13

A few years earlier Beethoven had composed his "favorite child," his one opera, *Fidelio*, but it had not been very successfully received. He now turned his attention to its revision. His regard

84

for the Divine Feminine could therefore now be directed towards the opera's heroine, Leonore.

Among the opera's themes are a wife's courage and constancy to her husband, her rescuing him from the jaws of death. Hence the title, *Fidelio*, "faithful one." Obviously, there has been speculation that the character of Leonore represented for Beethoven one of the actual women whom he had known in his life. Whether this is so or not, Leonore became a symbol of the ideal woman, possessing in the opera a constancy and morality which was virtually saintlike. Beethoven always held a special love for this opera, remaining faithful to it as though to a wife despite its initial poor reception and the need for several reworkings.

Beethoven himself may have died feeling that he never had found his Leonore, but then the Divine Feminine is rarely to be found so fully incarnated within an individual as within this heroine. And Beethoven's love for any human woman was always, in its fundamental form, the search for the Divine Feminine. Ultimately, Beethoven's love was for the universal Mother-God who is everywhere, and in all peoples, including within himself as the blazing, creative sacred fire. But in this footstool kingdom of time and space, do we not all sometimes see the Universal Virgin more clearly and tangibly in the face of a sweet, charming girl?

There were fluctuations in Beethoven's attitude toward marriage, and as a young man he proposed, and did so again as late as 1810, but as though by divine decree, he was rejected. In 1817 he confessed to being "exceedingly glad" of these rejections in his earlier days, because, he said then, he did not wish to be married. However, astrology may well have played a part here, for Sagittarians can, as we have seen, be swift to fall in love but may obstinately resist being dragged to the altar.

According to the classic Alexander Thayer/Elliot Forbes *Life of Beethoven*,[14] just two years before his death the composer did express a longing for domestic happiness and regretted not having married. This then, after all, may have been his final thought on the subject. However, if, as I have suggested, he could not have brought forth his momentous artistic creations if he had married, then we can but be grateful that in this, too, he proved a faithful servant to God, to his mission, and to the benefit of the generations destined to inherit the fruits of his sacrifice.

The Final Years 10

IN 1812 CLOUDS began looming over Beethoven which eventually so lowered his spirit that much of his creativity dried up. As his letters testify, in the aftermath of the Eternally Beloved affair, he became confused and depressed, and then physically ill. Furthermore, after intense arguments between Beethoven and his brother, Caspar Carl, Carl went ahead against Beethoven's hopes and married an unprincipled young woman by the name of Therese Obermeyer, who was already living with him. This action offended Beethoven's morality, and because of his sense of responsibility towards his brother, caused him intense grief. Beethoven also loathed his brother's wife.

In November, 1815, Carl died and left to the composer the guardianship of his nine-year-old son, Karl. Beethoven deeply desired to take Karl away from his brother's widow, for he did not consider her capable of raising Karl properly, but she was equally determined to retain the boy. The ensuing legal battles absorbed so much of Beethoven's emotional strength that his composition of important works virtually ceased. He had promised his dying mother to look after the family and felt young Karl to be contained within the scope of that promise. He also loved the boy dearly.

Beethoven's health was greatly affected by his worry and concern for the future of the boy, as the court cases swayed first in his favor, then in the woman's.

He had not entirely stopped composing, but not until late 1817 did Beethoven take up the pen again for a work of true significance, and the first bars of the unique B-flat Major or *Hammerclavier* Piano Sonata began to emerge. Even so, compared to his former output, little was composed for two years; thus 1816–19 was the driest creative period of his life.

Another reason for the lack of creative output was that he had exhausted everything that he wished to express in his "heroic" period style as exemplified in the Third and Fifth Symphonies. A new musical direction was required, something which Beethoven himself was not fully able to imagine or bring forth until a time of gestation, thought, and gradual musical development had taken place.

The style which was to emerge was to be a major turning point in the history of Western music. Even the most radical of musical developments or revolutions are usually extensions, more or less identifiably, of other, previously developed styles. But Beethoven's works were radically advanced and original beyond any music which had preceded them to a degree unique in the history of Western tonal art. Within the field of music, they correspond to the kind of revolution or paradigm shift which in science was engendered by the likes of Galileo or Einstein.

As Beethoven's deafness worsened, he found the condition very difficult to come to terms with, and it precipitated periods of inner torment. A journal entry reads: "The best thing to do not to think of your malady is to keep occupied." By the time he was fifty, his deafness was practically total. He was virtually cut off from all sounds of the outer world, and conversation often had to be conducted in writing for him to understand. This, combined with his isolation from the love of a life-partner, comprised a threat to his inner composure and strength. Yet again, as years before at the time of the Testament, it was a threat he met and overcame—through his music.

With the worsening of his deafness, Beethoven's "otherworldliness" also increased. A number of tales have come down to us of his tragicomic behavior in these later years. Once he absentmindedly went out early one morning and walked on all day, lost in thought and without food. His dress was such that in the evening he was arrested as a tramp. "I am Beethoven," he said. "Of course, why not!" came the reply as he was taken and locked up. Beethoven's shouts and demands eventually forced the police to bring Herzog, the local musical director, who knew the composer. "That *is* Beethoven!" exclaimed the astonished Herzog, and in the morning the shabbily dressed composer was sent home by the Commissioner of Police in a plush magisterial coach.[1]

A number of the aristocracy who had supported Beethoven and arranged for concerts of his music had by now died or left Vienna. Rossini visited the master and found him living in appallingly poor and untidy conditions, with water leaking through the ceiling. During their conversation, Beethoven sighed and said, "I am an unhappy man." Rossini wrote afterwards: "The portraits we have of Beethoven reproduce his features accurately enough. But no brush, no etcher's tool, could reproduce the sadness of his countenance or the deep-set eyes hidden under heavy eyebrows which gave the impression that they could wound with a glance. His voice was tender and mellow." As he left and walked away, Rossini was moved to tears. Beethoven's words, "I am an unhappy man," would not leave his mind. He felt ashamed of the attention and financial support he was himself by that time receiving while Beethoven had become so neglected. That evening he tried to convince some of the Viennese aristocracy to become Beethoven's patrons, but they would not. They considered him a reclusive eccentric.

For hours a day Beethoven's awareness was now completely immersed in music, and he could be almost oblivious to the world around him. Unaware of the noise he was making, he would sit at a table writing down the notes while he beat time with his feet, muttering and singing loudly and disjointedly, intermittently waving about and gesticulating with his arms. A woman employed at one time as a cleaner burst out laughing at this spectacle—but was seen by Beethoven, who drove her from the room.

He still went for long walks in the fields, during which he would compose in a notebook, yelling and waving his arms about. A peasant, driving two young oxen, once came across the shouting, wildly gesticulating figure, and Beethoven did not hear or heed the peasant's calls to "be a little quieter." The oxen took fright and ran down a steep hill before the peasant was able to bring them under control. But yet again Beethoven approached, still shouting and waving his arms. Again the peasant's calls were to no avail, and the oxen fled home in panic. Beethoven was by now at that stage of deafness of not realizing how loud the sounds were which he was making. Often, when talking to friends in the street or in a tavern, his voice would be so loud that other people around would look, and the friends became embarrassed and not a little concerned when Beethoven loudly voiced, as he sometimes did, criticisms which were politically dangerous. But these episodes were all the symptoms of deafness and of total immersion in his art—not of irrationality. Dozens of Beethoven's letters from his last decade have survived and reveal a man still perfectly sane, self-composed, and sharply intelligent.

To the extent that he had indeed become otherworldly, his music now followed suit. In late 1818 Beethoven, now forty-seven, began work on the stupendous *Missa Solemnis*. His journal of the time records that he went to considerable lengths to familiarize himself with the various past styles of church music and examples of suitable verses before embarking on this Mass. His diary also contains this moving reconsecration of himself to the mission:

> Sacrifice again all the pettiness of social life to your art. O God above all things! For it is an eternal providence which directs omnisciently the good and evil fortunes of human men. [Eight lines by Homer follow on the necessity to live a good and productive life, since "short is the life of man." Then Beethoven continues:] Tranquilly will I submit myself to all vicissitudes and place my sole confidence in Thy unalterable goodness, O God! My soul shall rejoice in Thy immutable servant. Be my rock, my light, forever my trust!

It was in this deeply devotional frame of mind that he embarked upon his second and greatest Mass. The *Missa Solemnis* is universally acknowledged to be different from any Mass composed by anyone before or since and to be of exalted sublimity. It took him five years, much longer than he ever spent in active work on any other composition. He did not complete it until February 27,

1823. His survival through hardship with almost no new music to sell during those long years is a story in itself.

A major reason for his frequent poverty was that he was the first composer to work without a patron, a situation partly due to his deafness and his resultant inability to play or conduct properly. Though he sometimes longed for the stability and security of an appointed position, like marriage, it, too, eluded him for a lifetime. In retrospect, this freedom was necessary for him to be able to compose not to order, but as his inspiration and divine mission took him. It meant, however, that he could rely on no regular salary or institutional backing. As recounted in Chapter 5, three of the Viennese aristocracy had promised Beethoven an annual stipend of 4,000 florins, but these florins became very intermittent after the death or departure from Vienna of the aristocracy, and, further, a severe devaluation undermined the florins' value. Many of his greatest works actually brought him little financial reward, and he could certainly have made more money by deserting his sacred calling to cater more to the immediate and less advanced demands of his contemporary public. The Battle Symphony, which he considered trivial and not one of the Nine, brought him more money than most of his truly great works. Though the players viewed it as a musical joke and a gigantic professional frolic, its noise and boisterousness made it a superbly popular success.

91

That Beethoven continued with the *Missa Solemnis* in the face of trying financial hardship demonstrates the depth of his commitment to his art. That he eventually won the right to custody of young Karl, thus having him also to support, did nothing to improve financial matters. Karl had experienced as problematic an upbringing as Beethoven and was not particularly well-behaved. To be fair, however, much of the tension between the two arose from Beethoven's neurotically overprotective attitude. He may have had no wife, but Beethoven had suddenly inherited a child, who arrived just at that age when boys yearn to begin exercising their individuality and freedom. Out of all proportion, Beethoven would go out of his mind with worry for days over relatively trivial incidents. At the same time, the tug-of-war over Karl with his late brother's widow was real enough, and still more legal suits followed. Reputedly a woman of loose morals, Beethoven hated her and dubbed her the "Queen of Night" after the character in Mozart's *The Magic Flute.*

The disruptions of living with Karl and of being enmeshed in legal wranglings, which so interfered with Beethoven's output at this time, may have been karmic in origin. They also may have been the result of occult forces of opposition to his work. Beethoven had already had an incalculable impact upon Western consciousness during his second period. Now his supreme third-period works were hovering, as it were, just above the physical, just beyond the point of crystallization into the form of score sheets, publications, and performances. Most esoteric systems teach that the greater the Light one is destined to manifest, the more that Light is opposed by forces of darkness which work through any and all means to prevent the victory. Archetypically as well as in practice, we see this process in the attempted opposition to the birth and mission of Jesus Christ, all the way from Herod's attempt to murder him as a newborn through to the later plots against his life of the Pharisees and Sadducees. Almost invariably, spiritual Light attracts the opposition of darkness in some form or another. In the lives of most aspirants, opposition comes in more subtle forms, and is most effectively and entertainingly described in C. S. Lewis's *The Screwtape Letters.* It may be, then, that Beethoven's entanglement with Karl and the "Queen of Night" was partly karmic, but partly also a *Screwtape*-style "set-up" by nonphysical forces, which worked for a time to prevent his third period works from being created. But once more, Beethoven at last won through.

Though we must imagine that in privacy and solitude Beethoven must have experienced moments of spiritual union with the divinity and glimpses of exalted realms of consciousness in order to have composed his final, sublime works, a number of accounts state that the last ten years of his life included times of almost unrelenting solitude and sorrow. Again, the glory of the man is in that from the midst of these, the most lonely and trying of all his years, he was capable of sufficient detachment and spiritual attunement to receive some of the most advanced music the world has yet known.

During the five years spent on the *Missa Solemnis,* the religious nature of the Mass itself, combined with the deafness and Beethoven's inner advancement, drew him into his final, third creative period, to which the Mass belongs. As biographer Marion Scott has expressed it, in the first period preceding Beethoven's worsening deafness and the Heiligenstadt Testament, he saw the *material world* from the *material standpoint*; in the second, between the Testament and the legacy of Karl, he saw the *material world* from the *spiritual standpoint*; and in the third period extending until Beethoven's final illness in late 1826, he saw the *spiritual world* from the *spiritual standpoint*. [2]

During 1823 and 1824 he wrote the world-famous Ninth Symphony: quite simply Beethoven's—and the world's—greatest work of the genre. He had been largely absent from the concert scene and had completed no major new works before the Mass for a number of years. He was now also disillusioned with the musical taste of the Viennese and thought of arranging for the premieres of the *Missa Solemnnis* and Ninth Symphony to take place elsewhere. But in the winter of 1823–24, thirty of Vienna's leading musicians, publishers of music, and music lovers addressed a moving open letter to the composer:

> Out of the wide circle of reverent admirers surrounding your genius in this your second native city, there approach you today a small number of the disciples and lovers of art to give expression to long-felt wishes, timidly to prefer a long-suppressed request . . .
>
> Do not withhold longer from the popular enjoyment, do not keep longer from the oppressed a sense of that which is great and perfect, a performance of the latest masterworks of your hand. We know that a grand sacred composition has been associated with that first one in which you immortalized the emotions of the soul, penetrated and transfigured by the power of faith and superterrestrial light. We know that a new flower glows in the garland of your glorious, still unequalled symphonies. For years, ever since the thunders of the victory at Vittoria [the Battle Symphony] ceased to reverberate, we have waited and hoped to see you distribute new gifts from the fullness of your riches to the circle of your friends. Do not longer disappoint the general expectations!
>
> May the year which we have begun not come to an end without rejoicing us with the fruits of our petition and may

the coming Spring when it witnesses the unfolding of one of our longed-for gifts become a twofold blooming-time for us and all the world of art!

Vienna, February, 1824.[3]

Arrangements for a Viennese dual premiere began, but Beethoven often displayed indecision, changing his mind about it more than once. On one occasion he was only persuaded to agree to the concert once more by a friendly conspiracy among his friends. They arranged among themselves to call on him, each one arriving individually and apparently by coincidence. Then, as though spontaneously, the subject of the concert was raised and the group prevailed upon Beethoven to sign a hastily prepared concert agreement. Upon their departure, Beethoven realized that a plan lay behind the incident, and uncharitably wrote to the main protagonists of the genial plot: "I despise treacheries. Do not visit me again. Concert not taking place."[4]

Eventually, however, the venue and all details were settled. On May 7, 1824, the Overture Op. 124, the Kyrie, Credo, and Agnus Dei of the *Missa Solemnis*, and all of the Ninth Symphony would be performed at the Käruthnerthor Theater in what was to be the greatest public event of Beethoven's last decade.

There were two full rehearsals. During the second, on the day before the concert, whatever Beethoven managed to hear of the performance of the Kyrie left him dissolved in tears of devotion. After the rehearsal of the symphony, he stood at the door to personally embrace all the players as they left.

Then arrived the night of the concert itself. Beethoven stood in front of the specially enlarged orchestra and choir, and beat time. He was now so deaf, though, that the performers had actually been instructed by Umlauf, the *Kapellmeister*, to watch himself, who conducted from a less prominent position, and Schuppanzigh, who led the strings. The audience was extremely enthusiastic. After one movement of the Ninth Symphony (accounts vary, but it was probably the *Scherzo*), the solo singer, Fräulein Unger, seeing that Beethoven was gazing at the score in utter oblivion to the immense applause, stepped forward and turned him around. Seeing the clapping and the waving hats and handkerchiefs, the composer bowed.

As Schindler wrote for Beethoven in his conversation book (one of the scrapbooks in which people communicated with the deaf composer in writing) after the concert: "Never in my life did I hear such frenetic and yet cordial applause. Once the second movement of the Symphony was completely interrupted by applause—and there was a demand for a repetition. The reception was more than imperial—for the people burst out in a storm 4 times. At the last there were cries of Vivat!"

With the composition and performance of the Mass and the symphony under his belt, from mid–1825 Beethoven turned his attention to string quartet writing, capturing in his last five string quartets the sacred tones of the most rarefied imaginable regions of consciousness. In the opinion of many, they are the greatest of all his works.

His personal life, meanwhile, was still disrupted by outbreaks of disharmony with Karl. The troubles with Karl culminated in 1826 when, attempting to leave behind him a squalid life of deceit, sin, debt, and some secret crime unknown to this day, the nineteen-year-old shot himself in the head.

Karl was not killed, and eventually recovered. But the episode only increased Beethoven's apprehension for the boy's future, especially since he suspected that his own years might be drawing to a close. He was still protective towards Karl to a neurotic degree. Therefore he urged his now-wealthy brother, Johann, to will his property to Karl. After fierce quarrels between the two brothers, Beethoven left Johann's house one night in the beginning of December, and in freezing weather headed back to Vienna. His health had been fragile for some time, and the shock of Karl's suicide attempt seemed to have taken years from him. Now, he arrived in Vienna ill with exposure and went straight to bed. But he was not to leave his lodgings again: the illness first became pneumonia, then what we now know to have been cirrhosis of the liver.

The illness dragged on into his fifty-seventh year and throughout the winter of 1826–27. These were months of great pain and awful conditions for Beethoven, though the latter were not so new to him. He was tapped four times for dropsy in a careless and unsanitary way, when pint after pint of excess fluid would suddenly be ejected from his swollen body. Parasites found their way into his bed. New Year was welcomed in with a violent quarrel with Karl,

95

who then left to join the army and never saw his foster father again. Beethoven had little or no fear of death, but hoped at least that, if his finale were to come, he might have a little money or someone to care a little for him at the end. Money came in the form of a compassionate gift from the London Philharmonic Society, a gift of a hundred pounds, though, as it turned out, it was too late for him to use it. Various friends came to visit him, as did Schubert, who was moved beyond speech by the sight of the sick master.

Being too ill to compose, Beethoven spent much of his time during this winter reading the complete scores of Handel. He said more than once that he placed Handel above all others, calling him "the master of us all." After performing the fourth operation for dropsy, the doctor tried to brace Beethoven up by saying the coming of the spring would help cure him. With a smile, the composer replied, "My day's work is finished. If there were a physician could help me his name would be called Wonderful." And as the doctor later told in a letter, "This pathetic allusion to Handel's 'Messiah' touched me so deeply that I had to confess its correctness to myself with profound emotion."[5]

Johann Hummel, a pianist, composer, and an old friend of Beethoven's, traveled to be at his bedside. Beethoven joked with him about his wife, whom Beethoven had known when she was young and beautiful. His words seem to show that he still took it to heart that he himself had not married. On Hummel's second visit Beethoven smiled and said, "You are a fortunate man. You have a wife who takes care of you, who is in love with you—but poor me!" He sighed heavily.[6]

Hummel's wife at first had not come; she had not been able to persuade herself to see in his present condition the composer she had known as a healthy, strong man; but Beethoven begged Hummel to bring her to visit him. A week later the couple did visit Beethoven, and again on March 23. This was to be the last time. Ferdinand Hiller, who also visited with them, records: "He lay, weak and miserable, sighing deeply at intervals. Not a word fell from his lips; sweat stood upon his forehead. His handkerchief not being conveniently at hand, Hummel's wife took her fine cambric handkerchief and dried his face several times. Never shall I forget the grateful glance with which his broken eye looked upon her." After having the last sacrament administered, Beethoven quietly quoted the words, *"Plaudite, amici, comoedia finita est."*[7]

At last, late in the afternoon of March 26, the end came. Hüttenbrenner, a friend of Schubert, was keeping vigil by the side of the dying master. Keeping vigil with him, the only other person present was Johanna von Beethoven, the sister-in-law with whom Beethoven had battled for the guardianship of Karl. It is good to know that by the end, Beethoven and the former "Queen of Night" were reconciled. Hüttenbrenner records the following strange conclusion to the story of the composer's life. After Beethoven had lain completely unconscious for hours:

> there came a flash of lightning accompanied by a violent clap of thunder which garishly illuminated the death-chamber. (Snow lay before Beethoven's dwelling.) After this unexpected phenomenon of nature, which startled me greatly, Beethoven opened his eyes, lifted his right hand and looked up for several seconds with his fist clenched and a very serious threatening expression as if he wanted to say: "Inimical powers, I defy you! Away with you! God is with me!" It also seemed as if, like a brave commander, he wished to call out to his wavering troops: "Courage, soldiers! Forward! Trust in me! Victory is assured!" When he let the raised hand sink to the bed, his eyes closed halfway. My right hand was under his head, my left rested on his breast. Not another breath, not a heart-beat more![8]

Beyond this point we cannot take Beethoven's earthly biography. But I fancy I see him rising free and victorious from his worn-out bodily form, shed like one of his tattered coats. And amid the cloud-tossed sky, the soul that was Beethoven meets the divine coauthor of his music, who then speaks gently and lovingly to him: "Well done, good and faithful servant; thou hast been faithful over a few things, I will make thee ruler over many things."

And, the once and future King of music, this soul that was Beethoven, shall surely come again.

97

PART *III*

The Music

His symphonies are to him what the Sermon on the Mount is to the life of Jesus; his sonatas are the inner struggle of Jesus in the Garden of Gethsemane.

—EDMOND BORDEAUX SZÉKELY[1]

How to Use
Beethoven's Music

11

THE REMAINDER of this book examines the most important works of Beethoven in the order that he composed them. My goal is to enhance the reader's understanding, enjoyment, and effective use of Beethoven's major works. Though you may use Beethoven's music for your pleasure and spiritual attunement in whatever way suits you best, here are a few specific suggestions:

1. It is not necessary to study and listen to his works as I have discussed them, in their precise chronological order, but it is advisable to begin with the earlier and middle works, progressing only afterwards to the later, third period pieces. In particular I suggest that those who are not yet familiar with most of Beethoven's music will benefit most from his final five string quartets only when they are first quite familiar with his other music.

2. The following study of Beethoven's compositions tells a story in itself of his soul—as an archetype for the soul of any seeker, including you and I—treading steadfastly along the stages of the Path. Even if you do not yet know all the works and do not have recordings of them all, I recommend that you read the next chapters in order, so that each piece you listen to may be understood in its context within the whole progression.

3. There are several different degrees of concentration with which to listen to music. As you listen to Beethoven's works, why not try all of these? Three basic planes at which we can listen have been called by Aaron Copland the sensuous plane, the expressive plane, and the musical plane.[2]

The *sensuous plane* is listening to music for the sheer pleasure of the experience. We may not always even be concentrating on it or thinking about it. The *expressive plane* involves actively concentrating on the music and absorbing its emotional "meaning" or impact. Carried out with sufficient concentration, this becomes a meditation. Great music is a tremendous aid to some forms of meditation. In meditating with Beethoven's music, concentrate on its being a direct musical revelation from God. Focus on what the music—beyond any ability of words to convey—is telling us about the nature of God, about eternal Truth, and about the Path. Always meditate with the heart as well as the head.

The *sheerly musical plane* is a way of listening to music which takes practice for the relative newcomer to classical music. It calls our intellect and intuition into play *and can help to boost our intellect and intuition.* This is the plane of appreciating the musical elements themselves. In a way, listening in this way is a second form of meditation to music. At this level, instead of just passively sitting back and being engulfed by the "sound" and "experience" of the music, one concentrates on being actively aware of such elements in the music as its melody, harmony, rhythm, and timbre. And there are many other elements besides, including trying to be aware of the work's emotional "meaning" and its musical structure. Using this level, one tends to sharpen one's awareness of so many factors. For example, what instruments are being used at a given moment, and why were they chosen to play those particular notes? Is a melody appearing for the first time, or is it a repetition? If a repetition, is the melody *exactly* the same, or is it a variation, and if it is a variation, in what way is it different? What kind of emotion does a particular passage seem intended to convey? Do different orchestras or conductors play a piece differently, and, if so, which do you prefer? Are there other melodies playing simultaneous to the main one? And so on. These are the kind of factors Beethoven himself had to be aware of in order to create each piece, so in our own discovery of them, we are following and taking on the profile of his own mind. This process of intellectual and spiritual evolution is very real: as modern psychological research has demonstrated, what we experience changes the very brain itself at the neuronal level.

4. I strongly recommend the frequent and repeated playing of recordings of Beethoven's music even just as background music. This is important for three reasons. First, the music influences and uplifts your emotions and vibrations even if you are not consciously listening. Second, we become familiarized with the melodies and other musical elements even when music is just playing in the background, so that what might at first hearing seem like a strange, incomprehensible collection of sounds gradually becomes familiar and loved, its musical progression and melodic content known and appreciated.

Third, the sound of any great music, even when released by recordings, carries a great and very real spiritual energy or radiance which blesses and heals. This energy charges the room and immediate environment wherever it is played, affecting even the physical atoms of the walls and furniture and of the bodies of those who are in the room. Music also has a direct effect upon the aura, capable of literally transforming a person's entire day. Even when the music has finished, the room is still charged for up to an hour or more and will bless all who enter. This healing energy of peace, joy, and upliftment also radiates out into the neighborhood. Therefore, do play Beethoven's music frequently and repeatedly!

(I have friends who, like myself, have consecrated a room, or a small closet, as a focus of blessing where Beethoven's nine symphonies are played constantly on auto-reverse, twenty-four hours a day. The volume only needs to be moderate and can be turned low at night if necessary. The spiritual charge which builds up in such a consecrated place is unmistakable, and increases over time. The nine symphonies are particularly powerful for this purpose and ideally should be played continuously in sequence from the opening of the first to the *Finale* of the ninth for the optimum esoteric effect, then repeated. Of course, if this is not possible, any way of playing them is still positive.)

Some people, including this writer, find that the various forms of rock music have an effect opposite to classical music, being destructive to the astral atmosphere of the planet as well as to the aura of the individual listener. Rock has sidetracked those

103

Before 1802: The First Period

Beethoven was the Titan of the musical world. Other famous musicians may be compared one to another, but Beethoven brooks no comparison. He stands alone. He was the veritable Prometheus who was lifted up to bring down spiritual music from heaven—music that will enthrall and enchant mankind for as long as the world stands.

—Edmond Bordeaux Székely[1]

 SYMPHONY NO. 1 IN C MAJOR (1799–1800). OP. 21.

Through the power of sound to affect soul, mind, emotion, and even the very atoms of our physical bodies, Beethoven's art transfers matrices of freedom and progress to all who hear it. To study this music is a spiritual adventure, a very real growth experience. Chord by chord, according to our capacity to receive and contain the distillations of spiritual essence, we can follow Beethoven through to those final years during which he began composing his way through to a new world of mystical awareness.

He was the master of almost every form of music prevalent in his day and was prolific in many forms, when one considers the length and quality of so many of his compositions. But if we are forced to restrict ourselves to an examination of only his very greatest and most significant works, then we should begin, if we take them in chronological order, with the First Symphony.

Beethoven had composed considerable chamber music towards the close of the eighteenth century, culminating in the *Pathetique*

Sonata for Piano of 1799. It seems as though he was intent upon mastering each musical genre as a foundation upon which he could build in ways uniquely his own. Then, the more secure and confident he felt within the established styles of composition, the more novel were the ideas which began to come to him. In the First Symphony the unmistakable, musically adventurous signature of Beethoven is already present in every passage, but it is still easily the most traditionally based symphony he wrote. Critics acknowledge the stature of the First Symphony in comparison to symphonies by other composers, though not all rank it equal to Beethoven's own other eight. However, it is difficult to tire of hearing this work's wonderful life, zest, and breezy humor.

Each of Beethoven's symphonies are symphonies of life. In fact, they are symphonies of the beings of the elemental kingdom and according to my sources were inspired upon Beethoven by nine of the Elohim. Thus a creative, mutative power emanates from the sound of these symphonies, for the Elohim, according to scripture, are the cosmic beings and conscious, living aspects of the Godhead who were responsible for the creation of the universe itself. In English translations of the Old Testament many of the references to God (singular) are actually mistranslations of the Hebrew word *Elohim* (plural). The Elohim are the gods or the aspects of God to whom the original Hebrew version of Genesis credits the manifesting of the universe through the "seven days" of the Creation. Just as the Elohim created the universe through their servants of the elemental kingdom, so they also created the Beethoven symphonies through this unique and worthy servant of the human kingdom. Beethoven's music can thus easily be seen to be *cosmic* music.

106

The nine symphonies are a formal rendition of the three-times-three, or a Trinity of Trinities. In them we hear the power, wisdom, and love flames of the Trinity in the elemental or nature kingdom, in the hearts of the angels, and in the hearts of the sons and daughters of God.

In my meditations on the inner nature of Beethoven's symphonies, I have intuited that each symphony corresponds with one sign of the zodiac, beginning with Capricorn for the First Symphony, going around the "cosmic clock" to Aquarius for the Second, and so on through to Virgo for the Ninth Symphony.

The order of the signs of the zodiac begins customarily in astrology with Aries; but for some purposes, to begin with Capricorn proves not only more accurate but also more cosmologically sound. The terrestrial year, for example, begins with Capricorn at the winter solstice, the first calendar month of January corresponding roughly with Capricorn. The terrestrial year is in fact a cycle of manifestation, each three-month period or quadrant of the year corresponding to one alchemical element and one of the four lower planes of existence. Thus, Capricorn, Aquarius, and Pisces (approximately December 22 to March 21) represent the Fire element and the etheric or higher mental plane. All is fulfilled, and the cycle of the year's manifestation completed, in Sagittarius in December, which concludes the three-month period corresponding with the Earth element and with the physical plane. This same cycle of manifestation is in fact followed by all activities, human or divine, beginning in Capricorn and the higher mental plane, and descending in vibration through the mental plane, the emotional plane, and into the physical plane, each plane of existence being represented by three signs of the zodiac. Even the twelve hours of the day follow this sequence: from midnight to 1 A.M. and from noon to 1 P.M., we are under the influence of Capricorn, for the next hour under Aquarius, and so on around the clock. (This is *why* our clock has twelve hours.)

If we try to fit the symphonies into a sequence beginning with Aries, there simply is no "fit." No correspondence between each symphony and the resulting zodiacal sign is evident at all. If, however, we begin at Capricorn as does the terrestrial calendar year and the hours of the clock, then all falls astoundingly into place. Precisely how each symphony relates to its resulting corresponding sign of the zodiac will be described in more detail in the treatment of each individual symphony in the pages ahead, but an outline is given below.

I do believe the resulting correspondences to be valid, though I would caution that I cannot offer any final confirmation for the identifications. However, if we accept this scheme as accurate, we can use the significance of the zodiacal signs and their properties to reveal a multitude of esoteric facts regarding each symphony. For example, each zodiacal sign corresponds to a certain hierarchy of beings which embody and release its vibrations and to a certain chakra or energy center within our subtle bodies, and so forth.

Thus, if my supposition is correct, the nine Beethoven symphonies correspond to the following zodiacal signs, embody the following divine qualities, and energize the following chakras:

No. of Symphony	Sign of Zodiac	Divine Quality	Corresponding Chakra
1	Capricorn	God-Power	Crown
2	Aquarius	God-Love	Seat-of-Soul
3	Pisces	God-Mastery	Solar Plexus
4	Aries	God-Control	Heart
5	Taurus	God-Obedience	Third Eye
6	Gemini	God-Wisdom	Throat
7	Cancer	God-Harmony	Base-of-Spine
8	Leo	God-Gratitude	Seat-of-Soul
9	Virgo	God-Justice	Solar Plexus

Through the law of polarity, some symphonies would also relate to others since they are opposite each other across the astrological "cosmic clock": namely the First and Seventh, the Second and Eighth, and the Third and Ninth.

Returning, then, to the First Symphony, Corinne Heline, the late, highly inspired American esoteric author, wrote that it "is a harbinger of the beauties and glories of the Nine Degrees of Initiation by which man becomes superman and godman. In it Beethoven rises to heights and descends to depths in a way that few of his time could foresee or understand. Whoever comes to perceive the values incorporated in the inner structure of this symphony will place it among the finest inspirations of this magnificent musical genius.

"Beethoven's compositions fall into definitely conceived patterns. This great musician did nothing without clear purpose. Thus, for instance, it is not to be taken as accidental that the introduction to the First Symphony is made up of twelve bars, each of which one may take as opening the door to one of the twelve zodiacal signs whose forces were all to play their part in the music truly cosmic in its expansion and nature. The twelve bars are divisible into three phases of four bars each, each of the four heralding the strain which is to follow. The four form an amalgamation of the powers that flow through the four elements of nature, namely: Fire, Air, Earth and Water."[2]

To this I would add that the words *Fire, Air, Water,* and *Earth* are rarely meant literally in esotericism. Usually the terms refer to the four planes of existence: the etheric (or higher mental), mental, emotional (or astral), and physical planes.

Throughout Corinne Heline's interesting work on the Beethoven symphonies are numerous fascinating numerological and other esoteric details. For example, of the *Allegro* of the First Symphony she points out that it "consists of 288 bars, 288 giving the numerical value of nine which is the number of man and of Initiation."[3] She notes of the second movement that it "consists of 250 bars, the numerical value of which is seven, a number fundamental in human evolution. It keynotes the movement which is introduced in an unusual seven-bar meter. Later there is a return to the four-bar measure after which is employed a single bar to confirm the beginnings of individualization."[4]

The third movement of the First Symphony, a minuet, is already very different from the then-traditional concept of the minuet and is typical of Beethoven in its intelligent, witty contrasts and in the jubilant, racing tempo of the *Scherzo* (meaning "vigorous and playful in character"). The numerical emphasis of the sparkling *Finale* is upon eight, the number of the Rose Cross and of the initiation into Christhood.

109

Piano Sonata in C-sharp minor (quasi una fantasia) (1801). Op. 27/2.

Though this composition is commonly known as the *Moonlight* Sonata, this was not Beethoven's own title. It derives from poet Ludwig Rellstab, for whom the piece portrayed "a boat in moonlight." Perhaps it is best for each individual to decide what Beethoven is expressing in this beautiful and popular piece. Certainly the image of moonlight shimmering upon placid waters is very fitting to the unique, well-loved first movement, with its exquisitely poetic triplets, but there is no indication that this is what Beethoven himself envisaged. One source states that the image Beethoven actually had in mind was that of a girl praying alone at an altar.

The immediate impression of peace is misleading: beneath the surface of the music, disturbance and tension is not difficult to detect. On the original manuscript penned by Beethoven, the notes of the sonata appear as though "driven forward on to the paper by a whirlwind,"[5] as Marion Scott puts it. The famous first movement was a marked, yet also justified, innovation to the piano sonata medium. Traditionally the opening movement was a sonata-form *Allegro* (meaning "played at a brisk, lively pace"), but here, and not by any means for the last time during his career, Beethoven felt free to compose within whatever structural form best suited what he had to express. Though the first movement verges on the melancholy, it is more than this, for melancholia has nothing to do with the Will of God, and there is something about the movement's infinite simplicity combined with beauty that comes straight from the planes of Perfection. Behind the sadness, if sadness it is, Beethoven appears to be making some deep statement of Reality.

This is fifth ray music, expressive of the green ray, the divine qualities of which are truth and healing.

SYMPHONY NO. 2 IN D MAJOR (1801–2). OP. 36.

Beethoven's third, fifth, seventh, and ninth symphonies are usually considered to be his greatest, the even-numbered symphonies thought to be, though masterpieces, not as great as the odd-numbered ones. Certainly the odd-numbered symphonies are more crucial in stating the transformations which took place within the composer, and in them greater issues appear to be involved. But the even-numbered works are also masterful. Not only are they great in their own right, but we must realize that the nine should be considered, to no small extent, as an integrated series: without any one of them, the others would be "unbalanced." It is important to know all nine symphonies well enough to be able to recognize quickly to which symphony and which movement music which one hears belongs, for this level of familiarity indicates that this music of Creation and life-energy has been well integrated into the soul.

The total nine symphonies sound the mystic tones of the nine spiritual mysteries on the Path of Initiation. Symphonies no. 1,

3, 5, and 7 are masculine, or *yang* in nature; symphonies no. 2, 4, 6, and 8 are feminine, or *yin*. In nonesoteric terminology this fact is acknowledged also by mainstream musicologists, since it is in the odd-numbered symphonies that Beethoven makes his great, powerful, thrusting statements, while in the even-numbered ones he is more relaxed and at peace. The Second Symphony, then, is feminine in nature. According to my meditations, it expresses the tonal energies of the hierarchy of Aquarius, its spiritual keynote being God-Love. And this can immediately be heard to be true, for the work does indeed exude this divine quality. So beautifully does it exude light and love, that many have actually claimed this Beethoven symphony as their favorite. Whereas the First Symphony had at least paid tribute to the musical conventions of the day, the Second contains more of the daring inventiveness and unique individuality of the composer. For this reason Beethoven found it difficult to write; in it, he was entering unexplored regions of symphonic music. The introduction is extremely long for the day, and sudden innovations, modulations, and hints of the symphonies to come occur in many places.

Corinne Heline refers to the work in terms of visual light and color: "The first movement produces the effect of brilliant sunshine. The *Larghetto* sounds in subdued colors like the varied play of light and shadow on some clear surface. The *Scherzo* flashes and sparkles in vivacious gaiety and beauty, bursting into dynamic contracts in the *Finale*."[6]

111

> *Beethoven's music has always resisted the attitude of detached connoisseurship. It is an involvement, a challenge to the very substance of the mind, a perpetual assault upon our complacency, a symbol of the victory of consciousness over itself.*
>
> —Philip Barford[1]

SYMPHONY NO. 3 IN E-FLAT MAJOR (EROICA) (1803–4). OP. 55.

Beethoven's Third Symphony, the *Eroica*, marked a startling and profound turning point in his work. Nothing which had preceded it came close to its peaks of tonal expression, its depths of meaning. It was originally composed as a celebration of the life and victories of Napoleon. But Beethoven, as we have seen, scratched out the dedication to Napoleon when the latter abandoned his altruistic and selfless mission of uniting Europe and instead proclaimed himself Emperor of France. From the highest point of view, however, the dedication to Napoleon was never more than a rationale for the composition of the work, for truly its meaning and value go far beyond the worldly affairs of humanity.

The *Eroica* symphony is at once a record of Beethoven's personal experience and the archetypal blueprint for every soul reaching the challenges and trials, initiations and triumphs of this stage of the spiritual path. It is the first major work to follow the period spent by Beethoven at Heiligenstadt when, afflicted by deafness, he suffered to the farthest reaches of his soul and emerged with the Heiligenstadt Testament. The Testament itself tells of the death of the mortal ego and the victory of the Real Man which took place in him at this time. It is this initiation which is recorded in every note of the Third Symphony. As the Testament records, although the prospect of continuing his life merely for the sake of himself as a man was unbearable to him, Beethoven determined not only to live but to commit his life to absolute, active service. He redefined the purpose of his existence as being *solely* for the sake of altruistic service to humanity, a service that he would render through his art. Music, as his divine gift to the world, became his absolute *raison d'être*.

Continuing the arc of the symphonies around the circle of the zodiac, the *Eroica* comes under the vibration of Pisces and indeed is Piscean through and through. The inner spiritual keynote of Pisces and of this Third Symphony is God-Mastery. The Piscean dispensation is that of the individual overcomer, and the archetypal story of the individual overcomer is rendered in tone form by the *Eroica*. In Pisces, as in the *Eroica,* the individual mortal struggles to become the victorious Christ, the perfect example of such a victor under the Piscean dispensation being, of course, Jesus. But first one must pass through the dark night and the crucifixion, represented within the *Eroica* by its funeral march.

Beethoven's contemporary composer, Rossini, wrote, "At Vienna I heard for the first time one of his symphonies, the *Eroica*. Henceforth I had but one idea: to make the acquaintance of this great genius, to see him, if only once."[2] And in the words of Marion Scott, "The *Eroica* symphony is one of Beethoven's supreme works; it is one of the supreme treasures of the world."[3] Its importance overflowed the field of music to affect consciousness, society, life itself. British musicologist Wilfrid Mellers sees the symphony as "the work that was to prove a watershed in European history as well as in Beethoven's own development."[4]

At a time when most of the symphonies had been completed (but not the Ninth), Hofrath Küffner, who was then living with Beethoven, asked him during a meal out, "Tell me frankly which is your favorite among your symphonies?"

"Eh! Eh!" Beethoven replied in good humor. "The *Eroica*."

"I should have guessed the C Minor."

"No; the *Eroica*."

Beethoven knew that it was with this work that he revolution-ized the symphonic medium for all time to come. And the themes it conveyed were also the most personal and close to his heart.

The first movement of the *Eroica* is very long, yet marvelously compact and moving. It is saturated with the psychological key-notes of heroism and the determination to overcome. At one point, for a brief moment, the brass section sounds out several powerful chords which omnipotently express the culmination of this phase of the struggle, a mixture of towering intensity and near-triumph, but then the moment passes, and the heroic struggle resumes. At another point, doubts querulously express themselves in the woodwinds, but then again the unstoppable main theme comes marching through. Writes Marion Scott: "In the great episode of the *Eroica* first movement Beethoven uses his beautiful melody in distant keys and its orchestration, divided between woodwind and cellos, lightly held together by the other strings, is indescribably sympathetic. The moment of actual return to the first subject is one of his most astounding strokes. The orchestra is hushed almost to nothing. Against a tremolo in the violins held on dominant harmony, the horn enters with the first theme in the tonic of E flat. By academic precedent it was all wrong; psychologically it was gloriously right and immensely daring."[5]

We have surmised that the zodiacal keynote of this symphony is Pisces. The esoteric, divine quality of each zodiacal sign also has its perversions or opposites. The failure to express the positive Piscean quality of God-Mastery results in the particularly Piscean negative attributes of doubt, fear, human questioning, and records of death. It is these Piscean aspects which appear in the second movement, which is a funeral march. Yet this funeral march is not, ultimately, a record of death, nor does it succumb to doubt and fear. Through the valley of darkness, the hero struggles continuously to fasten his gaze upon the higher goal of the resurrection. At worst, the funeral march is negative and melancholy only to provide contrast for the triumph to come.

Every commentator has sought to explain and understand this movement. Does it refer to the death of Napoleon? Quite possibly. Can it be derived at some level from the sufferings and contem-plations of Heiligenstadt? Yes, this is at least equally likely. But it

115

is also an expression of the tribulations of all souls, the song of a world in pain as it struggles with mortality. As St. Paul wrote, we "die daily" in seeking to cast off our old selves and give birth to the new. Throughout this movement's somber, tragic tones arise notes of heroism, compassion, and even the first gleams of a future glory.

When, years later, Beethoven heard that Napoleon had died in reality, the one-time emperor was hero no longer in the eyes of the composer. In 1809, when Napoleon had besieged and bombarded Vienna, Beethoven was there and once shouted out in anger that if only he could command armies as well as he could write music, he would show them a thing or two! Each of the two men had a great potential destiny which was theirs to fulfill, if only they willed to. One of them succeeded, and the other failed. As it was, when news of Napoleon's death came to Beethoven, his only comment was a sardonic "Well, I have already written his Requiem."[6]

The surging rhythms and beautiful melodies of the third movement relieve the tension, to say the least. But that such a delightfully happy *Scherzo* should follow the funeral march has perplexed commentators since the time it was first performed. One of the greatest mysteries in all of Beethoven is the poetic meaning his tones are intended to convey here. No worldly, literally programmatic solutions seem adequate. (For example, Berlioz' suggestion that the *Scherzo* represents funeral games such as those in the Iliad, at the grave of the dead warrior.) Under literal assumptions, the death and funeral of the hero would surely come in the final movement.

Ultimately, only esoteric insight can provide the clue. Since the second movement does not represent literal death at all, but rather an episode of soul-testing, there follows the music of spiritual victory. After the dark night of the soul comes the light. In the words of David, "Sorrow endureth for the night but joy cometh in the morning."[7]

Beethoven is benevolent and relaxed in the final movement. Conflict has been resolved in victory. Strength, enthusiasm, self-mastery, and all that is endowed upon the Piscean-style conqueror has now been assimilated by the soul.

Wagner wrote at length about the inner, spiritual meaning of this symphony. He saw it as expressing the growth and final rounding off of the "full-fledged *man*," the *Finale* depicting "the

116

whole man," the "total Man, who shouts to us his avowal of his Godhood."[8]

PIANO SONATA IN F MINOR (APPASSIONATA) (1804–6). OP. 57.

"During a walk," recalled Ferdinand Ries, "during which time we became lost, to the point of not getting back to Dobling until eight o'clock, Beethoven hummed the whole way and sometimes started to shout out tones without, however, singing. On arriving back, he set to work on the *Finale* of the Sonata in F Minor—the *Appassionata*."

The *Appassionata* was the culmination of Beethoven's lengthy early period of piano sonata writing, being no less than the twenty-third piano sonata to which he gave an opus number. Yet following it, he was not to write another for some five years. Again, as with the *Moonlight*, the title is not Beethoven's own. Apt the title is, however, the first movement so brimming with fiery passions, as is also the dynamic third movement. Between them lies the *Andante*, a curiously lovely piece in which all thought and conflict is held in virtual suspension. If we were lying in a canoe floating gently down a placid river, we could not exude more contentment than does this interlude. But then, from the calm and serenity, we pass into the sometimes almost ferocious passages of the *Finale*.

When asked to explain the sonata's meaning, Beethoven enigmatically replied: "Read Shakespeare's *Tempest*." Though the music is certainly tragic, it displays no obvious connection to *The Tempest*, and it is most unlikely any literal, programmatic connection exists. So the composer's reply was deliberately elusive in meaning and remains a mystery.

117

FIDELIO (1805, REVISED 1806 AND 1814). OP. 72.

Fidelio was Beethoven's only opera. Probably no other of his works brought him so much sorrow and disappointment, as for a period of almost ten years one factor after another opposed its being performed and its success. But after extensive revision, it finally emerged as a mature and great exposition of the operatic musical form. Beethoven himself considered it his one composition most "worthy of being preserved and used."

In 1823 or 1824 Beethoven stated, "My 'Fidelio' was not understood by the public, but I know that it will yet be appreciated." A couple of years later, as he lay dying, he told Schindler: "Of all of my children, this is the one that cost me the worst birth-pangs, the one that brought me the most sorrow; and for that reason it is the one most dear to me. Before all the others I hold it worthy of being preserved and used for the science of art."[9]

Virtually all operas are concerned with the relationship between men and women. Esoterically, they tell the symbolic story of how twin flames (male and female souls who were created together in the heart of God) become separated by the negative karma of the one or the other. Though the female may remain faithful, the duo may be let down by the male (*Madame Butterfly)*. Or it may be the male who is treading the Path immaculately, while the female partner outpictures imperfection (*Lohengrin)*. In *Thais*, by Jules Massenet, the story opens with Athanael, the male, living in monastic seclusion and prayer, and Thais, the female, living the life of a sensational, erotic courtesan, only for the opera to conclude with Thais having repented and turned to God, yet Athanael fallen and given over to desire. Of all of the great operas, it is in *Fidelio* alone that both male and female protagonists pass their initiations to perfection, making no negative karma whatsoever.

Many commentators have noted this opera's purity, its freedom from worldliness. Typical of Beethoven's idealism, he had refrained from writing music for any more profane libretto. For instance, though he much admired Mozart's music, Beethoven thought Mozart's operatic materials too frivolous and would not himself compose to such words.

The essential outline of the plot of *Fidelio* is as follows: For two years Florestan, a Spanish nobleman, has been secretly imprisoned in a mountaintop fortress by the regional governor, Pizarro. His whereabouts are unknown to others. But Leonore (often in translation spelled Leonora), Florestan's young wife, in searching for him, has dressed herself as a boy and penetrated the fortress to find out if Florestan is imprisoned there. She says that her name is Fidelio (a name taken from Shakespeare). From Rocco, the jailer, she learns that there is a secret prisoner of state, whose rations of food and water Pizarro ordered weeks before to be cut to almost nothing. She suspects that this prisoner may be Florestan, which indeed it is.

Pizarro had been hoping that the reduced rations would kill Florestan. But on discovering that a minister plans to make a surprise inspection of the fortress, he realizes that he must kill Florestan immediately and hide the body. Rocco is first asked to do the deed. He refuses but agrees to dig a grave in the lowest dungeon in preparation. He goes down with Leonore to accomplish this.

The lowest dungeon is exceedingly dark, damp, and miserable. It is here that Florestan is kept. Hearing Florestan in the darkness, Leonore recognizes the voice of her husband. When Pizarro comes with a dagger to kill him, Leonore bars the way and reveals her identity with the dramatic, powerfully rendered words: "*First kill his wife!*" When Pizarro does advance with the dagger, however, Leonore produces a pistol which she had earlier secured. At that very moment a trumpet call sounds from the tower above, announcing the arrival of the minister. Pizarro has to go immediately to meet him, leaving Leonore and Florestan (who sing the rapturous duet, "Joy inexpressible").

119

Soon afterwards, in front of a gathering of local people, the minister states that he has come in order to ensure that the King's justice is administered according to the just law. For his imprisonment of Florestan, the minister has Pizarro arrested. Florestan is still enchained, and the minister gives to Leonore the key, that she herself might be the one to loose him. The many other prisoners have been reunited with their families, and at the *Finale*, the entire group of the main characters, the freed captives, and the locals sing a jubilant and powerful song of emancipation and renewal. This song actually leaps out of the margins of the preceding plot, concluding the opera on a universal, transcendent note of freedom and hope.

There are, however, a large number of mysterious aspects to the plot of *Fidelio*. Various things are not clearly explained, but only an unspoken impression conveyed. This was partly due to the fact that the theme of the repressive, unjust government and of the gaining of freedom from such a regime was a very sensitive one in Austria and with its censors at the time. The creators of the opera had to go to great lengths to convince the authorities that the libretto was concerned only with a limited and specific period and with a place elsewhere in Europe.

Among those questions which are not clearly answered in the libretto are these: Are Leonore and Florestan entirely alone in their opposition to the unjust Pizarro, or is Florestan perhaps associated with an opposition movement? Is there a dawning of rebellion among the populace at the same time as Leonore's penetration of the fortress? (In several places a simmering uprising among the people seems to be hinted at.) And who, precisely, is the minister, Fernando? Why has he come now, and of what nature is the national regime? Have there been changes at the top in favor of greater justice? Under the Austrian government of the time, these things could not be clearly spelled out.

In the prominence Beethoven placed upon the music of *Fidelio*, which was unusual for the day, and in its style, the opera was a precursor to the music-dramas of Wagner. Beethoven spent long months carefully composing the work. There are no less than sixteen sketches for the opening of Florestan's air alone.

At first the opera was flawed. This was partly due to the original libretto's weaknesses and also to the fact that Beethoven was new to the medium. Unfavorable political conditions did not help: the first performance had to be postponed when the police censor's department objected to the text. With an adjusted text, the first performance went ahead in Vienna on November 20, 1805, but French troops had taken the city only a week earlier, so that the premiere and succeeding performances were practically unattended. Poor reviews and Beethoven's falling out with the theater's manager added to the woes.

Beethoven returned to *Fidelio* again and again, always seeking to improve it, and Stephen von Breuning, his friend, condensed the original three acts to two. The final incarnation of the opera emerged on May 23, 1814, to be met at last with acclaim.

Like his symphonies, Beethoven's opera is also an expression of his own emotions, beliefs, and aspirations. It is a work of immense moral power. Though on the surface its story is that of Leonore and Florestan, the opera actually embodies meanings and ideals which are of universal, including contemporary, significance. Chief among these are the themes of: 1) the Divine Feminine, and 2) the attainment of exalted and spiritual liberty.

120

The character of Leonore is Beethoven's ideal of a woman. She proves faithful to her husband through two years of adversity, and one feels she is prepared like Florestan to act in the cause of justice and truth not only to free her personal beloved but in support of universal rights.

In fact, Leonore is the ideal of womanhood of the enlightened age of Aquarius. Through the ages of Aries and Pisces, the role of woman was subdued by the patriarchal climate of the times. In Aquarius, as we already see beginning, woman is resuming her rightful role as man's equal consort—different from man, possessing different characteristics and potentialities, but equal. Lacking woman's input, the enlightened society of the future cannot successfully be manifested. Moreover, Leonore's fidelity, purity, courage, and idealism embody the essence of the Divine Feminine, which God desires all females to manifest.

Indeed, these qualities are those required for all souls of both sexes to cultivate the Divine Feminine within themselves. Only through the raising of the Divine Feminine, known in Hinduism as the sacred kundalini force, may humanity be liberated from its dungeon of karma and mortality, as Florestan is freed from his chains. Not that Beethoven was necessarily conscious of this symbology within *Fidelio*, yet the miracle is that it is present in the opera nonetheless.

121

Just as the energy of the Divine Feminine acts in the world as the creator and preserver of all that is worthy, so too it is the destroyer of all that stands in the way of evolution by being outworn or evil. At the dramatic moment in which she reveals her true identity, Leonore exclaims, "First kill his wife!" Then she continues, "Yes, I am Leonore," and turning to Pizarro, declares, "I am his wife, I have sworn solace to him, and destruction to you!" Thus, the incarnation of the Divine Feminine as Kali, the constructive destroyer, is here also taken up by Leonore. She is prepared to act, to use force in order to defeat evil and defend the good.

Florestan is also a man of the coming enlightened time; he is prepared to act courageously for the causes of truth, freedom, and all high ideals, and is incapable of passivity in the face of injustice, despite the consequences. Yet it takes Woman to free him. Leonore is also a symbol of the individual human being's personal inner flame of the Mother-God; or of the archetypal Eve atoning for the Fall of man which she caused originally through impurity, now destined to raise him up once again through unadulterated faithfulness. Leonore's descent into the deepest dungeon of the fortress is very like the archetypal descent of myth and fable into the underworld (the lower astral plane of esotericism) for the sake of rescuing those caught there.

Through the intercession of woman (Leonore), fallen man who is nevertheless still a son of God (imprisoned Florestan) receives the body and blood (Leonore's bread and Rocco the jailer's wine) of Christ, through which he may attain liberty and everlasting life.

Another major theme of the opera is freedom and its attainment. It is evident that this freedom is not only physical but also spiritual. "Men climbed towards the light," sing all the people in the final cantata melody. While Florestan is incarcerated, he has an ecstatic vision of Leonore, not as a wife, but as an angel summoning him to liberty in heaven. When Pizarro exits from Florestan's dungeon, his murder attempt foiled, Rocco takes Leonore's and Florestan's hands, presses them to his breast and, in a most significant gesture, points to heaven, signifying that this is the destined goal of these twin flames.

But freedom is not only a quality to be enjoyed one day in heaven. Humanity must strive actively to keep or to attain it within the world of time and space. Leonore, in producing the pistol with the intent of using it if necessary, saves the lives of herself and her beloved and buys time for Florestan to be liberated. At the very moment she produces the pistol in self-defense, the saving trumpet sounds out, symbolic of heavenly intervention. But it is as though Leonore's demonstration of individual willingness to move in active defense of truth and justice is necessary to bring forth this divine intervention. Without the physical action, help from above would not have come.

The trumpet, actually heralding the arrival of the minister, also heralds in the new era. The minister's decisions are like local forerunners to the archetypal Day of Judgment. Florestan is freed; a gracious amnesty is given to all the other prisoners; and Pizarro is arrested. Wrongs are righted, and the guilty are enchained. The new regime is Utopian and is greeted by a rousing *Finale* which has been called a precursor to the choral *Finale* of the Ninth Symphony. This transcends the allegory and fiction of the body of the opera, concluding the work in hopeful, powerful praise of liberty and brotherhood.

During the course of the opera's various revisions, Beethoven composed, besides the original, three replacement overtures. Of the total four overtures, the first three are named after the original title of the opera, as *Leonore No.'s 1, 2,* and *3.* (Opp. 138, 72a, and 72 respectively.) The fourth overture, the *Fidelio Overture*, is the one usually used in modern productions. However, following the practice inaugurated by Gustav Mahler in Vienna in 1904, *Leonore No. 3* is often played today before Act Two.

Of the three Leonore overtures, by far the most significant is the third. *Leonore No. 3* is a lengthy and magnificent tone-poem in which all the main elements of the operatic action are incorporated. The music takes us, in various sections, through the suffering and incarceration of Florestan, Leonore's struggle to free him, her success, and the final, jubilant sense of universal triumph. Its trumpet calls, which in the body of the opera announce the arrival of the minister and salvation, are renowned among music lovers. Within the music of this overture, through the tonal representation of Florestan and Leonore, the twin energy currents of yang and yin mingle as Divine Masculine and Divine Feminine, Alpha and Omega. The overture's conclusion is one of Beethoven's greatest musical expressions of the sense of ultimate and absolute victory.

123

The *Fidelio Overture*, though not of the intrepid scale of *Leonora No. 3*, is satisfying in its own right. It was composed in 1814, and unlike the three C Major Leonore overtures of 1805, it is in E Major. Loud, extravert chords contrast with the several much quieter passages representative of Leonore, her fidelity, and her compassionate heart.

Grand as *Fidelio* may be, it was Beethoven's first and only opera, and one senses that had he lived longer, he may well have gone on to write still greater works of the genre. One senses, too, from the grand and inspiring impressions left upon us by *Fidelio,* as well as by the operas and music-dramas of Wagner, Puccini, and many others, that this is an art form still destined to prove of immense importance in the centuries to come.

PIANO CONCERTO NO. 4 IN G MAJOR (1805–6). OP. 58.

Beethoven's first three piano concertos were written between 1798 and 1800. But by 1805 vast changes had taken place within his soul, resulting in a fourth concerto for piano which was unmistakably greater than any of the previous three. Its structure was completely novel; for example, the piano, alone, opens the work.

The first movement has an unearthly beauty, lyrical and restrained. The second, it is said, Beethoven composed with Orpheus' plea in the underworld in mind. The piano, as Orpheus, movingly pleads with the orchestra, the underworld spirits, which are at first inflexible but are gradually brought to a change of heart by Orpheus' magic sounds. The final movement expresses this success in its captivating, rhythmic theme.

I remember well the strains of this concerto drifting across the wide expanses of lawn, palm grove, and sandy beach when, years ago, I stayed near Madras, India. Each evening I would walk along a deserted but well-kept pathway which passed near to an unusual circular bungalow with a wide patio. Here some Europeans, presumably retired, were living out their days in quiet, meditative seclusion. Being apart from the usual noise and bustle of India, the house and its expansive, well-kept grounds were an oasis of peace and serenity. Each evening as I passed, there would be some music playing. Its sound was not so much *in* the home but rather emanating *from* it, as though to shed its radiation throughout the surrounding regions. This music was frequently Beethoven's Piano Concerto No. 4. It is impossible to describe the impression the music made in this setting. It seemed to transform the environment into a region from another world. Even the land of India became still more magical and mysterious. The fiery sun sank down into the Indian Ocean, and the air turned swiftly from deep blue to turquoise and vermillion as, sensing it their time of day, new fauna came into prominence among the palms, the grasses, and the great banyan tree, and the piano of eternity wove its tapestry of longing with the orchestra of infinity.

VIOLIN CONCERTO IN D MAJOR (1806). OP. 61.

This is the only concerto composed by Beethoven for the violin, yet how typical of his genius that this should also be considered

124

by many to be the finest concerto for the instrument that there is! Its formal structure is impeccable, the whole work rich in elegance. The long first movement is sculptured throughout in collaboration with the tonal character and possibilities of the instrument. The wonderful melodies of the first sections, effective in that special, emotive way unique to the violin, return to us at last, like long-lost lovers, in the recapitulation. The tenderness and wistfulness of the second movement are absolute, expressed in a dialogue of complete agreement between the soloist and the orchestra. The third movement is deliciously happy and lively, built upon a main theme which is like a folk melody. In its use of the horns, the *Finale* is at times reminiscent of French hunting music. Such is the grandeur and scope of this concerto, and so important is the role of the orchestra that it has sometimes been referred to, only half-jokingly, as the "tenth symphony."

Symphony No. 4 in B-flat major (1806). Op. 60.

This is a symphony of spiritual happiness—the happiness that comes with attainment. Poised between the two staggering *yang* peaks of the Third and the Fifth, the Fourth Symphony is a rich, verdant valley of *yin* expressiveness. Indeed, from biographers' studies of Beethoven's notebooks, the basic ideas for the Fifth Symphony came to him following the completion of the Third. But something held him back from composing all of the Fifth until this gentler B Major work could insert itself into the divine scheme of alternating *yang* and *yin* symphonies.

In the opinion of esotericist Corinne Heline, the spiritual key-notes of the four movements are, respectively, Serenity, Happiness, Beauty, and Peace.[10] What more could we ask for?

The first movement opens with the somber, expansive tones of eternity. How strange these sounds, used at the very beginning of the symphony, must have seemed to the people of the day! Then the somber void abruptly alters into what might be called the *vitality* of serenity. Of this first movement, Berlioz said, "One is seized, from the first bars, with an emotion that by the end becomes shattering in its intensity!"[11] The work culminates in a jovial fourth movement which tells of the peace of victory. Here, the orchestral sections gleam and swirl as various individual instruments come to

125

the fore and then once more recede in a marvelous synthesis of the orchestral medium.

MASS IN C MAJOR (1807). OP. 86.

This was Beethoven's first Mass. Though he composed it within the general structure traditional for Masses, Beethoven also added numerous creative ideas which lift the Mass in C Major high above those of most other composers. Beethoven knew that in order to "sing the new song" of a new era, certain innovations can be justified. Nevertheless, changes to established musical styles are crucially important developments, to be implemented only after forethought, and with caution. As the philosophers and sages of the great civilizations of ancient times were aware, changes in music eventually manifest as changes in thinking and lifestyle: "As in music, so in life." It was due to this awareness, by then held only half-consciously, that the world of music retained a considerable conservatism until the 1800s.

Therefore even this Mass, which was relatively straightforward compared to the *Missa Solemnis* which followed it over a decade later, was to Beethoven's contemporaries an unexpected and disconcerting departure from the norm. The work had been commissioned by Prince Esterhazy, and after its performance in his castle, Prince Esterhazy's first words to the composer were "but . . . my dear Beethoven, what have you been up to, writing this?" However, from the advantage of our own retrospective viewpoint, we can see that the work contains many superb passages of song and orchestration. One of the most telling qualities is the way in which the words are set to music, Beethoven extracting their full impact and depth of meaning by his strokes of musical genius.

SYMPHONY NO. 5 IN C MINOR (1804–8). OP. 67.

The Fifth is the most popular symphony of all time. E. T. A. Hoffman calls the Fifth "a Rhapsody of genius," while Neville Cardus enthuses that "not a note is uncharged with power and expression." One of the greatest qualities of the work is exactly this—its compactness. Not a note could be missed or changed without the whole work failing to remain the C Minor Symphony so many love to hear. The symphony is faultless in conception and flawless in construction.

So familiar has this masterpiece become that we rarely stop to realize today how unusual it is for a work based upon such deep spiritual themes to also become the most popular. Yet this was always Beethoven's conscious mission, "to approach the Godhead more nearly than other mortals and by means of that contact to spread the rays of the Godhead through the human race." In 1801, let us recall, he had written, "I shall seize Fate by the throat; it shall certainly not bend and crush me." These words were deeply felt, and the same concept was expressed by him in several letters written over that same general period. We know that around this time of the Heiligenstadt Testament, he had faced a great dark night of the soul but then found light in the very resolution itself to press on, never to give in, to overcome all. Yet the strengthening of one's personal, individual willpower is one thing; the *submission* of that will to the greater Will of the Supreme is quite another. After all, exceptionally strong willpower and resolute determination is present among a fairly large minority of humanity, such people usually becoming successful in one field or another such as business, science, art, or politics. But the individual who has surrendered all of his or her inner qualities into the hands of God, determining to do only God's Will, is of another, far rarer, and far more important breed. The drive and forceful will of such a person is not directed toward personal success *per se*. Rather, such a soul is an instrument through which the Universal Plan can manifest.

127

Even the great majority of people who do live their lives in direct altruistic service to others have not really surrendered to the Will of God, though they invariably believe that they have. In actuality they are fulfilling their own ideas of what needs doing and of what they should be. The difference, though seemingly subtle, is actually vast, placing the two classes of people worlds apart. The difference between those who are altruistic and who do serve others but are not aligned to the Will of God and those who are truly aligned is the difference between the neighborhood vicar and those such as St. Francis of Assissi or Mahatma Gandhi. And those such as Beethoven also, for it was due to his ever-increasing alignment with the One Above that his tremendous symphonic expression of God's Will was able to flow through him.

The tug-of-war between the desire to do one's own will, to serve oneself, and the desire to serve the greater Will of the Supreme is in fact the central problem of life itself. The surrender of one's outer life and one's inner qualities—the genuine surrender—is the greatest challenge of the spiritual Path. All other challenges and all other testings of the soul stem from this one. Yet the decision to become a handmaid of the Lord, to serve God and humanity wholeheartedly, is no simple decision like a New Year's resolution. It actually involves millions of decisions: to do the Will of God, the perfect thing, at every moment of every day. It is not that the same soul, unchanged, orients itself toward a new set of activities, but that gradually, painstakingly, the very fabric of the soul itself must be transformed and realigned.

Only one problem stands in the way of this self-transformation. This problem is the "Catch 22" of the spiritual Path. The one problem is the self itself. In the Bhagavad Gita we read: "Oh, let the self exalt itself, not sink itself below: Self is the only friend of self, and self Self's only foe. For self, when it subdues itself, befriends itself. And so when it eludes self-conquest, is its own and only foe."

128

This struggle to surrender to the Higher Self and to the Will of God is the spiritual theme of the C Minor Symphony. As Beethoven wrote, "Fate" must not "bend and crush" the soul, but the soul must not kick against or flee from its cosmic destiny either. Only that which is nonaligned with the Creator is ever ultimately "bent and crushed." The key to Reality and to self-realization is avoiding being bent and crushed by cosmic law by becoming one with that very same law of Reality.

As scripture records, in words also put to music by Handel in his *Messiah*, "But who may abide the day of His coming? and who shall stand when He appeareth? For He is like a refiner's fire."[12] The Will of God is indeed a refiner's fire, and it is a fiery energy that permeates the entire universe. As this fire burns and burns on, eventually all that is within us and all that we have brought forth that is imperfect must pass into the flame of transmutation, but that which is already perfected shall be left untouched, for it is *already* a part of God's flame. In the symbology of the alchemists, it is the gold, symbolizing the perfected soul, which is untouched by the fire, whereas all that is dross is consumed.

When it comes upon us, this flame, this Will of God, comes suddenly, because in reality it has always been here, for it is Reality itself. This is the meaning behind Christ's parable of the wise virgins: those who were the wise among them "kept their lamps trimmed," or, in other words, kept their chakras shining pure and preserved themselves for the appearance of their Lord, their own Higher Self, within themselves at any time. For this Reality comes unexpectedly, "as a thief in the night."

And thus come the sudden, thundering opening chords of the Fifth Symphony (*da-da-da*-daaa). They are the divine intervention of God into the world of time and space. They are, in a sense, the Second Coming of Christ—in the sudden opening of the symphony, coming when least expected. The right arm of the Almighty, as it hammers down in these four opening blows, is a thunder of love that terrifies the human ego which thought it could dwell forever apart from the One. The Fifth's opening chords are a hammering love that will hammer into nothingness all that is unreal, including the separate human self. Therefore all that is unreal trembles at the coming of this resolving Light.

All this and more is contained within the tones of the Fifth Symphony, which are first ray tones. The seven rays, often spoken of in esotericism, are the seven aspects or frequencies of God's energy and consciousness which manifest outwardly in such phenomena as the seven colors of the rainbow, the seven rows in the periodic table of elements, the seven notes of the diatonic scale in music, and the seven basic geometrical types of crystals. Beside these outward manifestations, each of the rays also contains particular spiritual qualities and is represented by particular heavenly beings who embody and transmit these qualities. The qualities of the first ray are divine will and divine power, and it is these qualities radiating from the Fifth Symphony which emanated directly out of the consciousness of the Elohim of the first ray.

129

The four opening blows and their repetition in the lower chord are probably the most famous, not to mention the most dramatic notes in music. Around the time they were composed, Beethoven told his pupil Czerny that the notes were inspired by a yellowhammer's song which he heard while walking through a park. But years later he was to say of them, "Thus Fate knocks at the door." This "Fate" is the soul's divine destiny and the operation upon the soul of karmic law. The bars which follow sound the same notes in less momentous mode, and in minor rather than in major, perhaps indicating not God's Will but human will, as if the individual is suddenly confronted head-on with Fate and is not willing to surrender. As the movement progresses, the tonal phrases relevant to the Greater or Absolute and the lesser, the individual soul, weave in and out, the Fate theme hammering down sometimes with gentler, sometimes with omnipotent force, while the human monad moves out of its way, comes back again, and tries to get the feel of the Fate which is confronting it. The Fate theme repeats in variation *hundreds* of times in the opening movement (and indeed is present in all the movements).

In the development (the movement's midsection) the musical tones strain upward in pitch, the tension mounting, until the Fate motto bangs out a relief and opens the way for the recapitulation. Then the oboe begins a cadenza in minor tones which exudes sympathy and compassion. But almost as soon as the instrument has begun, the relentless elemental musical forces sweep in once more and plunge on to the *Coda*. By this movement's close, the soul has to some extent bent the knee and begun to realize that the Will of God is good and that obedience to that Will does not mean bondage to some rigid, mechanical regime but rather implies the freedom to soar into an infinite reality.

In telling of the quest for resolution with Divine Will, the Fifth Symphony is also, musicologically, a quest for a final resolution of minor chords into major ones. The "story" of contrast between the minor and major, culminating finally in major at the *Finale*, is a strategy which exerted an immense effect upon the composition of music and was thereafter followed by other symphonists throughout the nineteenth century.

The Fifth Symphony comes under the direction of the cosmic hierarchy of Taurus, the sign which has the spiritual keynote of God-Obedience. In the four movements of this work, we hear the challenge to the soul of becoming aligned and obedient to the Will of God in each of the four elements of being: Fire, Air, Water, and Earth. These four elements relate respectively to the higher and intuitive mental faculties, to the more concrete mind, to the emotions, and finally to the level of physicality. So that in the Fifth Symphony the discovery of freedom through obedience is stepped down from one movement to another throughout the different levels or planes of being.

The third, emotional-plane movement is truly an enigma. Whatever Beethoven had in mind when composing this uncanny and sometimes menacing music is a mystery. The *Trio* conjures the image of a huge giant taking vast, lumbering strides in enormous Wellington boots; "monstrous, portentous" exclaims one critic, while another refers to this section as "a fugal dance for elephants." More recognizable is the return of the "Fate" motif of the first movement, the four hammer blows recurring here under various orchestration and at times sounding softer and more reflective. Then the *Finale*, the fourth movement, brings everything through into victory on the physical plane. Brilliant, startling surges of C Major chords send the mind racing to the stars, blazing through fully forty such chords until the close.

In the magnificent, victorious music of the symphony's con-clusion, Beethoven seems certain that he has found the way to ultimate salvation. The key is to so identify with the Supreme and with cosmic law ("Fate") that the soul and the Inner God become one. As the final sounds of this symphony echoed around the hall, Lesueur cried to the young Berlioz: "Ouf! Let me get out; I must have air. It's incredible! Marvelous! It has so upset and bewildered me that when I wanted to put on my hat, *I couldn't find my head.*"[13]

131

SYMPHONY NO. 6 IN F MAJOR (PASTORAL) (1807–8). OP. 68.

"No one can love the country as much as I do. For surely woods, trees and rocks produce the echo which man most desires to hear."[14] These words of Beethoven's are added to by his English pianist friend Neate, who testified that he had never known a man who enjoyed nature so much, or who took such a great delight in flowers, in clouds, and in everything natural.

Beethoven's perception of nature went beyond the purely phys-ical, however, being a mystical perception. He recognized the om-nipresence of God throughout all of life, and once wrote: "In the country I seem to hear every tree repeating 'Holy, Holy, Holy.'" It was this perception of the beauty of nature which is both physical and mystical which he desired to express musically in the Sixth Symphony.

The Sixth was composed soon after the completion of the Fifth, and to the Fifth's overwhelmingly powerful *yang* nature, the Sixth acts as a complementary *yin* creation of feminine loveliness.

The programmatic nature of this symphony—that is to say, its specific, storylike meaning—is almost unique in the work of Beethoven and anticipates the work of Liszt and the other symphonic poets. (This made the *Pastoral* a natural choice for Walt Disney to use in his famous and inspired production of 1940, *Fantasia.*)

Many critics make the error of describing this work only as the representation of a visit to the countryside. But in reality it transcribes the harmonious triangular relationship between the Soul, Nature, and God. Beethoven himself wrote that the symphony represents "an arrival at a knowledge of God through Nature." The Soul and God are the real protagonists in this work, but it is through the intermediary of Nature that they meet.

As we have previously noted, Beethoven understood that the different musical keys each express specific psychological states and energies. He chose the key of each of his works with the greatest of care. For the *Pastoral,* he chose F major. In *The Secret Doctrine* Madame Blavatsky states that F is the musical keynote of earth and that its color is green.[15]

The first two movements are more repetitious than almost anything else Beethoven wrote, but deliberately so and repetitious in the best sense. Rather than offering to us the beautiful melodies of these movements only to quickly snatch them away again, Beethoven allows them to linger to our heart's delight. This conveys the genuine feeling of experiencing nature. Just as the hills and babbling brooks are seemingly eternal and the boundless sky infinite, just as a walk across the dales or through the woods is not accomplished in a moment, just as Mother Nature has her own time scales and moves at a pace different from humanity, so these movements allow us to feel ourselves genuinely present amid the timeless natural scenes which the music evokes. As Beethoven himself said of this symphony, it is "more an expression of feeling than a painting."

The first movement is described by Beethoven as "impressions upon arriving in the country." For myself the movement

132

usually describes an open and expansive terrain, such as rolling grassy hills, though it can be adapted according to one's own personal inner vision to scenes of woodland or any other pastoral surrounding. It is superb meditation music. In this as much as in any of the movements, the innate Divinity which Beethoven perceived in nature is gloriously described. The joy and bliss of being in the countryside which is expressed by the music is never less than spiritual. At one moment in particular, the main melodic theme which has already delighted us numerous times unexpectedly rises in pitch suddenly to soar off into an experience of absolute, transcendent bliss.

It is difficult to conceive how even an immortal being could have described in musical tones the experience of sitting by a river better than has Beethoven in the second movement, the "Scene by the Brook." The feelings of peace and serenity and of the eternality of the flowing waters are overwhelmingly effective. The composer cleverly uses the strings to convey the impression not only of the main, leisurely flow of the body of water but also all the smaller crosscurrents and eddies. Again, we cannot forget Beethoven's words that the symphony represents "an arrival at a knowledge of God through Nature," for there is in the eternal, flowing waters, so superbly described by Beethoven, an experience of the everlasting, immutable, patient, but omnipotent flow of the cycles of the Supreme. Towards the end, the strings are hushed, and we hear the clear songs of a nightingale, a quail, and a cuckoo (put in, Beethoven said, as a joke). Then the strings enter once more, gentle and heart-meltingly compassionate, and the movement concludes.

The third movement opens with a gathering of rural folk at a country dance. Then comes the warning rumble of thunder, and soon the dance is abandoned as a summer storm begins to rage. The storm passes on, fading into the distance; the music quiets; the air has been cleared. Then, almost imperceptibly at first and then more radiantly, the listener not only sees but *feels* the sensation of the warm sun shining through and its settling upon the rapidly drying grass. This takes us into the final movement, outwardly a lovely shepherd's song of thankfulness and communion with nature, but also important because esoterically it is also the musical expression of the vibrations of Shambhala.

133

PIANO CONCERTO NO. 5 IN E-FLAT MAJOR (EMPEROR) (1809). OP. 73.

In the opinion of almost all lovers and critics of music, this last piano concerto of Beethoven's is also the finest. Again, the name *Emperor* was not Beethoven's own for this work, but one can readily understand how it came about, for the concerto is splendidly royal in its magnificent, regal tones. Composed soon after the Fifth Symphony, the "da-da-da-*daaa*" signature is again used here.

As in the Fourth Piano Concerto, the introduction to the first movement brings in the piano before the orchestra, but now the pianist is given much more daring notes to play. Then the orchestra enters, and the music leaps ahead with great dynamism. This first movement also introduces several notable changes into the traditional concerto form. As he had already shown, never one to consider innovation for its own sake, Beethoven was ever one to adapt tradition to his own needs without hesitation, or to by-pass tradition altogether when the music he sought to bring forth demanded it. At times his new wine could not be contained within traditional old bottles.

It was then the custom in concertos for the soloist to improvise a cadenza towards the end of the first movement, but in this concerto Beethoven omitted any real cadenza of the traditional form. In his previous four piano concertos, Beethoven himself performed on the opening night and thus had not taken the trouble of writing out the piano's part in full. However, by the time the *Emperor* was first performed, Beethoven was too deaf to play the part himself, and he did not trust another soloist to improvise a cadenza which might be unsuitable. Therefore he wrote out a pseudocadenza in full. In doing so, as it turned out, he signaled the end in general of the practice of having an improvised cadenza.

The second movement is in the key of B Major and is a work of inexpressible beauty. A martially rhythmic *Rondo* closes the concerto. In fact, the work was written in the year of Napoleon's invasion and has been called by musicologist Alfred Einstein the "apotheosis of the military concept" in Beethoven's music.[16] According to Einstein, Beethoven's audiences "expected a first movement in four-four time of a 'military' character; and they reacted with unmixed pleasure when Beethoven not only fulfilled but sur-passed their expectations."[17]

PIANO SONATA IN F-SHARP MAJOR *(1809). OP. 78.*

This composition opened a new period of piano sonata writing in Beethoven's life after a gap of several years. He considered this sonata to be much better than the *Moonlight*, and along with the *Appassionata* it was his favorite until the mighty *Hammerclavier* a decade later.

This sonata is full of lyrical beauty, and the number of move-ments—two only—along with its key of F-sharp Major, are among a number of the unusual features it displays. In its wonderful serenity and economy of form, this sonata hints at certain key elements of the third creative period which was yet to come.

SYMPHONY NO. 7 IN A MAJOR *(1811–12). OP. 92.*

135

Following a gap of four years in Beethoven's production of symphonies, the *yang* Seventh and the *yin* Eighth were composed in quick succession. Work on them was actually conducted simul-taneously, and they were completed in 1812. The mutual charac-teristic of each of them is an unparalleled, virtually unrestrained, buoyant good humor.

Of the Seventh Symphony, Beethoven said that it was "one of my most important."[18] In this symphony there is no longer any sense of struggle before the victory. Rather, triumph and unfet-tered joy are taken for granted virtually from the first bar until the end. There is in this composition no sense of conflict, the Seventh being one of the few major works of any kind by Beethoven in which this is so. The struggles and trials of the Third and the Fifth are now largely things of the past. The path to union with the Godhead now lies relatively clear ahead. The Seventh was completed in the same year from which comes his journal note: "Almighty One, in the woods I am blessed. Happy everyone in the woods. You speak through every tree. O God! What glory in the woodland! On the heights of peace—peace to serve Him."[19]

So dancelike is this symphony that the Ballet Russe of Monte Carlo once used the entire work to accompany their art of motion. In 1908 Isadora Duncan also danced to all but the first movement. Wagner and Liszt each considered this superb work to be the "apotheosis of the dance."[20] To this Corinne Heline adds:

> The innermost spirit of the dance enacts rhythmically the ascent on the initiatory path which concludes in divine at-one-ment with Light Eternal. From this standpoint of interpretation the Seventh Symphony is truly an Apotheosis of the Dance . . .
>
> There is such a mystical power infused into this symphony that it has the magic of awakening in the soul of an aspirant a vision of the steps that lead progressively up the ladder of attainment. More than that, it actually radiates tonal energies that impart a strength to the soul on the initiatory path to take those steps until the quest is finally consummated in the supernal glories of the realm Elysian.[21]

Each of the four movements is brilliant. The first is marvelously worked out and orchestrated, and, after a masterful slow introduction, continues with the uncanny "gigantic stairs" theme which has an unbelievably uplifting effect, as though Beethoven were no longer content to raise his audience to heaven gradually by means of increments of tone but somehow devised a means for the instruments to invoke invisible helpers who catch the listeners under the arms and physically lift them up swiftly from one exalted plane to another. To the spiritually clairvoyant, the music form created by these sounds on the higher planes must be extraordinary and surely must seem exactly like some kind of fantastic staircase!

In the second movement Beethoven changes keys from A Major to A Minor, the better to go within. Minor keys always have an inner, *yin* effect. Though the second movement of symphonies was traditionally a slow one, Beethoven here achieves the beautiful effect of a second movement more subdued than the first not by composing in slow tempo but by composing an *Allegretto* in low orchestral coloring. The third movement builds a dazzling, hurtling tower of omnipotent energy; this section has always been one of the most popular of Beethoven's movements. The more exuberant major key melody is interspersed with a slower theme which swells and undulates in the string section like a mighty ocean. Then we enter into a *Finale* of unfettered joy, which one might liken to a colossal explosion of light and which is also an overwhelming outburst and affirmation of spiritual emancipation.

SYMPHONY NO. 8 IN F MAJOR (1812). OP. 93.

The Eighth was to Beethoven "my little one," a phrase signifying not merely that it was in some ways on a less grandiose scale than the Seventh but also that he had a soft spot for it in his heart. On one occasion he said that he thought the Eighth was actually a better work than its twin. One cannot help but wonder, however, whether he was really serious in saying this. The Seventh is one of his greatest creations and ever since its first unveiling has proved the more popular of the two. The Eighth contains its own particular qualities which are more subtle than the glories of the Seventh, but still it is difficult to view it as a greater symphony than its predecessor.

Is it possible that in saying that it was better than the Seventh, Beethoven, tongue in cheek, was putting the icing on a symphony which was already meant to be something of a joke, albeit a beautiful and accomplished one? Paul Henry Láng believes the Eighth Symphony to be "an essay on humor in music, a parody on the symphony itself." Once introduced to the idea, it is not easy to disagree with it. Pointing to the third movement for example, Láng notes that it is significantly inscribed "Tempo di minuetto" and that it "pokes fun at Beidermeier docility." Continues Láng:

> Everything goes wrong in this movement: it has difficulty in getting started with its overemphasized and heavy-footed tentative lines; then the horns, trumpets and timpani, missing their cue, hurl their ponderous tones at the wrong places and get entangled in the cadence. The *Finale*, one of the longest Beethovenian movements, romps about with unrestricted merriment. Suddenly, in the midst of the swift but subdued flow in C major, the full orchestra crashes in with a resounding C sharp and pandemonium follows.[22]

For all its jocularity, the Eighth nevertheless is a genuine and lovely symphony, bearing the true Beethoven stamp. Basil Deane

137

warns us that it is also a concentrated work. (It is actually the shortest of the Nine.) It demands, in Deane's opinion, "a more sophisticated response from the listener than any other symphony of the series."[23]

The Eighth is truly the feminine counterpart for the glorious, powerful Seventh Symphony, for whereas the Seventh sings of the power and transcendence of soul-freedom, the Eighth speaks to us of that emancipated soul's happiness and gratitude.

Tremendous placidity and contented humor are present in each of the four movements. The story behind the cheeky second movement, an *Allegretto Scherzando*, is that the piece was originally written by Beethoven in honor of his friend Mälzel, the inventor of the metronome. Evidence for this lies in the jest that the entire piece is built on top of a jocular, incessant, metronomelike beat!

The third movement combines humor with moments of real beauty, neither detracting from the other—the two moods fit together perfectly. This movement sings the laughter of victory. The fourth movement is also a lot of fun and is often acclaimed as the best of the symphony. It has an atmosphere of heavenly fantasy, with much tomfoolery and many deliberate false starts among the violins, and it closes with a *Coda* which is practically half the movement in length. As a climax to the total work, this ending is just perfect. All the movements are remarkably compact and contain even less sense of conflict than is found in the Seventh Symphony.

138

WELLINGTON'S VICTORY, OR THE BATTLE OF VITTORIA (1813). OP. 91.

Usually called "the Battle Symphony," this composition is not actually a symphony at all and was not considered by Beethoven to be a part of the stream of his real artistic output. On June 21, 1813, Wellington won the Battle of Vittoria, and Mälzel suggested to Beethoven that he write a piece to celebrate the victory, which would bring in money by pleasing the English. For once the intractable composer agreed to such a scheme. Mälzel, already referred to as the inventor of the metronome, was an enterprising individual who had now just invented a kind of primitive mechanical orchestra called the orchestrion. The idea was that Beethoven should write music for this medium, which he did. Having done so, he thought his composition good enough to expand and score for full orchestra. Nevertheless, in Beethoven's own estimation, the work was never intended to be more than a moneymaker. He composed it very quickly—even hurriedly—and with an ironic disdain gave his contemporaries exactly what he knew would please their senses. "It is certain that one writes most beautifully when one writes for the public, also that one writes rapidly,"[24] he dryly jotted into his sketchbook.

The melody of "Rule, Britannia" is the motif of the British while "Malbrouck" represents the French—a tune better known to English ears as "We won't go home till morning"! After much fanfare, bluster, and even orchestral cannon shots, "Rule, Britannia" prevails, and a triumphant march leads into a special treatment of "God Save the King."

This piece is in essence a primitive piece of program music, and musicologists have never rated it higher than did Beethoven himself. One, Paul Bekker, called it "an example of his work in its crude state."[25] The piece did its intended job, however, and did so beyond any of Beethoven's expectations. Viennese audiences raved over it in its orchestral form, and it brought in considerable and much-needed cash. In fact, financially it was one of the greatest successes of Beethoven's life.

139

Beethoven himself considered the Battle Symphony to be a joke, but ultimately a more cosmic joke was on him, which is why we include the piece here. He may have composed it hurriedly, and it may be musically unsophisticated, but in terms of esoteric significance, the Battle Symphony is most important. Even working in a hurry, and even without seriously meaning to, Beethoven in this work captured the very keynote of the quality of victory itself. The energy released at inner levels when this music is played is actually comparable to that from the nine symphonies, and the work is excellent for clearing a room or hall of negative vibrations, replacing them with those of glory and light.

It is necessary, then, to put worldly, musicological sophistication aside while listening to this piece, which could be better called the "Victory Symphony." If we listen with the purity and innocence of the childlike mind, then we may attune ourselves to this music's true origins—in the heart of the sun, in Elohimic consciousness, and in the heart of the Ancient of Days. Wherever this music is played over and over again, the sign of victory as a mighty V at inner levels descends to part all darkness.

Following the composition of the Battle Symphony, one of Beethoven's own long inner battles commenced. It is true that with the Seventh and Eighth Symphonies, it seemed as though, after a decade of "heroic" music (in which the protagonist was archetypally portrayed as beset by difficulties, facing them, and overcoming them), Beethoven had won through to a new level of freedom and peace. But music is not always an outer expression of the natural inner state of its composer. It can be more, possessing a universal significance and being strangely inspired upon oneself from an unknown Source. This process may be a prophecy of that which can be and of that which is to come. It can result from something experienced but not retained, glimpsed but not yet grasped. Already the greatest living composer of his time, having forged a series of unique musical works expressive of the most fundamental and crucial challenges which face the living individual, and having composed his way through to entirely new altitudes and vistas of soul-freedom, in his own life Beethoven was, however, undergoing as many difficulties as ever.

140

To the extent that he continued to compose, the works of the next few years were of only secondary importance compared to those of the decade 1802–1812. Given this passing of several years without a great work, and the by-then common knowledge that he was almost totally deaf, some could not help but wonder among themselves: *did Beethoven have anything more to say?*

Time passed. And some thought not. But they could scarcely have been more wrong.

Hammerclavier, Missa Solemnis, *Diabelli Variations and* Choral

Above all he projected into his art not his own sufferings or his own life but the ideals which he set against them in himself.
—THE LAROUSSE ENCYCLOPEDIA OF MUSIC[1]

PIANO SONATA IN B-FLAT MAJOR (HAMMERCLAVIER) (1817–19). OP. 106.

This, Beethoven's twenty-ninth piano sonata, is the longest he ever wrote. It is also the greatest. It was written many years after the more immediately understandable *Moonlight* and *Appassionata* sonatas. By 1818 Beethoven was in many ways a different man and his music, a different music.

Marion Scott wrote of the *Hammerclavier*: "Op. 106 is a terrifying sonata—technically of immense difficulty, exhaustingly long, and mentally the toughest thing he ever wrote, except perhaps the Quartet in B-flat Major, Op. 130. The contrapuntal devices and the intellectual power Beethoven put forth overwhelm one like the statements of an astronomer about the universe . . . After more than a century Beethoven's *Hammerclavier* Sonata and his Quartet, Op. 130, are just becoming fully intelligible."[2]

141

I totally agree with this view of the *Hammerclavier's* importance. There may be works by Beethoven in which other qualities such as beauty, lyricism, and even sheer power abound more greatly, but taking an overview of his entire output, the *Hammerclavier* is to me the first of three works in particular (the others being the *Grosse Fuge* and the first movement of the String Quartet in C-sharp Minor) in which he forces the boundaries of music, sometimes physically and always psychologically, to the most uncanny and unforgettable frontiers.

The *Hammerclavier* is the second of Beethoven's last five piano sonatas which are usually viewed as being a group of works distinct from the earlier ones. In these last five the scale of thought and the breadth of the music are at times virtually symphonic. They also predict elements of the five late string quartets (the subject of the next chapters). For example, fugue form (in which melodies do not progress from a beginning to an end but repeat cyclically) is employed to evoke atmospheres and meanings lyricism alone could not contain, and fugues are also combined with sonata form, creating a revolutionary style of intense complexity. The other four late piano sonatas are Op. 101 in A Major, which preceded the *Hammerclavier*, and Op. 109 in E Major, Op. 110 in A-flat Major, and Op. 111 in C Minor which was completed in 1822 and is considered by some to equal the *Hammerclavier* in importance.

The nickname *Hammerclavier* is of no importance. Beethoven did not give it this name, but merely in rather strange German, wrote that it was a sonata "for the Hammerclavier," the word meaning literally "keyboard with hammers," as opposed to the harpsichord which does not hammer, but plucks. He was, in other words, indicating that the sonata was for the pianoforte. He also wrote the same on the scores of the previous sonata and the subsequent sonata, but somehow with Op. 106, the words managed to stick as a name.

The mighty fugue of the fourth movement is the most discussed part of the *Hammerclavier*, but the rest of the work is also of much importance. From the first movement it is evident that Beethoven is now of a mind to push the piano sonata medium over a horizon which it had not before even approached. This sonata-form movement is gigantic and very complex, leaving one wondering what can possibly follow it in the subsequent movements. As

142

it happens, the second movement is relatively straightforward. But the next piece, an *Adagio sostenuto*, is the first of a number of truly revolutionary musical conceptions which Beethoven was to bring forth in his final years. The *Adagio* is a radical development not because any of the components of the piece are new in themselves, but because of the daring extremes to which he takes them. The form is more or less that of a sonata, there being two main subjects, but the length of the piece, its carefully measured pace—slow almost to the point of quiescence—and the impression it conveys of almost static tension are unparalleled.

Actually, words are insufficient to describe this movement. As with the entire sonata, the reader who has not done so really must listen to it. Do so when you can give it your close, uninterrupted attention: the *Hammerclavier* is far from the kind of tonal art we can appreciate as background music.

Several of Beethoven's most important late works hold something startlingly novel waiting for us in the last movement. In the *Hammerclavier* this is the most fantastically dramatic and taxing of fugues; or rather, the fugue is not "in" the movement, but it *is* the movement and is difficult to the extent that it has struck horror into generations of otherwise able pianists. Prior to this last decade, Beethoven's harsher critics said to themselves, "Beethoven is incapable of writing a fugue." Now, in one movement, he created an incredible, multifaceted "art of fugue" in which is employed almost every fugal device music possesses. But at the same time the movement is, as Philip Barford puts it, "vastly more than the rattling of academic bones."[3]

143

The fugue itself is preceded by a fifteen-bar *Largo* which forms the perfect, and indeed essential, preparation of the listener (who is still enveloped in the stillness of the third movement) for the dynamism which is approaching. As for the fugue itself, what are we to make of it? Let us remember this sonata's place within Beethoven's chronological development. It was composed some years after his main second period expositions and in itself initiated a gradual resurrection from his dry period.

If during the preceding years Beethoven had found himself at the end of one phase of musical and spiritual development, then it was in Op. 106 that he began at last to find the way ahead. But his path ahead was still not well-defined. J. W. N. Sullivan, who was among the most perceptive of all commentators on Beethoven, felt this sonata to be "the expression of a man of infinite suffering, of infinite courage and will, but without God and without hope . . . The sonata is the complete expression of an important stage in Beethoven's spiritual development, but it was only after passing through this stage that the wonderful new world lay open before him, and that all his greatest work was achieved." Continuing, Sullivan referred to the curious austerity of the first movement and its "cold harmonies" which "no longer convey the warm human confidence of a man who knows that victory lies at the end." Sullivan did not feel that the sonata belongs to the third period or even to the second in its spiritual content. Rather, it "stands alone, a great and grim memorial to the long and painful journey between the two worlds." And he was surely right in speaking of it as expressing "the completely naked Beethoven, relying upon nothing whatever but his inner resources . . ."[4] Sullivan was correct in placing the *Hammerclavier* neither in the second period, nor in the third, but rather between them. For the *Hammerclavier* exhibits the musical styles of the third period, but virtually nothing of its mysticism. There could be no mysticism, for it was a time in Beethoven's life when he had not only lost or given up his Eternally Beloved, but was also embroiled in legal battles over the guardianship of his nephew, as well as being increasingly prey to isolation as a result of his deafness. It may well have seemed, then, that he was forsaken even by God. In the end, there was no solution to be found in mundane life, but rather the way out and upward was destined to be found by him in music itself, and once again through selfless service to humanity.

144

During his second creative period Beethoven had been developing and advancing in preparation for the mighty final works he was destined to compose in his fifties. But before the culminating triumph of the spiritual Path comes the dark night of the Spirit, and it is this dark night which we find in the *Hammerclavier*. This does not mean that it is a sonata of "darkness," but that it is the song of the solitary soul, surrounded by difficulties, struggling to maintain its hope and integrity. This trial typically comes at a time when the soul has been seemingly deserted by the Divinity, as is the nature of the initiatory period of the Path known as the "dark night" (depicted within the life of Jesus Christ in his call from the cross, "My God, My God, why hast thou deserted me?"[5]). Even the very form which Beethoven chose for this music—a sonata for a single instrument, the piano—conveys not only the symbolism but even the very atmosphere of the completely solitary being.

During the "dark night of the Spirit," the treader of the Way must undergo the trial of preserving his or her faith and *raison d'être* even when heavenly illumination and the sense of the nearness of God have been utterly withdrawn. The individual in this condition has only his or her inner resources upon which to rely. The absolute, stoic refusal to surrender, even when the reason for continuing is no longer clearly perceived, as expressed in Beethoven's tones, reaches its violent climax in the fugue, of which Sullivan writes: "We are presented here with a will to live which is inexpressibly furious and inexpressibly bare. It is the expression of the final refusal of annihilation, even if no hope and no object be left in life."[6] It is as though a mighty struggle is taking place to break through from darkness into a region of light—perhaps even into the masterworks of the third period. At times it seems as though the notes are actually trying to break through the limitations set by the instrument itself.

145

The *Hammerclavier* is indeed, then, a halfway point between the second and third creative periods. The third period works of Beethoven's last years are notable for their distinctive stylistic features, their unorthodox structures and novel musical ideas, and their spiritual sublimity. Of these three, the stylistic features are largely present in this sonata, and the unorthodox structures and novel ideas partly so, but the spiritual sublimity not at all. The time for this third factor, as important a feature of the third period as any developments of style or technique by which it is expressed, had not yet arrived.

Nevertheless, Op. 106 expresses exactly what it was intended to express. It remains Beethoven's most outstanding piano sonata and offers infinite scope for study. To play the work oneself or to listen to it is a tremendously stimulating experience for the third eye chakra, the spiritual center in humanity most stimulated by the piano.[7]

Beethoven himself said of this staggering creation: "Here is a sonata for you that will keep the pianist busy, and which will be played fifty years hence."[8] Fifty years later pianists were still echoing his words.

MISSA SOLEMNIS IN D MAJOR (1819–23). OP. 123.

We have compared the *Hammerclavier* sonata to the "dark night of the Spirit," an experience described most explicitly by the Catholic mystic, St. John of the Cross, in his *The Dark Night of the Soul*. We might extend the parallel further, for Beethoven did not conclude his output following this work, but went on to write his own *Spiritual Canticle* and *Living Flame of Love*. In 1809 he had written: " . . . in the old church modes the devotion is divine . . . and God permit me to express it someday."[9] A decade passed before that "someday" arrived, but when it did there began to take shape in Beethoven's mind and sketchbooks a creation which is still unsurpassed in its field. The *Missa Solemnis* is a monumental religious work which is one of the wonders of the musical world. It is also one of the most moving and uplifting musical creations for meditation in existence.

146

In 1819, at the age of forty-eight, Beethoven began work on the new Mass—his second—for the occasion of the installation of Archduke Rudolph as Archbishop of Olmütz in Moravia. But the gigantic proportions of the work caused the date of the installation (March 9, 1820) to arrive and pass long before the Mass was completed, for Beethoven's new work was hugely ambitious, months being consumed in each stage of its creation. When it was finished at last, Beethoven himself said that it was "the greatest work I have completed so far."[10]

The background preparation and research for the *Missa Solemnis* was deep and painstaking. Beethoven delved into the works of sixteenth-century Italian composer Giovanni Palestrina, the early liturgical composers, and also the religious works of J. S. Bach, C. P. E. Bach, and Handel. The result was neither a duplication of the old, traditional Mass, nor the classical style of Mass usual in Beethoven's day, nor a completely novel and innovative musical creation. In his desire for perfection and magnificence, Beethoven succeeded in fusing some of the best elements of many different styles of music, utilizing whatever style was the most apt for this or that portion of the text. But fuse these elements he did. The Mass conveys no sense of disunity but rather one of organic wholeness.

Years before, Beethoven had dedicated his life utterly to God, and now, for over four years, this dedication was channeled almost exclusively into his Mass in D. His friend Anton Schindler wrote that while he was working on it, Beethoven's "whole personality seemed to take on a different form. Never before or after have I seen him in such a condition of oblivion to everything worldly."[11] As an example, Schindler records one visit to Beethoven's house at this time:

> In the living room, behind a locked door, we heard the master singing parts of the fugue of the Credo of the *Missa Solemnis*—singing, howling, stamping. After we had been listening for a long time to this almost awful scene, and were about to go away, the door opened and Beethoven stood before us with distorted features, calculated to excite fear. He looked as if he had been in mortal combat with the whole army of contrapuntists, his everlasting enemies.[12]

Composed for four soloists, a large chorus, and large orchestra, the work was gigantic in every sense: vast in scope, an hour and a half in length, and as broad in texture as music could be. Beethoven sincerely saw it as music that could be used in the Mass ceremony despite the number of performers required, but at the same time he realized that his Mass was also a great deal more. A "Divine Heroic Symphony," he once called it. The *Missa Solemnis* is fundamentally a kind of *Eroica* or Fifth Symphony in liturgical form, but still more vast, and culminating in a victory far less personal than in these works—a triumph which is sacred in nature and universal in scope.

For their part, Roman Catholic authorities have never been happy with the work, questioning how committed to the Church and its traditions the *Missa Solemnis* really is. Though the work conforms to the traditional form of the Mass to a large degree, it is plainly a considerably subjective Mass compared to the norm and one in which Beethoven does not spare on occasion to give us his own view of the world and of divinity. Acknowledging the work's nonliturgical uses, Beethoven had the *Missa Solemnis* first performed with the Gloria and the Sanctus and Benedictus missing (since the concert, which was also the premiere of the Ninth

147

Symphony, would otherwise have been overlong). The remaining movements he termed as "Three Grand Hymns with Solo and Chorus Voices." This premiere also took place in a concert hall, not in a church. Moreover, Beethoven later offered to write a German language version so that Protestant communities could perform the work—hardly a conventional offer to make regarding a Roman Catholic Mass!

There are also unconventional aspects within the Mass itself. Rather than composing a work expressive of uncontrasted, uncompromised, automatic religious faith, Beethoven invokes certain elements of doubt and discord which must be faced and overcome before absolute faith and triumph is achieved. It is of interest to note that he sometimes emphasizes different lines and words from those usually and conventionally stressed. For instance, as Denis McCaldin points out, the sentence *"Et unam Sanctam Catholicam et Apostolicam Ecclesiam"* ("And [I believe] in one Holy Catholic and Apostolic Church") is all but lost and submerged within the surrounding musical texture.[13] By comparison, in the Masses of Haydn, for example, this line was the occasion for the majestic octaves of his confession of faith. In any other musical genre, such a change might have gone unnoticed, but within a form as sensitively doctrinal as the Mass, the idiosyncratic aspects of the *Missa Solemnis* have long been controversial.

Passing to a description of the Mass itself, each of the five toweringly impressive movements are sublime and moving pieces of musical experience in and of themselves. Certainly, each fulfills Beethoven's criteria regarding his motives for writing the work, as he described them to Andreas Streicher: "My chief aim was to awaken and permanently instill religious feelings not only into the singers but also into the listeners."[14] If music raises individuals into contact with God, if it genuinely leaves them transformed and transfigured after hearing it, then it is music fitting for the coming enlightened time. The *Missa Solemnis* is among the greatest of all compositions for achieving this.

Beethoven was striving for perfection more than ever in this work, which is part of the reason for its taking over four years to complete. He worked slowly and carefully. Until the very end, the entire work was still under constant review and subject to alterations and revisions. The result was worth the effort. We can only agree with Prince Galitzin who, when he had first heard the *Missa Solemnis*, was moved to enthuse to the composer in a letter: " . . . this whole work in fact is a treasure of beauties; it can be said that your genius has anticipated the centuries and that there are not listeners perhaps enlightened enough to experience all the beauty of this music; but it is posterity that will pay homage and will bless your memory much better than your contemporaries can."

Beethoven was never one to do anything in his art for no reason, but in the *Missa Solemnis* in particular an extremely painstaking degree of attention was placed upon creating the most fitting music not only for every line but even for every word of the text. This is powerfully evident even from the very beginning of the Kyrie. The word itself, *Kyrie* ("Lord"), is sung to masterfully majestic and devotional tones. First its melody enters instrumentally only, at the very opening of the Mass. Then the chorus comes in, intoning "Kyrie" three times, followed each time by a similar intonation from a soloist. Here, the chorus is like the people of the world and the soloist the priest, the whole series of calls to the Lord forming a magnificent opening invocation and the calls coming in threes in representation of the Trinity. Compared to the writing for "Kyrie," the subsequent "elyeison" ("have mercy on us") is fittingly more muted, its melody humble and prayerful. Then, after the manner of earlier times, the invocation to Christ which follows is less dramatic than the "Kyrie" section, musically forming a kind of interlude before the "Kyrie" returns to complete the arch.

What can one possibly say of the second movement, the Gloria, other than that it is indeed glorious and immensely so? Its opening has tremendous power and impact, and then we are underway, caught up in mighty, flowing *Allegro* passages. Again, the music is very closely suited to the text; the rhythms, melodies, and modes changing and scintillating according to the meaning of the words. The second of the three sections of the movement is one of more subdued texture, but at its close there is a powerful instrumental impression of divine omnipotence. The bulk of the section consists of ethereally serene and otherworldly fugal treatments of the text, which are interspersed with more linear and "symphonic" punctuations expressed primarily through the brass.

The third section returns again to the power and glory, the music building up and up in force. With the words *"gloria Dei*

Patris," a mighty fugue begins, which leads up to the greatest peak of the movement. Into the fugue is brought the text and music for "Amen," with which Beethoven weaves a superlative interlocking musical texture. Far from being the mere closing word of the movement, the "Amen" becomes part of an entire fugal section! This magnificent section was surely and quite literally inspired. In its diversity of treatment, which in fugue is like the details of a single, sustained intonation, the multiplicity of "Amens" are transformed into one continuous voice, the Word itself: the OM, the AUM, the AMN, the AMEN—call it what humanity will—it is one and the same and is here given forth in an exultant series of threes (for the Trinity). The fugue concludes with the most powerful three intonations of all, the orchestra and chorus decreeing the Word together in tones of inimitable magnificence, and for one seemingly eternal, omnipotent moment, the climactic "Amen" is sustained by the soloists alone after the orchestra and chorus suddenly halt. It is surely one of the most breathtaking moments, not only in the *Missa Solemnis,* but in all of music.

150   The text of the Credo is very long and again is rendered a musical treatment with a word-by-word consideration of the textual meaning. With the mention of the Holy Ghost, for instance, the flute immediately enters as its symbol. More than anything, there is the moment when out of silence comes the sudden, great upsurge of ascending lines with the Resurrexit. Then, following the reference to the resurrection, is a return of the original Credo ("I believe") theme with which the movement began, affirming that through the resurrection of Jesus Christ, humanity's faith is sustained, strengthened, and enhanced.

The Sanctus is comparatively subdued, being above all a careful preparation for the Benedictus. The Benedictus, despite the brevity of the text, is a large and sublime work of tonal artistry. Compared to the awesome power of much of the rest of the Mass, the Benedictus is, however, less massively orchestrated, at times verging on what sounds in comparison like chamber music. One of the most memorable moments precedes the singing of the text. The flutes and violas play a strange but lovely melody; this stops; there is not a sound, and then a lone violin enters and continues with its remarkably beautiful melody as the singers and the other instruments reenter. Karl Czerny, a composer and a pupil of Beethoven, recorded that Beethoven conceived this movement while regarding the "starry heavens" and reflecting on the music of the spheres.[15]

And so we find ourselves at the opening of the Agnus Dei. More than any other movement, this is less liturgical and more an expression of the composer's independent viewpoint. Of the five movements of the *Missa Solemnis*, only this is in a minor key, B Minor, which to Beethoven was a key conveying an atmosphere of darkness. Note the unusual inclusion of the sounds of warfare and strife (the drums and fanfares of trumpets). These follow the opening section which is headed by Beethoven as "Prayer for inner peace." The sounds of strife form part of the second section, constituting a contrast to the desire for outer peace. In the third section comes a return of the inward peace theme, this time in F Major. Then yet again discord enters in another section expressive of strife and the desire for peace in the discordant outer world. But finally the voices of the chorus and their calls for "Pacem" silence the strife and invoke a new harmony, the movement and the entire Mass then concluding in a majestically triumphant *Coda*.

Why did Beethoven bring in the discord? And why so late in the Mass, rather than concluding with an entire movement of unqualified triumph and salvation? Upon these very questions Beethoven has in fact been misjudged on various occasions since the *Missa Solemnis* was written. The solution, surely, is that the final and ultimate victory is always accompanied by the greatest conflagration of darkness. At the personal level, adeptship is preceded by the dark night of the Spirit, the crucifixion; and on the global scale, the New Jerusalem or New Age is inevitably preceded by Armageddon, the time of trouble, "Judgment Day," or whatever we desire to call that period of the flushing out and manifestation of all remaining residues of planetary discord in order that it might at last be exposed, confronted, opposed, consumed, and rejected forevermore. These then are the sounds of discord within the Agnus Dei. Far from being an unnecessary, nonliturgical secular invasion of the holy interior of the Church, they are a part of a deeper understanding of what the ultimate salvation really entails.

For some the *Missa Solemnis* is the greatest creation of any genre that Beethoven ever composed. Certainly, in the writing of

151

this Mass, Beethoven more than ever lived up to his own desire to "approach the Godhead more nearly than other mortals and . . . spread the rays . . . through the human race."

Thirty-Three Variations in C major on a Waltz by Anton Diabelli (1823). Op. 120.

Dedicated to Antonie Brentano, who we have seen was almost certainly the Eternally Beloved, these variations were Beethoven's last major work for the piano. And what a way to finish! Often considered Beethoven's companion piece to Bach's *The Art of Fugue*, they demonstrate his complete mastery of the variation medium.

The origin of the work is typically Beethovenian. Diabelli the publisher wrote to fifty-one composers of the day requesting a variation each on a waltz he had composed. Beethoven declined, calling the tune a "cobbler's patch." Eventually Diabelli received thirty-two variations from different composers, including Schubert and the eleven-year-old Liszt, and again asked Beethoven for his, to make the total thirty-three. But then in a sort of show of power, Beethoven went on to demonstrate his virtuosity by writing a further thirty-three variations himself.

Musically, so much could be said about these variations that the reader is best referred to the music itself. Suffice it to say that much could be written about each and every one of the thirty-three—of how some hark back to the polyphony of the sixteenth century, while others anticipate the styles of such later composers as Debussy and Webern.

Esoterically, there is a profound significance in the number of variations. Thirty-three is in fact the number of times a particular important form of initiation occurs on the Path. Thus, to complete the deep symbology present in the life of Christ, the record states that he lived for thirty-three years before taking the initiation of the ascension. According to some esoteric teachings, the earth must undergo a Dark Cycle of thirty-three years of the accelerated return of personal and planetary karma (from April 23, 1969, to April 22, 2002) before a New Age can appear, each year being a year of planetary initiation. The thirty-three initiations, both personal and planetary, are represented in a total of thirty-three chapters to the book of Revelation, only two-thirds of which have so far been released to humanity, and one-third retained. And there are a total of thirty-three vertebrae in the human spine (before some of the lower ones become fused in adults)—one vertebra for each initiation by which the kundalini energy must ascend the spinal altar. Though it is unlikely that Beethoven was consciously aware of the significance of the number, the knowledge came through him from the Universal all the same in this music of initiation. Hear it!

SYMPHONY NO. 9 IN D MINOR (CHORAL) (1822–24). OP. 125.

Still it stands unchallenged, this Everest of the symphonic medium. Beethoven's Ninth is quite simply the greatest symphony ever composed. In it he created yet another revolution for music; the Ninth was unprecedented not only musically but also spiritually.

As his last completed symphony, the Ninth followed a gap of ten years in Beethoven's symphonic writing. Yet during those years his mind often dwelt upon the medium: the Ninth was germinating throughout all the years of work on the *Missa Solemnis* and even earlier. The first ideas for the *Scherzo* date from as early as 1815. Further sketches for the Ninth are in Beethoven's notebooks of 1817. The following year he took up work on the first two movements in still more detail but then put these aside to compose the *Missa Solemnis*, which as it happened was to keep him occupied for over four years. The idea for the choral movement also came to him during his work on the Mass, which also used soloists and a choir, but the text was not yet chosen, and the movement was at first designated for a further, tenth symphony. Only at a very late stage indeed, in 1823, was the decision made to incorporate a choral fourth movement into the Ninth.

The text for the movement, Schiller's "Ode to Joy," was a poem Beethoven had first planned to set to music as far back as the age of twenty-two, and the finished movement of 1824 was not a little reminiscent of the choral music composed by Beethoven at the age of nineteen! So it could be said that the Ninth Symphony is the result of an entire lifetime of musical maturation, being the culmination of a number of ideas conceived over a wide span of years, as well as being the final, crowning fulfillment of the developments of the previous eight symphonic works.

The Ninth Symphony has often been compared by academics to the Third, the *Eroica*. Stylistically the *Eroica* is indeed in many ways the most similar to the Ninth, though the Ninth is more sophisticated. Insofar as the extramusical themes of the Ninth are concerned, the symphony is also seen as being similar to the *Eroica*, but with the victory and triumph expressed on a more exalted and universal scale. All this is most interesting, for, as we have seen, the nine symphonies each express the energies of one sign of the zodiac, and the Ninth Symphony comes under Virgo, whereas its polarity on the opposite side of the astrological circle is the *Eroica*, coming under the influence of Pisces.

In astrology, signs in polarity to one another are always closely related. And like the *Eroica*, the *Choral* or Ninth Symphony opened up an entirely new era of symphonic music. The *Eroica* was the symphony which, twenty years earlier, had initiated the sequence of Beethoven's masterful symphonic works of the Heroic second period. The stupendous Ninth also opened up an entire range of hitherto unexplored symphonic possibilities. Though Beethoven himself did not live to explore these new possibilities further in symphonic form, they were nevertheless destined to be taken up by those who followed him, in the music of Brahms, Wagner, Bruckner, Mahler, and others. And yet the full continuation of the possibilities Beethoven opened up is still to come, in the enlightened music of composers yet to appear.

One esoteric keynote of this symphony is God-Justice, the keynote of Virgo. Though the virtue of Justice may not be immediately apparent within the work, to refer to the esoteric concept of the seven rays—the great rays of creation which govern all matter and all thought—Justice is a seventh-ray virtue. The Ninth symphony certainly expresses many qualities which are also of a seventh-ray nature, including spiritual and material emancipation, joy, redemption, destiny, and heroism.

Esoterically, the symphony is particularly effective for the development of the crown chakra and the assimilation of true illumination. Its spiritual sublimity is the musical expression of samadhi, and this state of cosmic consciousness is anchored, through the four movements, in each of the four planes—etheric, mental, emotional, and physical.

The four movements are of such mighty stature that each of them stands as an epoch-making piece of music in its own right. Whereas the other symphonies convey the general impression of being symphonic works in four movements, the Ninth tends to seem more like four musical creations combined into the form of a symphony. Atmospherically, the movements differ greatly, apart from the stature of grandeur which they share, the *Scherzo* being the most perfect *Scherzo* imaginable, the *Adagio* being calm and serene to the limits of the form's possibilities, and so on. But closer inspection and more studied listening seems to reveal that the movements and their chief themes do indeed have certain elements in common—the arpeggios of the chords of D and B-flat, for example.

The amazing fact is that here, in one symphony, the three purely instrumental movements are *each* arguably the greatest symphonic expositions of their form that there is, not only in Beethoven, but in the entire Western musical tradition. The opening *Allegro* is the musical expression of the Presence of God at the etheric (or, in Theosophical terminology, "higher mental") level. Somehow, without Beethoven even needing to spell it out for us, it is plain from the unique, exalted tones of this movement that its major spiritual theme is that of "Destiny" or at least something very much like it. In a sense the movement and its Destiny theme fulfill a function akin to the opening of the Fifth Symphony with that work's similarly inclined "Fate" theme. But in the *Allegro* of the Ninth, sixteen or so years of further musical and spiritual growth are exhibited, the artistic techniques being now supremely sophisticated and the spiritual themes also now more mature. The opening melody, which for want of a better term I will call the "Destiny" theme, gives us an unearthly awareness of vast reaches of universal space and the sense of some kind of Power or Presence which pervades all, yet which cannot clearly be perceived or understood by mortal beings. But then, from the ill-defined dimensions of the beyond, this overshadowing Something seems to approach more closely and, almost before we know it, is upon us in full, omnipotent force, "hurtled at us with the force of Jove's thunderbolts," as Ralph Hill puts it.[16] This momentous opening is

155

then restated, and the full subject is transferred, still *fortissimo*, to the key of B-flat. In rising sequences the Destiny theme marches on remorselessly until we reach the second subject-group, in which some commentators find some faint resemblance to the "Joy" theme of the *Finale*.

This movement is clearly reminiscent of the confrontation between the Will of God and the will of the lesser self in the first movement of the Fifth Symphony, yet here the conflict is far more sophisticated: the arena is one of a higher spiritual plane altogether, the themes and their intertwinings are far less straightforward, and the "conflict" is not necessarily quite that at all. Musically and in the feelings and impression which the tones give us, the movement is a staggeringly grand fresco of such captivating magnificence that the involved listener loses all sense of time or of selfhood. Though the movement is one of great length, to say this is almost meaningless, for it actually possesses a quality of timeless eternality. Only at its conclusion do we descend back down to "real" time at all. Complex? Masterful? A *tour de force*? No; human adjectives could never adequately describe this music.

156   The *Scherzo* is an immaculate tonal rendition of the Divine Presence at the level of the mental plane. Its immediately effective characteristic is one of racing energy and physical exuberance, but the mental plane aspects of the movement are actually its most basic. The energy is that of unstoppable, divine omnipotence; the various subjects rush forward to exhilarate and stimulate the mind, possessing a kind of unrelenting, Bach-like mathematical beauty and precision. As the movement proceeds, we find, as so often in Beethoven's third period works, a combination of different structural techniques, a fusion of sonata, scherzo, fugue, and other forms. Then, at length, the music appears to be approaching its close, but to our mild surprise one of the main subjects, which we have already joyfully heard several times, begins as though to take off completely once again, only to break off abruptly, literally in midstride. Movement's end!

There follows the Ninth's absolutely unique *Adagio*, a work as extended in length as it is towering in metaphysical height. Amidst an atmosphere of unutterable serenity, we are first introduced to the beautiful first theme and then to the wonderfully lovely second theme, the rest of the movement to follow being basically a set of variations upon these two. The long, sustained chords and slow, deeply mystical melodies create an all-encompassing impression of consummate beauty and pious awe. The most fundamental feeling conveyed by this music is of a sea of Divine Love, supremely pure and perfect. The movement is, in fact, an exalted tonal expression of the divine quality of Purity and its flame.

Altogether, the three instrumental movements of the Ninth give us:

First movement: God the Father; Fire; etheric plane; omnipotence.

Second movement: God the Son; Air; mental plane; omniscience.

Third movement: God the Holy Spirit; Water; emotional plane; love and omnipresence.

The *Finale* of the symphony is a musical expression of spiritual joy and freedom. The text is based on Schiller's poem, "Ode to Joy." It has been said by some that this "Ode to Joy" was actually and originally an "Ode to Freedom" but that the text had to be changed due to the delicate political climate in which Schiller lived. While there is no direct historical evidence for this story, it could well be true, since, in writing the Ode, Schiller had himself been inspired by earlier Masonic poetry which frequently concerned itself with freedom and liberty. In any case, true joy is itself a spiritual state of consciousness having nothing whatsoever to do with mere human happiness. Joy is the result of spiritual freedom; joy is the invariable result of attainment, which is the only real freedom that there is. Therefore, in a sense, the fourth movement is indeed also an "Ode to Freedom."

Esoteric sources I am aware of have stated that the *Finale* is in fact the musical keynote, inspired upon Beethoven, of Gautama Buddha. Certainly the movement expresses the Consciousness of God now anchored fully in the physical plane. This entering into the physical plane is not only symbolized but literally *accomplished* by the fact that the movement introduces the human voice into the medium of the symphony for the first time ever. The use of the voice such as in speech, prayer, chant, and song is an immensely important esoteric occurrence which is fraught with significance. Volume upon volume could be written on this subject, but suffice it to say that the human voice, in its use of the throat chakra, is the most powerful means that there is of bringing about tangible manifestation. It is for this reason that almost all magical practices involve the use of the voice. In one way or another, speech *creates*. Words result in *change*. This is why Jesus cautioned his disciples: "But I say unto you, That every idle word that men shall speak, they shall give account thereof in the day of judgement [the time of their return of the karma]. For by thy words shalt thou be justified [raised in attainment], and by thy words thou shalt be condemned [lowered in attainment]."[17]

In speaking words of goodness, truth, and beauty in matter, human beings precipitate the Word of God into the material realm. This, precisely, is the inner meaning and significance of the first, path-breaking introduction of voices into the symphonic medium in the *Finale* of the Ninth Symphony.

Because this movement expresses the Earth element and the physical plane, the music is static in structure and "down to earth" compared to almost any other of Beethoven's works. The first three movements are fantastically complex, musically advanced, and otherworldly. The *Finale* is exactly the opposite; in the words of Antonín Sychra, "from the very beginning, from the shaping of the theme, he is seeking an adequate, suitably fitting realization in sound of completely concrete concepts."[18]

Then comes the "Joy" theme itself. At first the song is one of the brotherhood of humanity and is thus, perhaps, too merely human in its theme; but later the words direct themselves to heaven and, in some tremendous musical passages, the movement ends with the words:

> Be embraced, ye millions!
> For the universe, this kiss!
> Brothers—above the canopy of stars
> A loving Father surely dwells.
> Millions, do you fall upon your knees?
> Do you sense the Creator, world?
> Seek him above the canopy of stars!
> Surely he dwells above the stars!

The inclusion of a choral *Finale* was a late decision by Beethoven which he made when the other three movements were already almost complete. In finally accomplishing his decades-long idea of setting the "Ode to Joy" to music, he used an overwhelming variety of musical techniques, including fugue, variation, march, chorale, and recitative. You may find it helpful as you listen to this movement to keep in mind the basic elements of the movement in the order of their occurrence. These are outlined by Antonín Sychra as:

1. The introductory dramatic fanfare for the full orchestra
2. The baritone recitative
3. The *Hymn to Joy*—the main theme
4. The orchestral march designed as a *ritornello*
5. The chorale "*Seid umschlungen, Millionen*" ("Be embraced, ye millions")
6. The middle section of the chorale, "*Ihr stürzt nieder, Millionen*" ("Millions, do you fall upon your knees?")
7. The combination of the chorale with the theme of Joy
8. The climax of the theme of Joy in the line "*Und der Cherub steht vor Gott*" ("And the angel stood before God")
9. The climax of the entire *Finale* with the heightening of the instrumentation by the addition of piccolos and especially with the fanfares in the *Maestoso*.[19]

In the introduction of the movement, the main themes of each of the previous three movements enter but are each discarded in mid-melody. Then the "Joy" theme is introduced for the first time. With the coming of the baritone recitative, the movement prepares to give forth its own unique tonal expressions. Joy and freedom—or rather, the joy of spiritual freedom—pours over us in splendorous surges as the music builds up to greater and greater heights. Corinne Heline has stated that in this magnificent choral movement, "it was the triumphant music sounded forth by the Cherubim and Seraphim in celebration of the Mystic Marriage Rites of the Ninth Mystery which Beethoven has recorded."[20] As the music proceeds, one climactic peak after another is scaled, until we arrive at the final lines of the text. Here there occurs an inexpressible burst of second-ray light and exultation.

The first three movements correspond to the Trinity—Father, Son, and Holy Spirit. The significance of the choral *Finale* is that it creates what is called "the squaring of the circle." In esoteric symbology the triangle and the circle each represent the realms of Spirit, and therefore also the Trinity, whereas the square represents the planes of matter. The choral *Finale*, in being added to the previous three movements, brings the whole work and its force of energy down into crystallization in the physical realm and, therefore, squares the circle. (The same principle of the three, representing Spirit, and the four, representing matter, is symbolized in the Great Pyramid: a side view reveals the triangle or Trinity; a top view, the square.)

As the three instrumental movements represent God as Father, as Son, and as Holy Spirit, so the choral *Finale* represents God as Mother: Mother = *Mater*, *Ma-ter* = Mother (*Ma*) plus Earth (*terra*), or "God as matter," in all of its forms, including the Lifeforce itself and the Goddess Kundalini who invigorates that Life and who sings through the soloists and the chorus every time the Ninth Symphony is performed.

Finally, if the nine symphonies correspond to the nine signs of the zodiac and their energies from Capricorn through to Virgo, what then of the remaining three signs? The answer may well be that there are still more symphonies to come before the cycle is complete. Perhaps it will not be completed until the appearance of a new, enlightened music at some time in the future. Certainly Beethoven did not consider the symphonies to have ended. When he died, he had already begun the Tenth and even had sketches for an Eleventh.

For the time being, of course, we must take and use the Nine as a completed cycle, for they are all that we have. Yet it is worth remembering that the Nine which have been brought down into time and space are by definition finite, whereas the Source from which they were derived is infinite. There is certainly more from where they came from. When will we receive it, and when will more be heard?

Spiritual blessings and initiations (which, in a sense, is what the Nine are for humanity) are only given in sequence, each being delivered only when the previous ones have been well-incorporated and assimilated by the soul. Thus, more music from the Source Beethoven tapped can only come when humanity is ready and prepared. And a key feature of this preparation is for us to incorporate Beethoven's mighty music of the spheres and to assimilate it into our beings even as we do the body and the blood of the Cosmic Christ or the enlightened consciousness of the Universal Source.

The Late Quartets: An Overview

Beethoven's late music communicates experiences that very few people can normally possess. But we value these experiences because we feel they are not freakish. They correspond to a spiritual synthesis which the race has not achieved but which, we may suppose, it is on the way to achieving.

—J. W. N. Sullivan[1]

 AS WE HAVE SHOWN, Beethoven's art can be seen as a portion of the music of the spheres stepped down in vibration so that human beings might hear and experience it. Realizing this himself, it is no wonder that he said during his final days, "Strange, I feel as if up to now I had written no more than a few notes," for the spring from which he drew his inspiration was infinite. Moreover, looking not only at music but at the entire field of artistic endeavor, Beethoven stands out as an artist who continually, steadfastly, unrelentingly progressed, doing so even until what seemed the crowning victory of all music, the Ninth Symphony, was itself surpassed by the final five quartets which followed it. Beethoven has been called "the Shakespeare of music." But no other artist working with paint, clay, the written word, or musical notes seems to have entered, or at least captured in art, the transcendent levels of awareness from which he drew the inspiration for the late string quartets. By Beethoven's standard are the achievements of all other artists of all other mediums measured. It might be said that to find comparisons to Beethoven's message, it is necessary to look to the works of the acknowledged mystics, such as St. John of the Cross, St. Catherine of Sienna, or the ancient authors of the Upanishads. In my view, not even Shakespeare or Michelangelo can be said to have tapped the levels of Spirit from which Beethoven and the great mystics speak to us.

As we have seen, Beethoven's creations are far from being purely abstract "sounds." Rather, the greatness of his works rests not in their purely musical content, though this in itself is dazzling, but in their spiritual content. They are sacred songs of the Path to God. Like all enlightened music, Beethoven's compositions do not seek merely to entertain or to please or to soothe or to raise up from depression or to convey a worldly social message, though certainly they can do all of these things; rather, they are designed to rush the intent listener into the bosom of the Beloved.

Beethoven's final and highest rendition of the path of spiritual music are the five late string quartets. Beethoven had desired to compose one or more new string quartets from at least as early as 1822. Then, on November 9th of that year, Prince Galitzin wrote to him requesting "one, two, or three new quartets." But first Beethoven had to complete the *Missa Solemnis* and the Ninth Symphony. These finished and performed in May, 1824, he was free to turn once again to chamber music. Upon doing so, he found his creative font to be so overbrimming that not only did he compose the maximum of three quartets commissioned by Prince Galitzin, but he also went on to compose two more. These last five string quartets took two-and-a-half years to write. They were Beethoven's final works, and their overwhelming greatness and vital importance in the overall scheme of Beethoven's musical and spiritual progress demands that we look at them in some detail.

Even without Prince Galitzin's initial commission, it is likely that Beethoven would at this point have turned in any case to the medium of the string quartet or at least to some form of chamber music. The *Missa Solemnis* and the Ninth Symphony had rendered through music the religious experience and had done so in all of the power and grandeur their very large symphonic and choral forms allowed, but the string quartet form was necessary for Beethoven to express the subtle and even more mystical musical ideas and spiritual states he now found to be his. He had already written eleven string quartets during the course of his life, but the last of these, Op. 95, had been composed as far back as 1810, fourteen years earlier.

The string quartet is an intimate, sincere medium of musical expression, probably more so than any other. In his symphonies Beethoven had magnificently portrayed the trials, tribulations, and triumphs of the victorious seeker on the Path, but within the broad, vast symphonic medium the seeker is always an archetype, whereas the string quartet gives us the real man of the heart. J. W. N. Sullivan, author of the 1927 book, *Beethoven: His Spiritual Development*, goes so far as to state that "the true Beethoven of any period is more accurately reflected in the string quartets than in the symphonies. Beethoven wrote string quartets only with great circumspection and with a very keen sense of responsibility. In these he is more rigorously faithful to his experience . . . than anywhere else in his music."[2]

Beethoven's previous quartets were the six of Op. 18, composed between 1798 and 1800, the three *Rasumovsky* quartets of 1805–6, the *Harp* quartet in E-flat Major (1809), and the F Minor composition of 1810. In the initial Op. 18 works, the quartet form and its classical style as developed by Haydn and Mozart was taken and mastered, the later works then increasingly displaying Beethoven's individuality and revolutionary musical ideas. We glean some insight into how radical Beethoven's imagination was for his time from the story of what he said when he gave the scores of the three beautiful *Rasumovsky* quartets of 1805–6 to Felice Radicati for his appraisal. Radicati, himself a violinist and a quartet composer, tells us: "I said to him that he surely did not consider these works to be music? Beethoven replied: 'Oh they are not for you but for a later age!'"[3] If even these second period works were not for his contemporaries but "for a later age," then what can we say of the final five? By the time of their creation, a fourteen-year gap in his quartet writing had seen Beethoven undergo the great, dark night of around the time of the *Hammerclavier* and his subsequent emergence into the third creative period with the *Missa Solemnis* and the Ninth Symphony. Consequently, the last five quartets were his third period expression of the quartet form and, as such, are unmatched to this day.

The emergence of his third period not only marked a spiritual revolution for Beethoven but also a true revolution of musical technique. Yet as a musical revolutionary, Beethoven never dispensed with the standards and traditions which had preceded him, as many

165

of today's self-styled musicians are apt to do. His concern was not to break from but to develop and expand the existing musical tradition. Knowing well the value of the great stream of classical music he was heir to, he never introduced the new for its own sake but only did so when it was fully justified as being a higher musical rendition of the spiritual experience than could otherwise have been achieved.

Beethoven acknowledges his indebtedness to the past (to Bach) within the quartets themselves by use of a code which had been used by composers since before 1700. In this simple code, every letter of the alphabet has a pitch equivalent. Thus, words or simple phrases can be encoded into the music. In the late quartets B-flat, A, C, and B-natural recur throughout. By the code:

$$B\text{-flat} = B$$
$$A = A$$
$$C = C$$
$$B\text{-natural} = H$$

166   Bach himself used this code, and Haydn had also written a piece based on B-A-C-H.

Beethoven's late quartets are not easy to understand immediately. One important key to their comprehension is to approach them through a previously established familiarity with Beethoven's earlier string quartets. Harold Truscott, in his book on the late quartets, sees them as combining and bringing to fulfillment *two* lines of musical evolution which Beethoven had been exploring: his third period sonatas and his earlier progression within the string chamber medium.[4] Indeed, elements of the third period trends are present even within the earlier and supposedly second period quartets, reminding us that the three periods of Beethoven's musical development were not, strictly speaking, time periods at all. Rather, they were three planes of musical/spiritual consciousness, each rising higher than the preceding one. Chronologically, their demarcation lines were, it is true, surprisingly abrupt, and yet they were not absolutely so. Even the earlier string quartets possess moments and elements which rise into the atmosphere of the third period.

The late quartets are now generally regarded as the crowning achievement of Beethoven's creative development. But it was not always so. To the majority of listeners and even performers, the quartets were incomprehensible not only in Beethoven's lifetime but for decades afterwards. For years after his death, these quartets were explained away as having been a product of his deafness and mental derangement. The last two of the five were not performed at all during what remained of Beethoven's life, and after his death it was a rare event indeed for any of the five to be performed either in Vienna or elsewhere. Not understood, the works were largely neglected for a century. It seems that the rest of the musical world needed to catch up at its own pace before the significance and meaning of the quartets could be recognized. Perhaps also, looking beyond the world of music, a *general* breaking down of an entrenched rigidity and a certain evolution of the consciousness of humanity was necessary. Whatever the reasons for their delayed acceptance, there can be no doubt that in his final quartets Beethoven explored musical realms quite beyond any that had been experienced before. And when the value of the quartets was at last recognized in the twentieth century, they influenced, directly or indirectly, almost every musician of the day.

As we attempt to follow the footsteps of Beethoven through the chronological line of his progressive musical/spiritual development, it is at this point that he moves above the tree line to ascend to high altitudes where the air is thin, and he is increasingly difficult to follow. The composer was now almost totally deaf, forcing upon him an even greater introspection and otherworldliness. Composing his previous Mass and symphony had taken him to new vistas of ethereal being—to new, profound heights of self-knowledge.

In the late quartets more than anywhere else, the signs of divine inspiration are apparent. If Beethoven was the outwardly unknowing, yet inwardly (in his soul-consciousness) willing, co-operator in the process by which the music of the spheres was stepped down into the world of tangible score and physical air vibration, it takes nothing away from his own achievement. Divine inspiration can only be received when one possesses the necessary knowledge, experience, and spiritual attunement necessary for the comprehension, development, and faithful annotation of the inspired concepts as they are given. Beethoven's late quartets could never have been given to us were it not for the previous innovations of Haydn, Mozart, and others, which became Beethoven's

167

starting point, and were it not for Beethoven's own determined, unrelenting enhancement of his musical abilities.

So superhuman are these quartets that not only the student of esotericism but even the more illumined of mainstream musicologists are moved to ask, as does Marion Scott: "How far was he the unconscious channel for these great works (and his ideas never came more freely than when composing them) and how far was he their arbiter? That cannot be argued here. Whatever the relation, he was a willing co-operator, not a trance medium."[5]

One major new feature of these great works is their emphasis upon the *sounds themselves*—not in relation to the other notes, but sound for the sake of the beauty, the value, and the mystery of *sound itself.* Western music, as compared to Eastern music, tends to be more concerned with where the notes are going and what impression they make when strung together harmonically or in sequence rather than with the inherent meaning or effect of individual sounds or general tonal effects. In this, Western music reflects Western civilization in its structured planning and goal-orientation. The Eastern mind tends to dwell more upon the inherent value of the present, and Eastern religion more upon the immanence of God. Western music tends to be listened to through the intellect; Eastern music through the inward soul. Not that an emphasis upon linear goal-orientation or the divine mentality is wrong in music, but it is always good to increase one's options and widen the scope of the musical experience. And the twentieth-century Western rediscovery of the worth of sheer sound itself, the sensuous beauty of the note being played, has its precursor in Beethoven's late quartets, in which the composer displays a very great awareness of the nonlinear, present-moment effect upon the listener of the tones themselves on all planes of being: the physical body, the emotions, the intellect, the intuitive faculties, and the Spirit.

A further essential quality of the third period quartets is well-described by Christopher Small when he writes: "Beethoven was the first composer of the European tradition to conceive the possibility of going out of linear time altogether. In the last quartets, sonata movements, movements which are based on drama and contrast, play a minor role, their place at the center of gravity being taken by fugues and variations. A fugue can induce a sense

168

of timelessness, as we can hear both in the huge fugue of the *Hammerclavier Sonata, Op. 106,* and in the *Great Fugue, Op. 133....* The fugue that opens the *C-sharp Minor Quartet, Op. 131,* is timeless in a different way; here we feel ourselves to be floating in an infinite space. Variations in these last works ... break down finally into static repose."[6]

The basic chronological and thematic relationship between the five late quartets is as follows. The first was composed individually and, in practice, acts as a kind of preparatory "bridge" to the more radically revolutionary works which followed, though it is a marvelously accomplished work in its own right. The next three quartets, though distinct in many ways, overlapped considerably in their periods of composition and are linked musically in many ways. Some commentators have gone so far as to refer to them as being the three parts of one single musical project. The final work, the Quartet in F-Major, is again more distinct in musical content. The five encompass a stunningly varied world of musical experience, possessing movements ranging in content from the tonal rendition of nirvana to a German country dance, from gentle, exquisite, heartrending emotion to the most energetic and superphysical of rhythms.

169

Since their importance demands that we examine them in some detail, I would suggest that the reader acquire recordings of the five late string quartets to study and enjoy in conjunction with the next two chapters.

The Late String Quartets

There is a quality in Beethoven strictly comparable with the teasing zaniness of the Zen masters.

—Wilfrid Mellers[1]

 STRING QUARTET IN E-FLAT MAJOR (1822–25).
OP. 127.

Jottings in Beethoven's notebooks include elements of this quartet as early as 1822, but only with the completion and performance of the Ninth Symphony was he free to concentrate on the quartet, finishing it in February, 1825. Of its premiere shortly afterwards, the *Leipziger Musikalischer Zeitung* reported that "the work was understood by very few and made a bewildering impression." Some of this bewilderment may well have been due, however, to the fact that the rehearsals in preparation for the performance had not gone well. Once the performers were more acquainted with the work, later concerts were more successful.

In terms of both musical technique and his state of conscious-ness, Beethoven was now considerably in advance of where he had been at the time of his previous string quartet of 1810. To some extent the new quartet served to reestablish his facility within the medium, but even here the inventive genius and sublimity of the music exceeds anything to be found in his earlier quartets.

The pure joy and happiness expressed in this E-flat Major quartet could only have been composed by one who knew God in an intimate relationship and by one who, at some level, felt deeply content and fulfilled in his life and service. Gone are the trials and fiery initiatory experiences of the Third and Fifth Symphonies.

Now there is only the bouncing, soaring song of holy joy born of spiritual union. In giving to us something of the happiness resulting from his closeness to God, through the music Beethoven takes us back to its Source.

At first the quartet is not as easy to understand (that is, to appreciate musically and to experience emotionally in tune with Beethoven's own feelings) as is his earlier chamber music, but detailed study and repeated hearings soon familiarize one with it, revealing a wonderful array of breathtakingly beautiful and captivating melodies.

The opening piece, an *Allegro*, is an absolute song of a movement. It begins with six bars of extremely broad and concrete chords, a *Maestoso* (majestic and stately) prelude in E-flat. The same recurs twice more in the movement, once in G and once in C. These three sequences of chords form the architecture of the movement, acting as portals which reroute the main musical lines into new keys and planes of expression.

The second movement is an *Adagio* in A-flat, in the basic rhythmic framework of 12/8, though the rhythm and the pace are by no means unchanging as the music proceeds. The two basic melodic themes give rise to the five variations and *Coda* which constitute the fundamental structure of the movement. Of the five beautiful variations, the third is very different from the others. Here, the harmonic possibilities are not developed; rather, the melody is reduced to its most basic harmonic structure. The key becomes E Major, the rhythm 4/4—the rhythm of the chakra or spiritual center at the base of the spine. In more ways than one, the third variation is the heart of the movement. However, all the variations convey a wide range of emotions which are nonetheless beautifully pure, rare in music, rare in the consciousness of humanity, and drawn from the intimate depths of the composer's heart. The *Adagio* reveals a number of similarities to the Benedictus of the *Missa Solemnis* and also echoes the works of Palestrina. The opening bars are absolutely sublime, the instruments entering one at a time as if from an ethereal mist, then moving smoothly and naturally into the most wonderful, delicate, and heavenly melodic phrases.

In contrast, the *Scherzo* is an extremely bubbly, light-footed movement of much good humor. The numerous short phrases serve to add to the general lightheartedness. Musicologist Joseph

172

Kerman calls this "one of Beethoven's most explosive pieces . . . crackling with dry intelligence."[2] From the first bars it is evident that this is Beethoven with a twinkle in his eye. He almost dares listeners unfamiliar with the piece to guess what comes next; that our guesses are invariably wrong only enhances Beethoven's joke.

The final movement is in combined sonata and *Rondo* form and marks a return to a minimum of intramovement contrast. The opening theme in its two parts forms the foundation of the movement. The air is one of graceful gaiety, and there are a number of unexpected rhythmic and harmonic changes as the music proceeds.

STRING QUARTET IN A MINOR (1825). OP. 132.

Upon the completion of his Op. 127, Beethoven already had numerous other ideas for the string quartet medium. However, the quartets which followed were like nothing that had ever been known or imagined before. In these works, Beethoven passed utterly beyond any semblance of familiar musical territory. For a hundred years the musical sense and the extramusical expression of these final works were a mystery.

The A Minor Quartet had its genesis during the composition of the previous quartet but was mainly written between March and August, 1825, when it also overlapped with work on the next completed quartet in B-flat Major. Due to an early misunderstanding regarding the order of composition of the middle three of the late quartets, the opus numbers did not emerge in proper sequence. The correct order in which they were composed is 132, 130, 131. The resolution of this error aided the understanding of the middle *Trio*, since their true order of development and the sequence of Beethoven's thinking then emerged.

One immediately apparent difference between the more traditional string quartet and Beethoven's Quartet in A Minor is that the A Minor has not four, but five movements. Within the music itself there are also numerous developments of the quartet form, along with an astonishingly broad contrast of emotions expressed between and sometimes within the five movements.

This and the following two quartets are interrelated in a number of ways: in the chronological overlapping of their composition;

173

in the kind of emotions and atmosphere expressed; in their avant-garde nature; in their progressive extension of the string quartet's number of movements; in their nonlinear movement structure; in technique and style; and, last but not least, in the fundamental fugue subject which links them all, a motto theme which recurs in various guises throughout all three quartets. In the opening of Op. 132 it manifests as:

Figure 1

The same subject returns in various forms throughout the work.

The interrelationship between the middle *Trio* of the late quartets should not becloud the fact that each is ultimately an individual work worthy of independent listening and study. Yet certain similarities between the three are clear. One important common feature is that the "meanings" or the overall feeling and psychological expression of the quartets do not proceed in linear, chronological sequence from movement to movement. In other words, there is little sense of the classical pattern of introduction, crisis, development, and resolution. Most of Beethoven's symphonies exhibit dramatic movement-to-movement meaning as conveyed by the music, but this is rarely the case in these three quartets. Here, the movement structure is nonlinear; it can best be described as spherical or simultaneous. That is, the movements of each quartet seem to convey different aspects of one central subject or a variety of different psychological states resulting from one central experience, the movements radiating out from this experience. Though in places Beethoven has still carefully structured the music and tailored the movements' endings so as to connect the movements together, in other places one almost feels that the order of movements in the quartet could be rearranged without significantly altering the impact or meaning of the music. This is particularly so in Op. 130. In the middle *Trio* of quartets, some movements lead abruptly into others with little or no apparent linear psychological or musical connection.

Beethoven's renunciation here of the linear form is a superbly apt stroke considering the rare, sublime nature of the works and the spiritual message which they are intended to express. The result to the studious listener is a forceful realization of the timelessness of the central experience of each quartet, the experience which gave birth to each of the movements. The physical world of daily life proceeds in linear fashion, along the time line of minutes, hours, and days, as future becomes present becomes past. But in the realm to which a person is raised during that rarest of life events, the true mystical experience of divine union, time and space do not exist. Time and space are of the world of effect; while in the mystical experience, the world of cause has been entered into. The key to understanding the last five quartets is that in them we have from Beethoven the widest possible variety of movements resulting from one central experience of divine union.

Each quartet contains at least one movement which gives us in tone form a rendition of the mystical experience itself or, at least, its immediate aftermath and its effect upon the listener. Other movements may not express the experience of the divine union itself, but each in their own way—whether they are profoundly beautiful or joyous or thoughtful or dancelike or comprised of Zen-like humor—express the *effects* and *results* of the original core experience of oneness. The composer has now, as it were, seen God face to face, and the world of *maya* or illusion has no further hold on him. Now everywhere and in everything, he perceives only different aspects of God's Reality of divine Goodness, Beauty, and Truth, and these various aspects are each rendered in all of the late quartets.

175

This effect is discernible within the A Minor Quartet. While the most solemn of all of Beethoven's quartets, it never becomes depressing. *Maya*, seen for what it is now, can no longer cloud the vision. Whatever sadness exists here is a sweet sadness of longing; the tribulations of life are known to be temporary phenomena of the world of time and space and are borne with patience; the solemnity is rendered musically in various beautiful ways, and through it emerge several episodes of a basic happiness which cannot be lastingly quenched. This A Minor Quartet remains, however, the most human of the middle three works. The pain is to some degree still a recognizably human pain; the episodes of relief, in their appearance in the world of time and space, still possess elements of straightforward human happiness.

The opening movement is radiant with a powerful, haunting beauty. Beginning with the fugue subject which links the A Minor, B-flat Major, and the C-sharp Minor Quartets, the basic structure of the movement is that of three expositions divided by developments of the opening theme. After a progressive buildup of mood and emotion is a conclusion of sheer brilliance and a peak of heavenly feeling. The sound is to J. W. N. Sullivan like a "celestial trumpet call," and the effect is as though rays of golden sunlight beam down at last through the overcast sky of the dark night of the soul. In this movement of large contrasts, it is clear that a prime psychological subject dealt with is pain. Musicologist Joseph Kerman believes that pain here receives its most objective treatment in all of Beethoven, the tones being expressive of pain itself and not just of psychological stances or reactions to it. At some points the mental anguish is so strong as to be almost tangible. The instruments sound out at times even dissonantly, giving the effect of tangible pain, and we suck in our breath through our lips as if our fingers had been burned with hot water. Yet still the musical treatment is beautiful; the pain is faced with the patience of the saints.

176

The second movement is in effect a kind of *Scherzo* and *Trio*. The movement that is to follow is to be the most important of the quartet, whereas this second movement and the fourth are not as fundamentally important as the first, third, and fifth. The second and fourth, therefore, serve the purpose of clearing the atmosphere before and after the central third movement. Again in the second movement there are elements of human suffering and exhaustion, but through it shine glimpses of something heavenly. The movement also contains the clear theme of a German country dance, a lovely section which was particularly well-received by early audiences to whom the rest of the quartet was largely an enigma.

During the composition of the A Minor Quartet, Beethoven became seriously ill and almost died. For a time, work on the composition was at a standstill, but when he was sufficiently recovered to write once more, Beethoven's next musical offering was the truly masterful third movement, headed by him as a "Hymn of Thanksgiving to God of a convalescent, in the Lydian mode." The slow music of gentle but deep thankfulness which constitutes the

"Hymn" theme consists of five phrases of four bars each. This theme recurs, punctuated by the secondary and more energetic theme which Beethoven headed "Feeling Renewed Strength" in a structure of ABABA, in which A represents the "Lydian Mode Hymn" and B the "Feeling Renewed Strength." It is interesting to note the prominence of fives here, five in occultism symbolizing that which is within, at the heart or core of things. The basic hymn is five phrases long and occurs in a movement of five sections, the movement being within a quartet which is itself constituted of the unusual number of five movements.

This movement, almost twenty minutes in length, is the psychological core of the quartet. It also introduces an original concept in music, being far from the traditional, classical quartet style. A superb, whimsically beautiful opening takes us into the ABABA structure, and the ending comes with a final third "Lydian Hymn" section which is actually a detail of the previous two but here is dwelt upon and extended with sustained notes and chords which produce a sublime peak of spiritual feeling. As the movement progresses, the role of the strong C grows in importance until here at the climax it asserts itself more powerfully than ever.

177

The short fourth movement is a straightforward and regular enough march, ending with a bridge section which leads into the fifth and final movement. Though it is not at all a composition of suffering, it lacks the exuberant victory of the Fifth Symphony or the pure joy of the previous Op. 127 quartet. With the bridge section comes the end of the march atmosphere and a return of melancholy.

The final movement is a *Rondo* with a lovely waltz melody, the main *Rondo* subject having originally been planned as the fourth movement of the Ninth Symphony. Here, it is transposed into the A minor key of this particular quartet and scored, of course, for only four instruments. Yet it retains more than a touch of the symphonic style. Interestingly, however, compared to the definitely third-period style of the first three movements of the Ninth Symphony, this movement is more akin to the style of the second period. If Beethoven had used it as he originally intended, the Ninth Symphony might have ended with something sounding as if out of the Fifth. Placed within the framework of the A Minor Quartet, however, it brings a satisfactory conclusion to the work;

psychologically it also creates a sense of the final overcoming, the music racing somewhat out of the earlier sadness and suffering. And yet in this work the final victory is, in the words of Sullivan, "so hard-won that we are left with none of that feeling of exultant triumph with which we have watched so many of Beethoven's victories, but rather with a feeling of slightly incredulous relief, of thankfulness still tinged with doubt."[3]

STRING QUARTET IN B-FLAT MAJOR, OP. 130, AND GROSSE FUGE (1825). OP. 133.

It is a wonder that a mortal mind could have conceived, contained, and transcribed a work so brilliant, original, and enormously complex as the B-flat Major Quartet. And yet, it was composed surprisingly rapidly. Though the earliest work on it was done in March 1825, almost all of the quartet was actually written between August and November.

This is the most enigmatic of all Beethoven's quartets. Even today, with all the advantages of the retrospective viewpoint and decades of scholarly debate, even a partial revealing of the quartet's many secrets requires considerable study. Little wonder that a reviewer of Beethoven's day called the final movement, the *Grosse Fuge*, "incomprehensible; a sort of Chinese puzzle."

For some reason Beethoven did not attend the premiere performance but waited in a nearby tavern! When the concert was finished, Karl Holz, Beethoven's friend in his last years, dashed immediately to the tavern to give the composer a complete report. Two movements, he said, had received tremendous applause and had to be encored, but upon hearing that these were the relatively straightforward *Presto* and *Alla Danza Tedesca*, Beethoven (typically) did not hesitate to verbalize his thoughts. "Yes, these delicacies! And what of the Fugue? That alone should have been repeated. Cattle! Asses!"[4] As we shall see, the startling Fugue with which the quartet ended was to cause Beethoven further problems. It is now quite clear that this *Grosse Fuge* is psychologically the fundamental movement of the entire work, musically expressing the central experience to which all the other movements relate.

In this quartet, more than ever, the nonlinear nature of the work is strikingly apparent. In his book on the quartets, Joseph

178

Kerman speaks of Beethoven's "drive towards dissociation"[5] in this composition, and agrees that probably "Beethoven was working toward some new idea of order markedly different from the traditional psychological sequence that he had developed in the earlier music. This new order is not easy to comprehend, because on the evidence of the Quartet in B, the idea was not entirely realized. In the few works that were now left to him to compose, he did not pursue the new conception but reverted to more traditional ideas of order."[6] Kerman goes as far as to call the quartet *"the truly radical work of the third period,"*[7] a viewpoint with much to support it.

Just as novels are a dramatic, linear art form, the action moving from A to Z through time, music had until then been structurally rather similar. But now Beethoven was exploring a musical structure more synonymous with the artistic experience of a painting. There is no chronological development to speak of; the art form just is. In the B-flat Major Quartet Beethoven gives us different details of the work to perceive and experience as though we were glancing here and there at the various details of the background of a painting. Then only at the end does he unveil the foreground subject matter—the *Grosse Fuge*—which gives coherence and sense to the previously sampled supporting details.

179

The previous quartet, Op. 132, was unusual for having five, not the usual four, movements. Now this next quartet had six. The first of them is the lengthiest with which Beethoven ever opened a string quartet. It alternates between *Adagio* and *Allegro* and also contains the fugue theme which haunts all the middle three of the last five quartets. A difficult but wonderful work of musical ingenuity, the movement contains a wealth of tonal allusions and references for those willing to search for them. Multifaceted in its sonata form, it again presents to us a spiritual joy and triumphant energy forged in the furnace of the trials and tribulations of the successful seeker on the Path. But as Sullivan points out, "This, to him, was one of life's dominant characteristics, but how lightly he touches on it! This movement has something of that note of reminiscence, of remoteness, that becomes so familiar to us in the last quartets."[8]

The second movement is the shortest of the quartet, though one of the sweetest. It is a *Presto* in B-flat Minor, the first violin coming to the wittily melodic fore in the *Trio*, as the other three instruments provide the strong background rhythm which makes the piece so racy.

The third movement is a very beautiful *Andante* (played at "walking" pace, steady and flowing). It is not a true sonata, since for it to be so, a second key would need to be explored, and here the key of D-flat is quite strictly adhered to. A number of brief musical references to the other movements remind us of the ultimate interconnectedness of them all.

The other movement of the quartet to be encored in the first performance follows, the *Alla Danza Tedesca* in G Major. Based upon a German dance, the result is music which smiles through tears.

The *Cavatina* is not a long movement, having only sixty-two bars, but Beethoven apparently spent much time perfecting it to his satisfaction. He disposed of and reshaped many earlier ideas and sketches. The result is a combination of superb simplicity, perfect expressiveness, and heartrendingly sincere emotion. To Marion Scott it was "one of his supreme inspirations."[9] Beethoven himself confessed that it moved him more than anything else he had ever written. Violinist Karl Holz reported that it cost Beethoven tears in the writing and that "merely to revive it afterwards in his thoughts and feelings brought forth renewed tributes of tears."[10]

And so we arrive at the final movement. Knowing what it must have meant to him, we can well understand Beethoven's disappointment at his contemporaries' incomprehension of the work. Probably the strangest and most advanced movement he ever wrote, the *Grosse Fuge* (Great Fugue) was a giant leap forward in Beethoven's musical courage and unique inventive genius. The Fugue was the Apollo XI landing of the art form, taking music to another world of landscape. More than any other Beethoven works, the late string quartets, with movements such as this one, demonstrate to us that so much in classical music, though composed in the past, belongs more to the present and to the future. If Beethoven's late string quartets are not New Age music, then nothing is. But indeed they are such music and shall be recognized for their sublime qualities more and more in the decades and centuries to come, as people evolve to the point of being able to appreciate them fully. In the words of Stravinsky, spoken a full century after Beethoven's

Grosse Fuge was composed, it is "an absolutely contemporary piece of music that will be contemporary forever."

As I have said, fugues became an important constituent of Beethoven's third period repertoire, since they lent themselves more readily to the expression of timeless experiences. But whereas fugues were traditionally built upon a single, unified theme, Beethoven here adopts a sonatalike form of contrast between two different fugal themes. The result is a huge, difficult, and unique masterpiece of artistic endeavor.

The opening introduces all the main thematic versions which are to come later, serving much like a table of contents. After a brief, slow beginning, the two fugal themes are brought forward and become the basis of the movement's structure of several sections. One of the themes is in its outline somewhat reminiscent of Bach, the other strongly—even violently—rhythmic with amazing wide skips. At first the two fugal themes seem to be in complete opposition to one another, and a resolution unlikely. First we hear as the subject the ubiquitous fugue motto of all the middle three quartets, then the rhythmic countersubject, but as the movement proceeds, the two switch places, first one acting as subject, then the other. In the third section the two clash in head-on confrontation, and the familiar fugue motto emerges the victor. Yet as the culmination of the movement approaches, the two achieve a majestic synthesis.

181

The negative reaction of the audience and the critics to this "Chinese puzzle" *Finale* was not the end of the matter. The players, Beethoven's friends, and eventually his publisher became concerned about it. They tried to persuade him that the *Finale* was too long, and he agreed to write an alternative sixth movement for the quartet. Thus the *Grosse Fuge* was replaced by a more familiar sounding and shorter *Allegro*, the Fugue becoming a separate and orphaned composition, receiving the opus number 133. Thus another of the great Beethoven controversies was born.

The question is, which of the two endings of the quartet is the "real" or rightful one, the *Grosse Fuge* or the alternative *Allegro*? Indeed, one only has to recall what a stubborn, self-assertive man Beethoven could be, rarely willing to compromise art for the sake of popular taste, to realize how strange it is that he should have agreed to the alternative *Finale* in the first place. He certainly knew that the *Grosse Fuge* was one of the most advanced and original creations of his life's work. Why, then, did he agree to the replacement? Four possibilities have been advanced:

1) He was mentally preoccupied with Karl's suicide attempt, which took place at this time.

2) The new *Finale* brought him a further fee of fifteen ducats. (It is true that Beethoven had become increasingly anxious in his later years about his financial affairs.)

3) He agreed that the *Grosse Fuge* was not the best or most fitting conclusion to the quartet.

4) He agreed out of sheer ironic disdain for his bemused audience.

The answer may be a combination of these four reasons. The first two may well have been contributing factors (though surely that only). And the romantic fourth reason would not be beyond Beethoven. However, some musical scholars have opted for the third reason, believing that Beethoven's decision was not ironic, but serious. They make the point that he may have been persuaded that good though the Fugue was, its length and its radical, startling qualities tended to swamp and render inconspicuous all that was good in the previous five movements. Personally, I believe the *Grosse Fuge* to be the only logical conclusion to the quartet and that Beethoven knew this. Without it, the other movements become dissociated and contain little overall dramatic logic.

The debate continues even in today's concert hall. The quartet is still occasionally performed with the second ending. Modern recordings typically end with the Fugue but may also contain the second ending as a kind of appendix. J. W. N. Sullivan, in his study of Beethoven's spiritual development, goes as far as saying that Beethoven never did, in a sense, replace the Fugue. Though he wrote a new *Finale* (under the pressure of others and for the money), he had faith that posterity—you, I, and the wise peoples of a later day of greater enlightenment—would know to restore the *Grosse Fuge* to its proper position. This has tended to happen: the Fugue is the most common ending in modern concerts.

Which leaves us with one final question: What is the Fugue's *meaning*? While one must beware of the foolhardiness of searching for meaning and a storyline in all music, it is impossible to believe that Beethoven had no extramusical ideas, qualities, or experiences in mind when he launched forth on this stunning work. We know for a fact that Beethoven rarely, if ever, indulged in his art purely for art's sake; rather, his works were intended to express an extra-musical meaning. At one time he actually proposed to write down the meanings intended in each work. Truly, this would have been a fascinating revelation, though ultimately one has mixed feelings about its wisdom. As it happens, his friends dissuaded him.

So we must still ask ourselves, what is the meaning of the *Grosse Fuge*? And for that matter, what indeed is the significance of the fugue motto which appears in each of the middle three late quartets? I recommend to the reader that a useful spiritual exercise is to familiarize yourself with this quartet and its Great Fugue until you are able to receive the answer intuitively within your own heart. In the meantime, here are some possible meanings others have suggested. Marion Scott, in her book on Beethoven and his music, wondered if the *Grosse Fuge* does not sing of "the struggle between body and spirit, and the ultimate triumph of spirit."[11] Others have seen in the Fugue a meaning similar to this, but more subtle. The two basic themes seem to represent, on the one hand, destiny and all that it requires of one, including submission and, on the other hand, individuality and assertion. In other words, we might very tentatively wonder if the two are similar to the two basic spiritual subjects of the Fifth Symphony. But whereas in the symphony the self-assertive ego only submits at length to its divine calling, here the submission to and alignment with the Will of God is more willing and complete. As Sullivan comments: "Beethoven had come to realize that his creative energy, which he at one time opposed to his destiny, in reality owed its very life to that destiny."[12]

183

ALTERNATIVE ALLEGRO FINALE TO OP. 130 (1826).

This alternative sixth movement was written after the five late string quartets were completed and so was actually the last music Beethoven ever wrote, being composed in late 1826. In style it is close to the final quartet, Op. 135, and tends to seem out of place in Op. 130. As much as the *Grosse Fuge* was a controversial *Finale* due to its length and radically avant-garde nature, so this alternative seems inappropriately straightforward and traditional, giving the quartet a human, not a metaphysical, conclusion.

Taken as a work in itself, however, like all of Beethoven's serious music, it is extremely enjoyable. It bursts with melody. As in the final completed Quartet, Op. 135 (which is examined below), the style is neoclassical, owing much to Haydn and the late eighteenth-century tradition. If as a conclusion to the quartet some find it unsatisfactory, this is not a view shared by all. In his book on the late quartets, Harold Truscott champions the piece with vigor, insisting that "it is quite as subtle as [the *Grosse Fuge*], and I believe it to be even more so . . . It is, without doubt, the most complex tonal design in the whole of these late quartets . . . [and] all but the greatest sonata movement Beethoven wrote for string quartet." [13]

STRING QUARTET IN C-SHARP MINOR (1825–26). OP. 131.

Upon the completion of the previous Quartet in B-flat Major, Karl Holz asked Beethoven which of his quartets he himself thought the greatest. Beethoven replied, "Each in its way. Art demands of us that we shall not stand still." [14] And Beethoven didn't.

Between November, 1825, and July, 1826, he wrote a fourth new quartet which was also to become the third of the middle *Trio* containing the common fugue motto. Upon its completion, this C-sharp Minor Quartet *was* held by Beethoven to be his finest. This evaluation from the master himself tells us in advance of close study that we are dealing here with something very, very special.

Interestingly, the keys of the middle three late quartets are, in order, A, B, and C, a fact which, assuming the coincidence was not by design, would certainly not have escaped Beethoven's own notice. As we have said, one controversy among musicologists concerns the question of just how related we should conceive Beethoven's "ABC" to be. The answer, surely, is given to us by St. Paul when he says of the Trinity that they are both three *and* one, or three *in* one. The three are separate *and* unified. We may even see in these three quartets a conscious reference to the Trinity. And since the Trinity is a fundamental feature of the world, so many universal qualities being triune in nature, the possible references become endless. Marion Scott, for one, suggested that the three works might symbolize body, soul, and spirit, or past, present, and future.

Whatever the answer, Beethoven's publishers, not sharing the composer's sense of humor, fell prey to somewhat less lofty thoughts when they first received the score of the C-sharp Minor Quartet. They themselves had requested a quartet from him, stipulating that it must be a new, original one. Beethoven, finding the jest all the greater due to the magnitude of the work, therefore scrawled on the score by way of introduction, "Cribbed together from this and that"! The publishers wrote immediately to demand an explanation, and Beethoven had to reply that the comment was only a joke.

As a matter of fact, there *are* in the quartet a number of conscious musical allusions to earlier compositions, a device Beethoven used to refer to previously expressed extramusical states, qualities, and conflicts. But here most other possible similarities with anything else cease. The publishers had requested a new, original quartet; we can but wonder whether they ever realized just how "original" the one they received was!

Whereas the traditional string quartet possessed four movements, Beethoven had given the A Minor Quartet five, and the B-flat Major six. Now he gave this one seven. Seven is the perfect number of numerology. It is also the number of the seven outer or exoteric rays in esotericism, which are the source of all creation and manifestation and from which are derived the seven major tones of the diatonic scale, the seven colors of the rainbow, the symbolic concept of the seven "days" of creation, the seven crystal systems of crystallography, the seven major hormonal glands (and their corresponding seven chakras), and so forth. It is even possible that in these seven movements Beethoven unconsciously rendered in tone form the divine qualities of each of the seven rays in numerical order through the movements from the first to the seventh. The divine qualities of the rays are, in order: God-Power, God-Wisdom, God-Love, God-Purity, God-Healing and Science, God-Ministration and Service, and God-Freedom.

185

Opus 131 also possesses other structural extensions of the quartet form; for example, in the choice of keys. Whereas the quartet traditionally had two main keys, the previous B-flat Major Quartet had four. Now Beethoven gave this quartet six. The number of different tempos, musical forms, and textures also increase dramatically in this work, yet the astonishing miracle of Beethoven's genius is in that from such pronounced and radical diversity emerges, paradoxically, a superb sense of *unity*. This brilliant unification is achieved in a number of ways. Not only is the work psychologically and musically unified, but he even stipulated that the entire work should be performed without pauses between the movements, thus making it, quite literally, one. And despite the large number of keys used, the six occur in an order so as to create (apart from the key of the sixth movement) a unified wave form (see figure 2). Finally, the seventh movement is in the same key as the first, thus ending where the music began, as though completing a cycle—the circle being the symbol of eternity.

Since six is in numerology the number of the Man, or the Son, and seven the number of Creation, the *six* keys and the *seven* movements of this *cycle* (eternity) can be deemed to represent the universal *Christ* in the *eternal Creation*. But wait, there is more. Looking at the movements' keys as laid out together in figure 2, we realize that we are seeing the mysterious motto fugue theme!

186

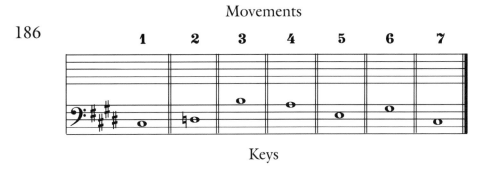

Figure 2

Marion Scott writes of this, "Still further, the motto theme with its characteristic interval of the sixth is now below the threshold of consciousness, merged as it were in the new order, but in its reversed form—with the *third* as its characteristic, it dominates the thematic matter of the Quartet. Thus the third (which might symbolize God since it is the number of the *Trinity*) and its inversion the sixth—Man—are seen like reality and its reflection."[15]

Again we ask ourselves, what does this mysterious fugue theme, which we have now encountered in one guise or another in so many places, stand for? The omnipresence of God? Whether for this or not, the fugue motto, being present even in the tonal structure of this C-sharp Minor Quartet, thereby becomes related to the *six* keys, the *seven* movements, and the *cycle* of eternity.

In this conscious, intricate play upon esoteric numerology and fundamental religious symbolism, Beethoven was following in the footsteps of Bach, whose music also contained such secrets. Mozart, too, had placed a rich harvest of inner meanings within his work, but in Mozart's case, his Masonic ideas and symbolism were not only within the numerology and interval structure of the notes but even in the words and the dramatic events of his operas. This kind of symbolism was later to be used extensively in drama by Wagner. How true it is that without a theoretical—and practical—understanding of esotericism and of the Path, so many great musical works are impossible to comprehend fully.

Though Beethoven's Op. 131 is the most difficult quartet of all to understand, it soon becomes apparent why Beethoven considered it his finest. As a feat of sheer mental concentration, it is staggering. It is also Beethoven's most metaphysical work of all. The same deeply mystical and sacrosanct atmosphere which Palestrina succeeded in creating with his ethereally serene vocal compositions is here more than reproduced by Beethoven through the medium of the violins, viola, and cello. It is above all in this quartet that we encounter the stylistic element Beethoven wrote of at this time as his "new manner of voice writing." Melodies, instead of being pronounced by one instrument (or set of instruments) from beginning to end, are built up *from a composite*, each instrument contributing a note or two to the phrase as a whole. The technique lends a wonderful organic life to the melody, the music seeming to possess an existence all its own, independent of the instruments. In a sense this technique, usually known as *open* or *pierced* work, adds a whole new dimension to the music. In order to hear this, the reader will need to listen under highly stereophonic conditions, with widely spaced speakers or with headphones, or to attend a concert where visual cues will aid in the location of the notes. To appreciate and follow this technique requires of the listener an extra level of concentration and understanding which is marvelously invigorating for the heart, third eye, and crown chakras.

187

Of the quartet's seven movements, four are of greater importance than the other three, these three being short and acting somewhat as transitional episodes. There is a certain build-up of tension throughout the work culminating in the concluding seventh movement, but this quartet is by no means like the previous one in which the final movement, the *Grosse Fuge*, provided the central psychological reference point for the whole. Rather, this time it is the opening movement which gives the central experience from which all the other movements are born. Like the *Grosse Fuge*, this movement, too, is a fugue and, indeed, is based once more upon the fugue motto, the rising sixth of the theme now changed to a descending third. But whereas energetic rhythm and contrast were so prominent in the *Grosse Fuge*, here there is a vast, endless, universal serenity as immutable and unreachable as the stars of heaven.

Wagner thought this "the most melancholy sentiment ever expressed in music."[16] Yet with time, it has increasingly come to be realized that this movement sings not of the melancholy but of the mystical. It is, indeed, the most transcendently mystical music in all of Beethoven. J. W. N. Sullivan called the movement, "the completely unfaltering rendition into music of what we can only call the mystic vision. It has that serenity which, as Wagner said, speaking of these quartets, passes beyond beauty. Nowhere else in music are we made so aware, as here, of a state of consciousness surpassing our own." Sullivan thought that to Beethoven, the passionless, remote calm derived from this mystic vision "was the justification of, and the key to, life. In the light of this vision he surveys the world."[17]

It is also in the light of this vision that the six movements which follow are composed. From the highest reaches of the spiritual realm, Beethoven now (comparatively) descends and, like the Buddha who refused to remain forever in the world of divine bliss while others were lost in *maya*, brings the message of this vision down into the etheric, mental, emotional, and physical planes of experience.

There results an *Allegro* of a superbly pure and divine beauty. Then next comes a short, transitional third movement which takes us into the *Andante*. In structure this slow movement opens with a two-part theme, takes us through six variations, and then ends with

188

a *Coda* which refers us back to the opening theme. The movement is central to the quartet not only since it is the fourth of seven, but also, to some extent, musically. In whatever relationships it holds with the slow movements of earlier works, the common qualities are here raised onto a higher level of significance as a result of the mystical vision experienced in the first movement.

The fifth movement is a *Scherzo* which Kerman has called "Beethoven's most childlike scherzo in his most mature and complex work of art."[18] This is no paradox, however, for without the wonderful innocence of the childlike mind, the kingdom (consciousness) of heaven is quite unattainable.

The sixth movement, an *Adagio*, is derived from the fugue of the opening movement and, though short, has a lovely, melancholy melody. Again in the final movement we encounter the fugue theme of the first, though in an inverted or reversed form. But now it is thrust into a movement which, after the carefully controlled atmospheres of the previous six, suddenly bursts into vigorous, dynamic action. The release of tension forms a perfect climax to the Quartet. All is fulfilled—not only conflicts raised in this movement but also in the others. Wagner saw in this music "the dance of the whole world itself: wild joy, the wail of pain, love's transport, utmost bliss, grief, frenzy, riot, suffering . . ."[19]

189

STRING QUARTET IN F MAJOR (1826). OP. 135.

This was Beethoven's final completed work. His sixteenth string quartet in all, it was followed only by the alternative *Finale* to replace the *Grosse Fuge* in Op. 130. This final quartet was composed between July and October, 1826, a trying period encompassing Karl's attempted suicide and Beethoven's penultimate illness. Much of the work was composed at Gneixendorf, where Beethoven took Karl for a holiday. A servant there left this graphic account:

> At 5.30 a.m. he was at his table, beating time with hands and feet, humming and writing. After breakfast he hurried outside to wander in the fields, calling, waving his arms about, moving slowly, then very fast, then abruptly stopping to scribble something in his notebook.[20]

In style this quartet and the alternative *Finale* are very similar. Well might one have wondered where Beethoven would go following his logarithmic advances in structure, style, and psychological impression in the previous three quartets. Yet another surprise is in store, for these final compositions are quite short, traditional enough in structure, and mark something of a return to classical style, with more than a few touches akin to Haydn and Mozart. Beethoven has returned, however, not in a circle, but in a spiral. He reenters traditional territory at a higher and more sophisticated level than he left it. The style is *neo*classical—much more than a mere repetition of earlier music.

In its own way then, the final work is as unexpected as its predecessors. Perhaps the earlier quartets' radical explorations depict an ongoing spiritual quest and restlessness which is finally resolved, once and for all, in the previous, C-sharp Minor Quartet. The F Major thus is the work of a man inwardly at peace. Beethoven's outer life had actually never been more trying than at this time. Trials of the emotional body and of raw, physical pain were more frequent than ever. But as we have seen from previous periods of his life, the inner man was able to separate himself from the difficulties and distractions of the outer world to a remarkable degree.

Harold Truscott, in his book on the late string quartets, advances the interesting idea that "this quartet is not a third period work at all, or a first or second period either, but the beginning of a new, fourth phase."[21] However neoclassical this quartet and the alternative *Finale* may be, from his notebooks it can be seen that the further projects Beethoven had in mind (which death prevented him from accomplishing) seem to have been at least as advanced as those of Opp. 132, 130, and 131, as though his next work would have been a continuation of the third period or, indeed, the beginning of a fourth period of even greater surprises and explorations. Of course, we can never really know what he might have gone on to do had he lived. Perhaps from this point Beethoven would no longer have been confined within the convenient margins of "periods" at all.

In this quartet then, we find ourselves back to the four-movement format. The opening *Allegretto* in F major sets the atmosphere of most of the work: brisk, melodic, relatively straightforward at first hearing, but with grim undertones beneath the

190

surface. The second movement, the *Vivace*, is noted for its sparse texture, but it is racy, joyous, and, as so often in Beethoven, superbly melodic. The slow movement—a very slow movement—has the heading "Sweet song of rest or peace" in Beethoven's sketchbook. Its structure is that of three variations on a very simple theme. At the opening, the instruments enter one by one, not unlike the opening of the second movement of Op. 127. The music is extremely placid, like a string quartet lullaby, smooth as a calm sea. But if we see in this movement a foreboding of the death that was to come, it is possible to see the same even more in the *Finale*.

To view the *Finale* as a Requiem is to go beyond the evidence, though. Even half a year later, after weeks of illness, Beethoven still hoped to recover and had made sketches for a tenth symphony, an eleventh symphony, another quartet, and several further ambitious choral works. But he certainly must have realized that his days were becoming numbered. Whether the subject was death or not, we are in any case left with no doubt that this movement expresses a very definite extramusical conflict through the music. The movement is headed "*Der schwer gefasste Entschluss*"—"The Resolution hard to take" or "The difficult Decision." The musical themes represent specific verbal meanings which Beethoven wrote beneath the notes. First come the three extremely grave, ominous notes marked by him as "*Muss es sein?*" ("Must it be?"): 191

Der schwer gefasste Entschluss

Muss es sein?

Figure 3

These are repeated a number of times and in variation. The theme had already been hinted at in the very opening tonal phrase of the first movement, played in the chord of B-flat minor, Beethoven's black key. Now, in its full appearance within the closing movement, the theme's gravity may possibly be tongue-in-cheek, and yet a very definite anxiety and even fear is conveyed. But then we are surprised by a sudden introduction of the movement's affirmative main theme, the six-note *Allegro* reply, "*Es muss sein! Es muss sein!*" ("It must be! It must be!")

Allegro

Es   muss sein!   Es   muss sein!

Figure 4

This positive, dancing affirmation goes on to set the pace and spiritual tone for most of the movement. Near to the end, further elements of doubt and anxiety creep in but then are dismissed for good, as the music ends more lightheartedly than ever with a passage in exuberant *pizzicato* (plucking of the strings) and a confident conclusion.

192   The words of the movement's thematic question and reply originated in a private joke. Dembscher, an agent of the Austrian War Department, who missed the first performance of the Op. 130 Quartet, offered that the second could take place in his own large house, and he would hear it then. Beethoven refused. Receiving from Holz Beethoven's negative reply, Dembscher stammeringly begged how he could be returned to Beethoven's favor. Holz told him that first he should pay the subscription fee for the *first* performance to Schuppanzigh, who had arranged the concert. Laughing, Dembscher asked, "Must it be?" When Beethoven heard the story from Holz, he wrote a humorous cannon with the words: "It must be! It must be! Yes, yes, yes, yes, it must be! Yes, yes, yes, yes, it must be! Yes, yes, yes, yes, come out with the purse! Come out! Come out! It must be!"

The phrase became a standing joke among Beethoven and his friends during the late part of 1826, as is evidenced from the conversation books. For example, when Beethoven's housekeeper came for the weekly house money, his friend Anton Schindler wrote, "It must be. The old woman is again in need of her weekly money."

Certainly Beethoven could be musically playful even at the most difficult of times. During his very serious illness experienced three quartets earlier, he found the strength to write a song with the musical/medical pun: "Doctor, close the door 'gainst death; Notes will also help in need." With the words "It must be" within it as the main thematic materials, some see the last movement of the F Major Quartet as a musical mock tragedy. This, though, may well be to misinterpret the mood of light-heartedness. Repeated private jokes have a habit of remaining prominently in mind. It is altogether likely for a character such as Beethoven's to have recalled the words and related them to some weightier matter which was preying on him. A number of biographers view the worded phrases as Beethoven's own question and answer to death. Certainly the opening question, "Must it be?," is sounded seriously enough. But, consciously or otherwise, Beethoven may have been posing a question still more crucial than that of the possibility of death. There is much truth in the oft-quoted statement that Beethoven had known how to die since he was fifteen years old.

"Must it be?" is an archetypal query—even the basic question of all human existence and consciousness. For instead of manifest- 193 ing a pointless universe of mechanical subservience, has not the Creator blessed the highest creation, humanity, with the precious gift of free will? Yes, God has, in order that we each might enjoy the opportunity of obeying God and cosmic law out of our own indi-vidual choice, whereby we grow in consciousness. And out of this free will, since not everybody makes enough of the right choices in life, there arise the opposites apparent on earth such as wisdom and error, good and evil, God-centered and self-centered existence.

Muss es sein? Must it be?

It is not reading too much into this to say that ultimately the question is asking: *Must* we obey our inner conscience? *Must* we be moral? *Must* we do all we can to become godly, pure beings?

Must it be? *Must* we obey God's Will?

Little more than a week before his end Beethoven wrote in a letter:

And what is to become of me, if my illness persists for some time?—Truly my lot is a very hard one! However, I am resigned to accept whatever Fate may bring; . . . to bear my lot, however hard and terrible it may prove to be, with a feeling of submission to the will of the Almighty.[22]

"Must it be?" is a very Gethsemanelike enquiry. (The gospels recall how immediately preceding his capture leading to his crucifixion, Jesus prayed so earnestly that his sweat was, as it were, great drops of blood falling to the ground, and he said, "Father, if thou be willing, remove this cup from me: nevertheless not my will, but thine, be done."[23]) Beethoven's alignment and his surrender to his destiny was by this time so complete that when the now-familiar challenge of the confrontation between the lesser will and the Greater Will recurs in this quartet, the question, "Must it be?" has hardly been raised before its querying and ominous tones are dismissed by a rush of dancing acceptance. The answer is joyful because to give it no longer requires the inner conflict of former times, when it was indeed "the difficult Decision." To that which almost all people would balk at, Beethoven—provided that it was the Will of God—was now indifferent. He had overcome the major challenge of life: "Choose ye this day whom ye will serve." The soul and its Maker had begun to become one.

The Late String Quartets and the Secret Rays

IT IS WELL-KNOWN among students of the divine mysteries that there are seven rays or creative emanations from God which are the basis of much of the phenomena of the universe. But in fact there are five other creative emanations or rays, making a total of twelve altogether. Twelve is a number which we all instinctively feel to be significant, since there are, in addition to the twelve rays, twelve signs of the zodiac (one for each ray), twelve months of the year, and twelve hours on the clock. The seven rays tend to be more associated with outer, tangible phenomena; the five with inner, less overt phenomena. The seven are masculine, *yang* or positive in polarity; the five feminine, *yin* or negative.

The seven proceed from out of the five. That is, the five are the cause; the seven the effect. If we master the seven and go within them, we find the five. The seven rays and the five are manifested tonally in the seven major and five minor keys of the diatonic scale. (It is said there are also five "minor" or "inner" colors which are invisible to our physical eyes, as there are seven visible colors of the rainbow.)

Though comparatively little is known of the five secret rays, occult sources reveal certain details, to which I would add a little more. Man and woman are themselves the talisman of the secret rays, the five-pointed star (symbolic of the rays and also of the human individual) having been made tangible in our two legs, two arms, and head. The secret rays and their spiritual qualities are contacted in true meditation, and the best physical posture for realizing them is the lotus position.

The soul on the Path must master the seven outer rays in his or her own environment and being. Only when the qualities of all seven—God-Power, God-Wisdom, God-Love, God-Purity, God-Healing and Science, God-Ministration and Service, and God-Freedom—are developed within, can the soul begin to manifest the fullness of the Christed one. Then, the seven rays having been mastered, the seeker must gain a more complete attainment in the five secret rays.

The increased capacity in the Adept to wield the energies of the secret rays is symbolized in the initiation of the crucifixion. The wounds of the crucified Jesus Christ are symbolic of the five secret ray chakras, located in the palms, the soles of the feet, and deep within the heart (this latter symbolized by the spear-wound to Christ's side). In the similarly Christed one, then, the secret ray chakras are opened, the opened palm chakras, for instance, greatly enhancing the power of the soul to radiate healing forces.

The development of the secret rays is a necessary level of attainment on the Path. The secret rays promote an action of detail, the final sculpturing of the mind and consciousness in the perfect image of the Divine. The secret rays are like the refiner's fire; they purge and purify. When an individual has said of himself or herself, "My work is finished," God sends forth the secret rays to show that person that the detail is not finished. For the Law requires perfection.

Here is the value and role of the five late string quartets of Beethoven to the spiritual aspirant. As the secret rays finish the subtle detail of perfection in the soul, beginning their work where the seven rays leave off, so do the beautiful, sophisticated, pious tones of the late quartets complete that subtle work of detail in the body, mind, and soul of the aspirant which the less subtle but powerful molding influences of the nine symphonies have left undone. The nine symphonies correspond to the Path from its early stages to the attainment of major initiations. Their sound

196

is a most powerful shaping factor on the consciousness which is open to them. But the quartets are often delicate and intricate, sublime and supernal to an extent rarely, if ever, achieved in the more "physical" music of the symphonies.

Each string quartet corresponds to one of the five secret rays. Now, the four fingers and thumb of the human hand are also manifestations of the five secret rays. And though at first this may not seem to tell us much, by the esoteric Law of Correspondence, the parallels can be quite revealing. Through thinking about the attributes of the fingers, we can glean clues as to qualities of the secret rays. Moreover, when we relate the fingers to the quartets, we discover some fascinating correlations. The most obvious correlation is that the fingers, in order, have the same relative lengths (in space) as do the quartets (in time) in their chronological order:

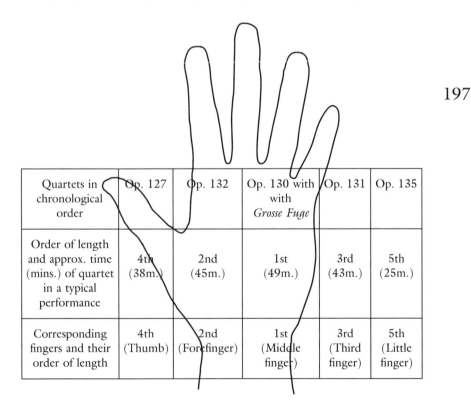

Quartets in chronological order	Op. 127	Op. 132	Op. 130 with with *Grosse Fuge*	Op. 131	Op. 135
Order of length and approx. time (mins.) of quartet in a typical performance	4th (38m.)	2nd (45m.)	1st (49m.)	3rd (43m.)	5th (25m.)
Corresponding fingers and their order of length	4th (Thumb)	2nd (Forefinger)	1st (Middle finger)	3rd (Third finger)	5th (Little finger)

Figure 5

The correspondences go further. The thumb is the most singular of all the five appendages of the hand. It is separate from the four fingers, and through its function as an opposing member able to grasp an object from the opposite side to the fingers, it enables the entire hand to perform a large variety of important tasks. The first late quartet, Op. 127, is also very different from the middle triad and from Op. 135. In addition, in a way that is sensed but difficult to describe in words, Op. 127, the "thumb quartet," has a distinct feeling of solidity and steadfastness about it, reminding one of the breadth and strength of the thumb. It also acts as a bridge and foundation to the four quartets which follow.

Of the four fingers, the forefinger points the way, even as the first quartet of the middle triad, Op. 132, points the way stylistically, thematically, and spiritually toward the other two quartets of this group of three. This finger also touches and works with the thumb more readily than does any other, as Op. 132 has more in common with the first late quartet, Op. 127, than to any of the middle triad.

198

The middle finger is not only the longest but also the strongest of the four fingers, as is the third late quartet, Op. 130, with its powerful and dynamic *Grosse Fuge*. It is the longest of the quartets and the strongest at least of the latter four.

The fourth quartet, Op. 131, is the most mystical of the works, imbued as it is with the sense of divine union and love. On its corresponding finger, fittingly, is worn the wedding ring.

The middle three fingers act in unison to provide almost all the necessary gripping force of the fingers; similarly, the middle three of the late quartets are so interrelated that some experts consider them to be a single musical project. The third and fourth fingers are the most difficult to separate using only their own interior muscles, even as the third and fourth quartets, Opp. 130 and 131, are the most alike in terms of structure and meaning.

The smallest finger is the shortest, most delicate and refined of all the fingers, qualities which remind us of the neoclassical final late quartet, Op. 135. One can almost see the Op. 135 Quartet extended outwards in perfect etiquette as the other four lift a cup of tea! In acupuncture, the important heart meridian ends at the tip of this finger.

When we absorb the music of Beethoven's late quartets, then, we are absorbing the invisible flames of the secret rays and are being initiated by their vibrations. *The symphonies are for the triumph of the outer person; the late string quartets for the perfection of the inner person.*

A great key to the realization of the divine qualities of each of the secret rays and their respective quartets are Gautama Buddha's Ten Perfections of the Law. The Ten Perfections are the qualities we need to master in order to succeed in the more subtle and refined challenges and initiations of life. When the spiritual aspirant says, "My work is finished," God tests that person in the Ten Perfections of the Law to show him or her that the detail is not finished. For the Ten Perfections of the Law are the *yang* and *yin* or masculine and feminine energies of the five secret rays. They correspond to the late quartets in this way:

Quartet	Op. 127	Op. 132	Op. 130	Op. 131	Op. 135
Alpha or *Yang* Perfection	Alms	Renunciation	Courage	Truth	Goodwill
Omega or *Yin* Perfection	Precepts	Wisdom	Patience	Resolution	Indifference

199

In readiness for that time when humanity might consider that its work is finished, God, through Beethoven, has sent forth the amazing late string quartets not only to show them those states of consciousness they have yet to attain, but also to help humanity attain them.

Future Music in Relation to Beethoven

 WE HAVE SEEN through the life and work of Beethoven what true music of the Spirit is like—that it should "strike fire from a man." We have seen what sincerity and intensity of dedication to the path to God Beethoven demonstrated in order to bring forth his music for humanity. What lessons, then, can be drawn from his example in order that others might again tap the sources of inspiration he found, in order to again bring forth such world-transforming creations? And what can we learn from his example of service to inform our work not just in music, but in all of the arts and, indeed, in whatever area of life we feel to be our sacred calling?

The most fundamental lesson that we can learn from Beethoven is that he was primarily motivated not by the desire to be technically or stylistically innovative but by the desire to serve humanity through art which was expressive of love, beauty, and truth. The motive behind any artistic creation determines the result, and Beethoven's motive was to lift humanity nearer to God.

As Wagner was later to express it, "I have found true Art to be at one with true Religion." By this he meant, of course, religion in its broadest and highest sense, as in the cultivation within each heart of that which transcends the limited human state. Thus, the purpose of true art is not merely to represent life as it already is, nor to flee life's reality in escapist thrills, nor, least of all, to degrade life; rather, the purpose of true art is to redeem life.

As it is stated in *Liki*, a part of the classic Chinese text, *The Wisdom of Confucius*, "the superior man tries to create harmony in the human heart by a rediscovery of human nature, and tries to promote music as a means to the perfection of human culture. When such music prevails and the people's minds are led toward the right ideals and aspirations, we may see the appearance of a great nation."

Music as something capable of helping to forge a great nation. What a goal for the artist to strive for! Yet how can we compare to this ideal so much of the music being created today? When leading jazz musician Ornette Coleman informs us, "It was when I found out that I could make mistakes [and call it art] that I knew I was onto something," he is in fact onto nothing but how to make mistakes. When the late Sid Vicious of the Sex Pistols declared, "You just pick a chord, go twang and you've got music," he had in fact got nothing except a twang.

202

The wisdom of the ancients informs us that all true art is a vehicle used by the Supreme in order to convey intimations of the Godhead to the beholder or listener. Art, as music, as dance, as painting and sculpture, as drama is the loving way of instructing humanity in the disciplines necessary for the bringing forth of the greatest creativity in the individual. Those who sing and those who play musical instruments become the harmony of all the earth, since music is not just an intangible art form, but it is literally an esoteric power source. If we are not materialists, then we should be open-minded to the possibility that this belief, once held to be true in many ancient cultures, is not groundless. And according to the ancient wisdom, the misuse of music by a sufficient number of people may result in the manifestation of inharmony at all levels of human affairs, leading to economic depression, war, and possibly even, ultimately, the shaking of the landmasses and atoms of physical reality themselves in earth changes.

What, then, is constructive, and what destructive music? I have often been asked my opinion on whether this or that rhythm, or instrument, or musical genre, or combination of chords is likely to have a beneficial or a negative effect on the listener. I have come to answer that such questions actually need to be approached from another angle, since there are literally an infinite number of musical components which could be evaluated in this way. Rather than analyzing every minute aspect of every composition, which would be impossibly complex, I believe it is more useful and more freeing to realize that music is always the result of the consciousness and the motive of the composer or performer.

Rather than examining the result, examine the source. To the extent that the consciousness and motive are impure—for example, if there is an element of pride and of a desire to impress—then the resulting music will be equally flawed. When the consciousness and the motive are pure, on the other hand, the resultant creation will automatically reflect that purity, and we need not concern ourselves with questions about the individual musical components.

So to forge, train, and mold oneself into the capability of expressing divine art is not so much a question of doing as it is one of becoming. This was clearly understood by Beethoven, who spent his entire life attempting progressively to purify his selfhood in order to compose still more transcendent music. One may study music for decades (and study is necessary), but if imperfect aspects of the ego remain untransmuted, then despite all of one's study, it may be impossible to bring forth the pure stream of unpolluted inspiration. Transformations in consciousness automatically lead to transformations in one's art, but without inner change there can be no meaningful improvement in what one creates.

Therefore, if a new and transcendent future music is to come into the earth, then to look to create a revolution only of technique is to miss the point entirely. (It is also to allow the untransmuted human ego to neatly sidestep the real issue.) For all sublime art depends first upon a revolution in consciousness, a sublimation of the artist's motive and intent.

How then is this to be achieved?

Once more we can take a lesson from Beethoven. Witness his utter dedication to the task—a dedication dependent upon self-discipline. The expansion, purification, and sublimation of consciousness can only be attained through discipline. Apart from motive, discipline is the next most important feature of Beethoven's life and music and is, unfortunately, all too often lacking in the artists of today. Yet it has always been true that those who are

203

the greatest artists, poets, and musicians, those who cultivate an inner fire of love to implement an idea of God, are those who have the greatest discipline of self, of the energies of consciousness, of life, and even of their use of space and time. Discipline is a grid, a forcefield that is necessary in order to have the flow of love and to retain the flow of love. Where there are undisciplined lives, love flies out of the window. As Beethoven expressed through his very life, the art of living love is to be creative, and the art of being creative is to be self-disciplined.

Many have wondered during recent years: "Where is the new Golden Age music? When and how is it to appear?" The answer is that, for the most part, it still has not appeared because in today's society so many have been unwilling to make the sacrifices and efforts required in order to create fine art, including music, through the disciplined mastery of the flame of universal love. Sadly, many whose destiny it might have been to be adepts of that flame of disciplined, living love have degraded that destiny or perverted that flame. Devoid of true peace and selfless love within, they are unable to create true harmony or joy in their art. Such individuals must refine the matrices of their personality at both conscious and subconscious levels, learning all that is to be learned from lives such as Beethoven's, if they are to gain mastery of their flow of thought and feeling. Until then, they will continue to create discordantly even if inadvertently.

Like Beethoven's creations, the future Golden Age music, if it is to appear, will not be the expression of self *per se* at all, being no longer so-called "self-expression," but rather a manifestation of Self—of that which is above and beyond the limitations and foibles of the more earthly part of ourselves. Such music will be attained only by focusing upon and becoming the very highest and most sublime part of our true nature as human beings.

One prime law is that the performer is there to express the music; the reverse is the way of the ego. To understand that the music transcends the performer in importance is the way of the Golden Age artist. When the motive behind the artistic endeavor is selfless, altruistic, and as uplifted toward the heavens as possible, then even the commonplace which holds that one can create as art only that which comes from within and what one has oneself felt and experienced may be miraculously transcended by divine inspiration.

In the past, individuals such as Beethoven who were outwardly of rugged nature but who had internal sensitivity and right motive were able to penetrate into the realms of glory and bring forth a portion of the harmony of the spheres in their works.

As the ability is mastered of precipitating beauty from Spirit to Matter, the consciousness increasingly penetrates the realm of First Cause, the harmonics of the Creation. Here, one's mind is imbued with a higher inspiration. Indeed, one is at the Source of all true art, and all that one wills into manifestation will bear the mark of timeless perfection.

How much music of *timeless perfection* is being composed today? This we must ask ourselves, for timeless perfection is the hallmark of that music which must come and which will be capable of playing a monumental role in the transfiguring of this world. The stream of serious, inspired music which included the works of the great composers of classicism and romanticism has all but dried up since early in the twentieth century. The reasons for this may largely be traced back to a change in the motives of composers around that time—away from the selfless and religious impetus and into the intellectual exploration of new techniques and ideas for their own sake. The spiritual motivation was largely supplanted by a materialistic frame of consciousness.

205

At the same time, popular music has also undergone revolutionary changes causing much of it to fall into lyrical and musical levels so low that they would have been quite unimaginable only a few decades ago. Even more importantly, these fallen forms of popular music have become more prominent and loom much larger in everyday society than any form of classical or more exalted tonal art. This is a fact which simply cannot be ignored and which, esoterically and sociologically, has devastating implications for the future of civilization. How can a future music of beauty, truth, and goodness be born in a world which beats overwhelmingly to the dehumanizing sounds of heavy metal and aggressive rap, and to the newer house, rave, hard core, and techno music (danced to while drugged on Ecstasy)? We may well ask. From where, indeed, is the new generation of composers of both serious and popular Golden Age music to arise on a planet which, nation by nation, has become gradually accustomed, year by year, to musical forms which clash with the harmony of the spheres?

Thankfully, all is not lost. Does not the light of a higher way sometimes appear in the most unexpected of places and times? It is interesting to observe that the mystical side of music and its power, while having largely been forgotten for a century, until around 1970, is again being discovered. Books, seminars, workshops, and therapies based on the inner powers of sound, of the voice, and of music are proliferating today.

This movement is especially reflected in the growth of music therapy. Various forms of music therapy have been found to be effective in treating clients of all ages for either physical or psychological problems. An expanding number of colleges and private organizations train people to practice music therapy. Such therapy is often effective where all other treatments have failed, and the true scope and potential of such methods is by no means yet fully realized.

In the early 1980s the movement known as "New Age music" also arose. At first this was limited to only a few performers and was notably lacking in melody and emotional engagement. It tapped, however, an unexpectedly large market of the generation of young adults who were tired of the noise and the lack of new directions in contemporary pop. By the end of the eighties, New Age music had become an established category of music represented on the racks of any sizeable music store.

The name *New Age music* is fundamentally a misnomer, since compositions in this category have always tended not to be art music—or even music at all—so much as placid and restful sounds which are pleasant to have on in the background. (Van Morrison hit the nail on the head when he once called such recordings "New Age Muzak."[1]) Nevertheless, much New Age music is an encouraging and beneficial escape from the other directions of contemporary musical creation and reflects the inner longing of millions of music lovers for a return to the harmony of the spheres in tonal art. In fact, the quality of such music has improved over the years, until some of its former performers are now producing true art music.

Some performers and record labels have even sought to highlight this development of their work into something new and truly worthy of artistic merit by disassociating themselves from the "New Age music" appellation. Where such new movements in music are ultimately taking us remains to be seen, but there may well be exciting things ahead. These future developments are, however, still in the realm of the unmanifest, and they need to become manifest in the now to release their transformational energy.

All who are the awakened ones look hopefully toward a new and golden era for humanity. Yet, just as both audible sound and cosmic vibration are the foundations of all of creation, so too the dissonant music which is so widespread today is the foundation of a state of consciousness incompatible with a dawning Golden Age. Esoterically, the basis for the restoration of the Christ consciousness in and among all nations is the restoration of right music and right sound. The point is not simply to suppress the dissonant music; it is, rather, to displace it creatively. When the music of the land changes, and only when and if it changes, *then* shall the visible, tangible transformation of civilization take place before our very eyes. Truly, there is no higher cause toward which those who are musicians, or who could be, might dedicate their lives.

What, then, can we expect to hear if future music becomes aligned once more to the tones of the All?

Over the last few decades, several concepts have evolved regarding the nature of the music to come which are inaccurate and misleading. One is that the future music will be "futuristic" in terms of being electronic, akin to science fiction, or avant-garde. Another is that it must be totally novel and revolutionary in terms of its style, structure, and musical elements. Even the instruments it will be performed upon may well be, it is thought, new instruments which are yet to be invented and which will emanate entirely new sounds and timbres.

None of this speculation is necessarily incorrect; it is just that it misses out what are by far the most important points of all: the intent behind the music, its purpose, and its effect. Some music in the future may well be electronically generated. Other music will not be. Some may well be entirely novel in structure and performed on instruments yet to be invented. Other music, however, will undoubtedly be created on the wonderful instruments we already have and will conform to the forms of musical composition as we know them today—everything from the symphony and the string quartet to the folk song and Gospel music.

None of these musical elements, or their lack, is critical to music becoming the music of the Spirit which is to come. After all, an electronic piece performed on a novel instrument in an unusually structured composition is essentially what musicians such as John Cage, Edgar Varèse, Morton Subotnik, and Karlheinz Stockhausen have been doing throughout most of the twentieth century. It is not "futuristic" musical elements that make a piece of music New Age. This is especially so since futuristic music, like science fiction speculations into the future world, is so often concerned with technology and intellectualism that the human spirit itself is swamped beneath ideas of mechanization and intellectualism gone mad.

Genuine New Age or Golden Age music can be composed in any form, using any instruments, but it will be defined as New Age according to its intent. It is *not* the medium (the instruments, the form) which makes any music New Age; it is the message, the consciousness behind it, which is communicated to the listener.

This spiritual renaissance and the quest of the individual for personal evolution is central to the New Age ideal and will be central to the future music. All other aspects of genuine New Age thought emanate from the spiritual quest. This is why, when asked which was the greatest commandment of all, Jesus, an archetype for New Age humanity, gave a synthesis of all of his teachings by answering:

208

> Thou shalt love the Lord thy God with all thy heart, and with all thy soul, and with all thy mind. This is the first and great commandment. And the second is like unto it, Thou shalt love thy neighbor as thyself. On these two commandments hang all the law and all the prophets.[2]

These are the great commandments of the spiritual life, and therefore of the coming age of the Spirit and also of true spiritual music. Music can be spiritually uplifting in a great variety of ways: it may be an overtly religious hymn or mass, or it may be mysteriously, almost unfathomably mystical. Often, it may bring one closer to the Godhead even though not expressing overtly religious sentiments, simply through the beauty of its melody, or through the divine, mathematical precision of the geometry of its rhythmic and melodic interplay. But certainly any music which bestows an actual spiritual force has *power*. It radiates purpose and drive. At times it may be quite complex. At other times its melodies haunt one with their otherworldly beauty.

Such will be the future music of the Spirit, and such is the music of Beethoven. His is genuine Golden Age music, already with us! Whenever he composed, Beethoven's intent and purpose was always the New Age ideal as expressed in Christ's two great commandments, and this intent underlies every note of the composer's creations. The Beethoven works discussed in this book exert an effect upon atoms, upon molecules, upon the individual's consciousness, and upon society at large similar to that of a magnet placed beneath a sheet of paper upon which iron filings have been scattered. Beethoven's compositions organize and harmonize, dissipating all unreality, transforming entropy into alignment with the Divine. With this music available to us, there is no need to lose our children to sound creations which point in the downward direction. We can play and discuss Beethoven with our young people. They can be raised in an environment in which such tonal art is always to be heard, so that they become one with its inner message from the earliest age. Indeed, our children should be God-taught by the rhythms, melodies, and harmonies of Beethoven even while in the womb, for burgeoning evidence exists for the importance and efficacy of prenatal learning. Our children should all know they are heirs to Beethoven's creations; after all, he himself always knew his life's work was aimed like an arrow at the future.

209

We should ponder deeply Beethoven's words, with which we close this book, on the meaning and function of his music and all good music:

> When I open my eyes I must sigh, for what I see is contrary to my religion, and I must despise a world that does not know that music is a higher revelation than all wisdom and philosophy. It is the wine which inspires one to new generative processes, and I am the Bacchus who presses out this glorious wine for mankind and makes them spiritually drunken . . . I have not a single friend; I must live alone. But well I know that God is nearer to me than to other artists. I associate with Him without fear. I have always recognized and understood Him and have no fear for my music—it can meet no evil fate. Those who understand it must be freed by it from all the miseries which the others drag about with themselves . . . Music is the only entrance into the

Appendix 1

TABLE OF WORKS DISCUSSED IN PART III

The figures in the left-hand column are the opus numbers under which the works were originally published. Bear in mind that the works listed below, which were relevant to discuss in the present book, are nevertheless only a small fraction of the whole. Beethoven wrote 138 works to which he assigned opus numbers, and far more than this without opus numbers. For example, I list below the four piano sonatas discussed in this book, but Beethoven was an adept of the piano sonata medium and also wrote another twenty-eight with opus numbers as well as five earlier ones without. Similarly, the set of piano variations listed below (those on a waltz by Anton Diabelli) were preceded in his output by nineteen other sets with or without opus numbers.

Op.		Page
	I. Symphonies	
21	No. 1, C Major (1799–1800).	105
36	No. 2, D Major (1801–2).	110
55	No. 3, E-flat Major (*Eroica*) (1803).	113
60	No. 4, B-flat Major (1806).	125
67	No. 5, C Minor (1804–8).	126
68	No. 6, F Major (*Pastoral*) (1807–8).	131
92	No. 7, A Major (1811–12).	135
93	No. 8, F Major (1812).	137
125	No. 9, D Minor (*Choral*) (1822–24).	153
	II. Concertos	
58	Piano Concerto No. 4, G Major (1805–6).	124
61	Violin Concerto, D Major (1806).	124
73	Piano Concerto No. 5, E-flat Major (*Emperor*) (1809).	134

212

Appendix 2

I. Piano Sonatas

All of them, but in particular Op. 13 (the *Pathetique*), Op. 53 (the *Waldstein*), Op. 90, and the late sonatas Opp. 101, 109, 110, and 111.

II. Violin Sonatas

The three Op. 30 sonatas, in particular the second one in C Minor; Op. 47 (the *Kreutzer*) and Op. 96.

III. String Quartets

The three Op. 59 quartets (the *Rasumovsky* quartets), Op. 74 (the *Harp*), and Op. 95.

IV. Other

Piano Concerto No. 3 (Op. 37), the ballet music *The Creations of Prometheus* (Op. 43), and the *Archduke* trio for strings and piano (Op. 97).

Notes

Chapter One: *The Importance of Beethoven Today*

1. Emily Anderson, ed., *The Letters of Beethoven*, 3 vols. (London: Macmillan, 1961), no. 1248.
2. Quoted by Marion M. Scott, *Beethoven* (London: J. M. Dent & Sons, 1934, rev. 1974), p. 155.
3. Ernest Newman, *The Unconscious Beethoven* (London: Parsons, 1927).
4. Quoted in David Tame, *The Secret Power of Music* (Rochester: Destiny Books, 1984), p. 19.
5. Wilhelm von Lenz, *Beethoven, Eine Kunst-Studie* (Hamburg: Hoffman & Campe, 1860), V, p. 32.

Chapter Two: *The Inner Power of Music*

1. Julius Portnoy, *Music in the Life of Man* (New York: Holt, Rinehart & Winston, 1963).
2. *American Journal of Psychiatry* 99:317.
3. For more detail see David Tame, op. cit., pp. 15–17.
4. For a more complete quotation see David Tame, op cit., p. 39.
5. John Michell, *City of Revelation* (New York: D. McKay Co., 1972).
6. Simon Frith, *Sound Effects* (London: Constable, 1984), p. 14.
7. Mick Jagger in *The Rolling Stone Interviews 1967–1980* (New York: St. Martin, 1989), p. 333.
8. Mick Jagger quoted in David Tame, op. cit., p. 153.
9. Plato, *The Republic,* trans. by A. D. Lindsay (London: J. M. Dent & Sons, 1935), pp. 84–85.
10. Quoted in David Tame, op. cit., p. 35.
11. Deryck Cooke, *The Language of Music* (Oxford: Oxford University Press, 1959).
12. H. P. Blavatsky, *The Secret Doctrine* (Wheaton, IL: Quest Theosophical Heritage Classics, 1993, orig. pub. in 1888), Vol. I, p. 633.
13. Dorothy Retallack, *The Sound of Music and Plants* (Marina Del Rey, CA: De Vorss & Co., 1973).

14. David Tame, op. cit.
15. Cyril Scott, *Music, Its Secret Influence Throughout the Ages* (London: Rider, 1958). Orig. pub. in slightly different form as *The Influence of Music on History and Morals* (London: Theosophical Publishing House, 1928).
16. Dane Rudhyar, *The Rebirth of Hindu Music* (Adyar, India: The Theosophical Publishing House, 1928).

Chapter Three: Whence Came the Music?

1. Quoted in Corinne Heline, *The Cosmic Harp* (Santa Barbara: J. F. Rowney Press, 1969), p. 39.
2. Ibid., p. 93.
3. A. Eaglefield Hull, *Cyril Scott: The Man and His Works* (London: Waverly Books, undated), quoted in David Tame, op. cit., p. 264.
4. Cyril Scott, *The Initiate in the Dark Cycle* (London: Routledge & Kegan Paul, 1932). The other two, earlier Initiate books are *The Initiate, Some Impressions of a Great Soul* (New York: Samuel Weiser, 1971, orig. pub. in 1920) and *The Initiate in the New World* (New York: E. P. Dutton, 1927). First published anonymously, these books are still in print and now attributed to Scott openly. For a biographical sketch of Cyril Scott and a discussion of the Initiate books, see David Tame, op. cit., pp. 263–71.
5. Cyril Scott, *Music, Its Secret Influence Throughout the Ages,* op. cit.
6. Van Morrison, interview by the author, April 1987.
7. Ernest Newman, op. cit.
8. Quoted in Corinne Heline, *Beethoven's Nine Symphonies Correlated with the Nine Spiritual Mysteries* (Santa Barbara: J. F. Rowny Press, 1971), p. 58.
9. Ibid., p. 56.
10. Quoted in Marion Scott, op. cit., p. 121.
11. Ibid., p. 123.

Chapter Four: Before the Eroica

1. See note 15 below.
2. Quoted in J. W. N. Sullivan, *Beethoven: His Spiritual Development* (London: George Allen & Unwin, 1964, orig. pub. in 1927), p. 44. From a letter by Beethoven at the age of sixteen.

3. Quoted in Marion Scott, op. cit., p. 18.
4. Ibid., p. 108.
5. Ibid., p. 40. For an alternative translation see Emily Anderson, op. cit., no. 30.
6. Revelation 3:15, 16.
7. Emily Anderson, op. cit., no. 53.
8. Letter from Cherubini to Zeltner, 1812, quoted by Wilfrid Mellers, *Beethoven and the Word of God* (London: Faber and Faber, 1983), p. 5.
9. Elliot Forbes, ed., *Thayer's Life of Beethoven*, 2 vols. (Princeton: Princeton University Press, 1964, rev. ed. 1967).
10. Quoted in Marion Scott, op. cit., p. 45.
11. Quoted in J. W. N. Sullivan, op. cit., p. 53.
12. Corinne Heline, *Music, the Keynote of Human Evolution* (Santa Monica: New Age Press, undated).
13. Quoted in Marion Scott, op. cit., p. 46.
14. Ibid., pp. 46–47.
15. The Heiligenstadt Testament appears in almost all Beethoven biographies under various translations, but was first published in the seminal biography by Alexander Thayer. The translation in the present volume is a collage of the better parts of former versions.
16. Quoted in J. W. N. Sullivan, op. cit., p. 87.

Chapter Five: Of Life and Love

1. Quoted in Marion Scott, op. cit., p. 56.
2. Quoted in Philippe Autexier, *Beethoven: The Composer as Hero*, trans. by Carey Lovelace (London: Thames and Hudson/New Horizons), p. 61.
3. Marion Scott, op. cit., pp. 97–98.
4. Quoted in Marion Scott, op. cit., p. 99.
5. Anton Schindler, *Beethoven as I Knew Him*, ed. by Donald W. MacArdle (London: Faber, 1966). Trans. of 3rd ed. of Schindler, *Biographie von Ludwig van Beethoven* (Münster: Aschendorf, 1860).
6. Maynard Solomon, *Beethoven* (London: Cassell & Co., 1978), p. 158.
7. Ibid., Chap. 15, "The Immortal Beloved." For readers desiring to learn more about the life of Beethoven, Solomon's is in my opinion the best general biography and is recommended.

8. Ibid., pp. 184–85.
9. Mircea Eliade, *Cosmos and History* (New York: Harper, 1959), p. 18.
10. Emily Anderson, op. cit., no. 373, trans. Elliot Forbes, ed., *Thayer's Life of Beethoven*, pp. 533–34, amended.
11. Anton Schindler, *The Life of Beethoven*, ed. Ignaz Moscheles (Boston: O. Ditson, 1841). Trans. of 1st ed. (1840) of Schindler, *Biographie von Ludwig van Beethoven*, p. 55.
12. Anton Schindler, ed. MacArdle, op. cit., pp. 102–04.
13. Marion Scott, op. cit., p. 75.

Chapter Six: Beethoven as a Sagittarian

1. Quoted in Marion Scott, op. cit., p. 63.
2. Quoted in J. W. N. Sullivan, op. cit., p. 53.
3. Ibid.
4. Originally published in Franz Wegeler and Ferdinand Ries, *Biographische Notizen über Ludwig van Beethoven* (Coblentz: K. Bädeker 1838).
5. Quoted in Wilfrid Mellers, *Beethoven and the Word of God* (London: Faber and Faber), pp. 364–65.
6. Derek and Julia Parker, *The Compleat Astrologer* (London: Mitchell Beazley, 1971).

Chapter Seven: The Religion of Beethoven

1. Emily Anderson, op. cit., no. 1248.
2. Michael Hamburger, *Beethoven: Letters, Journals and Conversations* (London: Thames and Hudson, 1984, orig. pub. in 1951), pp. 86–87.
3. K.-H. Kohler, G. Herre, and D. Beck, eds. *Ludwig van Beethovens Konversationshefte* (Leipzig, 1976), Vol. 1, p. 211.
4. Anton Schindler, *Beethoven as I Knew Him*, op. cit.
5. Written into a friend's autograph album in 1793. Quoted by Wilfrid Mellers, op. cit., p. 14. A different translation of the same in Emily Anderson, op. cit., no. 4.
6. Gustav Nottebohm, *Beethoveniana* (Leipzig: J. Rieter-Biedermann, 1872), p. 39.
7. Elliot Forbes, ed., *Thayer's Life of Beethoven*, op. cit., p. 501.
8. Beethoven himself sourced these lines only by writing: "From Indian literature." According to Marion Scott, op. cit., pp. 124–25,

Beethoven's copying of them is preserved on a manuscript page in the library of the Royal College of Music, London. Her translation, used in the present volume, is by J. S. Shedlock (amended). According to Wilfrid Mellers, op. cit., p. 292, the passages are found in "a diary of 1816."

9. The words copied out by Beethoven: "I am That which is. I am all, that is, that was, that will be; no mortal hath ever Me unveiled . . . He is alone by Himself, and to He alone do all things owe their existence."

   There are two claimed sources from which Beethoven took the lines. They do appear in Schiller's essay, "The Mission of Moses," from which a number of biographers, such as Maynard Solomon, state that Beethoven copied them. A fuller transcription was rendered by J. F. Champollion in his *The Paintings of Egypt,* and Anton Schindler stated that Beethoven took the words from here. In any event, the words are a little spurious. Of the three sentences, the first two are said to have been at the Temple of Isis at Sais, Egypt. They are apparently not there now, but are attributed to Plutarch, as copied down by him and published in *De Iside et Osir, IX.* As with all Egyptian hieroglyphics, they can be translated liberally with a variety of subtle differences. David Wood, in *Genisis: The First Book of Revelations,* The Barton Press, 1986), translates the middle sentence to include the name Isis: "I, Isis, am all that has been . . . " Interestingly, the words "I am That which is" is very close to, and may even be accurately translated as the name of God as revealed to Moses from out of the burning bush: "I AM THAT I AM"—a mantric statement infused with deep esoteric significance.

   Schiller's and Champollion's accounts of ancient Egypt, from which Beethoven chose a few lines to copy and frame, were not necessarily totally scholarly historical narratives such as we would expect today, and may have been partly idealized. Nevertheless, Plutarch may well have truly found these writings, now lost to us. And none of the above academic hair-splitting at all alters the basic facts of the mystical truths of the lines, or that to Beethoven they meant a great deal irrespective of their origin. That they meant so much to him gives us, in turn, insight into his own mental world.

10. 1 Cor. 3:16.
11. 1 Cor. 15:28.
12. John 10:34.

219

Chapter Eight: Beethoven and the Spiritual Path

1. J. W. N. Sullivan, op. cit., p. 37.
2. Michael Hamburger, op. cit., p. 29.
3. Ibid., p. 125.
4. Friedrich Kerst, ed., *Die Erinnerungun an Beethoven* (Stuttgart: J. Hoffman, 1913), Vol. 2, p. 72.
5. Michael Hamburger, op. cit., p. 45 in slightly different translation.
6. Emily Anderson, op. cit., no. 139.
7. J. S. Shedlock, trans., *Beethoven's Letters* (New York: Dover Publications, 1972, orig. pub. in 1926), pp. 193–94.
8. Gal. 1:16.
9. Matt. 5:48.
10. St. John of the Cross, *Living Flame of Love.*
11. Letter to Franz Wegeler, 1801, quoted in J. W. N. Sullivan, op. cit., p. 57.
12. *Napoleon's failure can be viewed as a setback to the real, inner destiny of Europe from which it has not even now recovered.* The present-day European Community is to date again based upon human ideas of political and economic expediency, not upon the Universal Christ in all. Moreover, contemporary moves toward European unity do not, as in the case of the United States of America, begin at the grassroots level with the people, then moving up, but are undemocratically being imposed upon the people from above. While the unity of all is surely what God desires, not only for Europe but for the whole world, this must be a true unity of the people, united heart to heart, a unity free of greed and national jealousy. Beethoven's homeland and the European Continent shall only know a true New Age union when there is attained a uniting founded not upon the desire for material gain, but upon the democratic and cooperative desire to fulfill a spiritual destiny together and in God.
13. Franz Wegeler and Ferdinand Ries, op. cit., p. 78. Beethoven actually changed his mind about the title of the Third Symphony and his opinion of Napoleon many times, as best detailed in Maynard Solomon, *Beethoven*, op. cit., Chap. 13.
14. *Light on the Path*, written down by Mabel Collins (London: Theosophical Publishing House, 1972), pp. 1–3.
15. Luke 18:19.

16. Michael Hamburger, op. cit., p. 138, translation amended.
17. J. S. Shedlock, op. cit., p. 14.
18. Ibid., p. 22.
19. Joseph Kerman, *The Beethoven Quartets* (Oxford: Oxford University Press, 1967), p. 375.
20. Heb. 12:5–7.
21. St. John of the Cross, *The Living Flame of Love.*

Chapter Nine: Bride and Bridegroom

1. Georg Schunemann, *Ludwig van Beethovens Konversationshefte* (Berlin, 1942), Vol. 2, p. 365.
2. 1 Cor. 7.
3. See Maynard Solomon, op. cit., p. 220.
4. Michael Hamburger, op. cit., p. 155.
5. Quoted by Wilfrid Mellers, op. cit., p. 19.
6. Elliot Forbes, ed., *Thayer's Life of Beethoven,* op. cit., p. 379.
7. Ibid., p. 253.
8. Quoted in J. W. N. Sullivan, op. cit., p. 92.
9. 1 Cor. 7:32, 33.
10. 1 Cor. 7:37, 35.
11. Quoted in J. W. N. Sullivan, op. cit., p. 86; translation amended in last sentence of second paragraph.
12. O. G. Sonneck, *The Riddle of the Immortal Beloved* (New York: Schirmer, 1927), p. 60.
13. Ibid.
14. Elliot Forbes, ed., *Thayer's Life of Beethoven,* op. cit.

Chapter Ten: The Final Years

1. Marion Scott, op. cit., pp. 80–81.
2. Ibid., p. 79.
3. Elliot Forbes, ed., *Thayer's Life of Beethoven,* op. cit., pp. 800–01.
4. Michael Hamburger, op. cit., p. 210.
5. Quoted in J. W. N. Sullivan, op. cit., p. 125.
6. Quoted in Marion Scott, op. cit., p. 86.
7. Elliot Forbes, ed., *Thayer's Life of Beethoven,* op. cit., p. 1048.
8. Quoted in Marion Scott, op. cit., p. 87.

Chapter Eleven: How to Use Beethoven's Music

1. Edmond Bordeaux Székely, *Ludwig van Beethoven* (San Diego: I.B.S. International, 1973).
2. Aaron Copland, *What to Listen for in Music* (New York: McGraw-Hill, 1939).

Chapter Twelve: Before 1802: The First Period

1. Edmond Bordeaux Székely, op. cit.
2. Corinne Heline, *Beethoven's Nine Symphonies Correlated with the Nine Spiritual Mysteries* (Santa Barbara: J.F. Rowney Press, 1971), p. 16.
3. Ibid., p. 17.
4. Ibid.
5. Marion Scott, op. cit., p. 94.
6. Corinne Heline, *Beethoven's Nine Symphonies Correlated with the Nine Spiritual Mysteries,* op. cit., p. 20.

222 Chapter Thirteen: 1802 to 1815: The Second Period

1. Philip Barford, "Beethoven as Man and Artist," in Denis Arnold and Nigel Fortune, eds., *The Beethoven Companion* (London: Faber and Faber, 1971).
2. Quoted in Corinne Heline, *Beethoven's Nine Symphonies,* op. cit., p. 26.
3. Marion Scott, op. cit., p. 164.
4. Wilfrid Mellers, op. cit., p. 18.
5. Marion Scott, op. cit., pp. 166–67.
6. As recounted in George Grove, *Beethoven and His Nine Symphonies* (New York, 1962), p. 54, in a different translation.
7. Psalms 30:5.
8. Quoted in Corinne Heline, *Beethoven's Nine Symphonies,* op. cit., p. 30.
9. Anton Schindler, *Beethoven As I Knew Him,* op. cit.
10. Corinne Heline, *Beethoven's Nine Symphonies,* op. cit., p. 33.
11. Quoted in Marion Scott, op. cit., p. 169.
12. Mal. 3:2.
13. Quoted in Marion Scott, op. cit., pp. 171–72.

14. Emily Anderson, op. cit., no. 258.

15. Helena P. Blavatsky, *The Secret Doctrine*, quoted in Corinne Heline, *Beethoven's Nine Symphonies*, op. cit., p. 43.

16. Alfred Einstein, *Essays on Music* (London: Faber and Faber, 1958), p. 247.

17. Ibid., p. 248.

18. Quoted in Marion Scott, op. cit., p. 172.

19. Quoted in J. W. N. Sullivan, op. cit., p. 83.

20. Quoted in Corinne Heline, *Beethoven's Nine Symphonies*, op. cit., p. 50.

21. Ibid., pp. 50, 55.

22. Paul Henry Láng, *Music in Western Civilization* (London: J. M. Dent & Sons, 1942).

23. Basil Deane, "The Symphonies and Overtures," in Denis Arnold and Nigel Fortune, eds., *The Beethoven Companion* (London: Faber and Faber, 1971).

24. Quoted in Marion Scott, op. cit., p. 70.

25. Paul Bekker, *Beethoven* (Berlin: Schuster and Loeffler, 1911), English trans. by M. M. Bozman (London: J. M. Dent & Sons, 1925).

Chapter Fourteen: Hammerclavier, Missa Solemnis, *Diabelli Variations, and* Choral

1. Geoffrey Hindley, ed., *The Larousse Encyclopedia of Music* (New York: World Publishing Co. 1971).

2. Marion Scott, op. cit., pp. 145–46.

3. Philip Barford, "The Piano—II," in Denis Arnold and Nigel Fortune, eds., *The Beethoven Companion* (London: Faber and Faber, 1971).

4. J. W. N. Sullivan, op. cit., p. 102.

5. Mark 15:34, Matt. 27:46.

6. J. W. N. Sullivan, op. cit., p. 103.

7. For an overview of which musical instruments particularly stimulate the seven chakras, see David Tame, *The Secret Power of Music,* op. cit., p. 277. Though the third eye chakra has ninety-six petals, or radiating lines of energy, these group into forty-eight on the left and forty-eight on the right, sometimes giving to the clairvoyant the appearance of only two large petals or "wings." This is why, in ancient Egypt, a Pharaoh who was treading the Path and had raised the kundalini to the third eye, thus activating the chakra, was said to

be a "winged Pharaoh." The grouping of the petals into two "wings" means that one wing and one hemisphere of the brain relates to each hand while the piano is being played: thus both wings of the chakra and both hemispheres of the brain are activated in piano playing.

8. Wilhelm von Lenz, *Beethoven, Eine Kunst-Studie* (Hamburg: Hoffman & Campe, 1860), V, p. 32.

9. Cited in Warren Kirkendale, "New Roads to Old Ideas in Beethoven's Missa Solemnis," *The Musical Quarterly* 56 (1970):676.

10. Emily Anderson, op. cit., no. 1079, dated June 5, 1822.

11. Anton Schindler, *Beethoven As I Knew Him,* op. cit., quoted in Wilfrid Mellers, op. cit., p. 293.

12. Anton Schindler, *Beethoven As I Knew Him,* op. cit., quoted in Marion Scott, op. cit., p. 80.

13. Denis McCaldin, "The Choral Music," in Denis Arnold and Nigel Fortune, eds., op. cit.

14. Emily Anderson, op. cit., no. 1307, dated September 16, 1824.

15. Cited by Wilfrid Mellers, op. cit., p. 343.

16. Ralph Hill, *The Symphony* (St. Clair Shores, MI: Scholarly Press, 1961).

17. Matt. 12:36, 37.

18. Antonín Sychra, "Ludwig van Beethovens Skizzen zur IX Sinfonie," *Beethoven Jahrbuch,* 2nd ser., IV, 1959–60.

19. Ibid.

20. Corinne Heline, *Beethoven's Nine Symphonies,* op. cit., p. 66.

Chapter Fifteen: The Late Quartets: An Overview

1. J. W. N. Sullivan, op. cit., p. 122.

2. Ibid., p. 80.

3. Quoted in Marion Scott, op. cit., p. 257.

4. Harold Truscott, *Beethoven's Late String Quartets* (Denis Dobson, 1968).

5. Marion Scott, op. cit., p. 274.

6. Christopher Small, *Music Society Education* (London: Calder, 1977).

Chapter Sixteen: The Late String Quartets

1. Wilfrid Mellers, op. cit., pp. 161–62.

2. Joseph Kerman, op. cit., p. 230.

3. J. W. N. Sullivan, op. cit., p. 120.
4. Quoted in Maynard Solomon, op. cit., p. 323.
5. Joseph Kerman, op. cit., p. 268.
6. Ibid., p. 322.
7. Ibid., p. 324.
8. J. W. N. Sullivan, op. cit., p. 115.
9. Marion Scott, op. cit., p. 270.
10. Elliot Forbes, ed., *Thayer's Life of Beethoven,* op. cit.
11. Marion Scott, op. cit., p. 271.
12. J. W. N. Sullivan, op. cit., p. 114.
13. Harold Truscott, op. cit.
14. Friedrich Kerst, ed., *Die Erinnerungen an Beethoven* (Stuttgart: J. Hoffmann, 1913), Vol. 2, p. 188.
15. Marion Scott, op. cit., p. 273.
16. Richard Wagner, *Beethoven* (Leipzig: Fritzsch, 1870). English trans. A. R. Parsons (New York: Schirmer, 1872).
17. J. W. N. Sullivan, op. cit., p. 117.
18. Joseph Kerman, op. cit., p. 338.
19. Richard Wagner, op. cit.
20. Quoted in "Beethoven," No. 1 of *The Great Composers* (Aldbourne: Marshall Cavendish Partworks, 1990), p. 16.
21. Harold Truscott, op. cit.
22. Letter to Moscheles, March 14, 1827, quoted in Marion Scott, op. cit., p. 85.
23. Luke 22:42. Similarly in Matt. 26:42 and Mark 14:36. Also John 12:27: "Now is my soul troubled; and what shall I say? Father, save me from this hour: but for this cause came I unto this hour"; and John 18:11: " . . . the cup which my Father hath given me, shall I not drink it?"

225

Chapter Eighteen: Future Music in Relation to Beethoven

1. Van Morrison, interview by the author, May 1987.
2. Matt. 22:37–40.
3. Beethoven, as recounted by Bettina Brentano in a letter to Goethe. It is generally acknowledged that Bettina Brentano elaborated and perhaps overpoeticized the language a little, but that the ideas expressed did come from Beethoven. Beethoven himself was shown

Bettina Brentano's letter and said, "Did I say that? Well, I must have had a raptus!"

4. Beethoven, as reported by J. A. Stumpff. The words reported by Stumpff are generally acknowledged to have become overelaborated in his transcription of them, but the ideas expressed will have been Beethoven's own.

Index

228

229

231

233

QUEST BOOKS
are published by
The Theosophical Society in America,
Wheaton, Illinois 60189-0270,
a branch of a world organization
dedicated to the promotion of the unity of
humanity and the encouragement of the study of
religion, philosophy, and science, to the end that
we may better understand ourselves and our place in
the universe. The Society stands for complete
freedom of individual search and belief.
In the Classics Series well-known
theosophical works are made
available in popular editions.